CHRISTIAN ECONOMICS

CHRISTIAN ECONOMICS

The Integration of Capitalism, Socialism, and Laborism

DALE ANTHONY PIVARUNAS

RESOURCE *Publications* • Eugene, Oregon

CHRISTIAN ECONOMICS
The Integration of Capitalism, Socialism, and Laborism

Copyright © 2018 Dale Anthony Pivarunas. All rights reserved. Except for brief quotations in critical publications or reviews, no part of this book may be reproduced in any manner without prior written permission from the publisher. Write: Permissions, Wipf and Stock Publishers, 199 W. 8th Ave., Suite 3, Eugene, OR 97401.

Resource Publications
An Imprint of Wipf and Stock Publishers
199 W. 8th Ave., Suite 3
Eugene, OR 97401

www.wipfandstock.com

PAPERBACK ISBN: 978-1-5326-5895-2
HARDCOVER ISBN: 978-1-5326-5896-9
EBOOK ISBN: 978-1-5326-5897-6

Manufactured in the U.S.A. 11/09/18

Dedication

I HAVE WRITTEN THIS book for common, ordinary people—actually the majority of people, not the rich and powerful people who constitute a very small minority of the people. The natural rights of the common people as partners in the economies to which they belong and co-own have been ignored and denied. Because of this, they have been exploited and cheated out of their fair share of the benefits of these economies. The production and the consumption by the common people are the driving forces of the economy, yet their share of the benefits from the economy is disproportionate to their contribution. That is unjust and needs to change.

This book is for the unemployed, the underemployed, those making minimum wage, those living in poverty, those who are having or have had their homes repossessed, those who are slaves to payday loans or title loans, students who have invested in a college education and have not found work that corresponds to their skills, women who do the same work as men but get paid less, those living from paycheck to paycheck, those who cannot afford to get needed medical care, and the tens of millions of people who have lost hope of ever achieving the American dream.

While the majority of people in the United States are Christian, there is virtually a total absence of Christian moral principles within the economic system. In fact, the US economy is currently driven by economic theories which hold that economic actions are and should be amoral as expressed in the statement 'it is neither right nor wrong, it is just business'. All Christian morality is based on the commandment 'love your neighbor as yourself'. This is certainly not applied to the unemployed, the underemployed, those making minimum wage, those living in poverty, those who are having or have had their homes repossessed, those who are slaves to payday loans or title loans, those who have been cheated through rent-to-own, lease-option or lease-purchase contracts and countless others suffering financially.

It is my sincere hope and prayer that someday Christians will act like Christians in their business, economic and political lives and that through their actions help to eliminate the economic and political injustices prevalent in the United States and throughout the world. May Christians be inspired by this book to truly be that light to the world and help society to put people before profits!

Contents

Introduction | 1

Christian Economics | 5

Origin of the Current Economic Crisis | 40

Part I: Causes of the Current Economic Crisis

Pricing | 49

Interest, the Price of Money | 65

The Distribution of Wealth | 78

A Refocused Tax System | 85

Redefining the Corporation | 90

Raise the Minimum Wage to a Living Wage | 92

Eliminate Unemployment | 94

Minimize Under-Employment | 96

Eliminate monopolies and oligopolies | 98

The Relationship between Capital and Labor | 103

Stock Markets | 110

Imports, Outsourcing and the Economy | 114

Home Ownership and the Mortgage and the Rental Industries | 122

Corporations | 141

US Foreign Policy and the US Economy | 154

Spending by the US Government and the National Debt | 160

War, Business, the Economy and Christianity | 164

The Role of the Government within the Economy | 169

Capitalism | 175

The State of the US Economy | 181

Economic Disaster by Design | 186

Part II: Christian Economics

The Principles of Christian Economics | 195

The Good of All the People, the Objective of the Economy | 198

Desired State | 203

What is Capitalism? | 205

The Little Red Hen | 209

Origin and Historical Development of Inordinate Capitalism | 215

The dignity and excellence of labor | 224

The Current Economic Crisis | 228

Christian Economics | 232

The Nation: A Community: One for All and All for One | 234

True Patriotism and the Economy | 236

The Balanced Distribution of Income and Wealth | 239

The Economy and the Living Body Analogy | 245

Basics of Christian Economics | 249

What is the Purpose of the Economy? | 250

Principle of Economic Self-Sufficiency | 253

Investment—Yes! Speculation—No! | 256

Property | 259

Price Management Principles | 262

Just Price Principles | 266

Labor | 269

Home Ownership | 273

Contracts | 275

Corporations | 277

The Balanced Economy Principle | 279

The Most Appropriate Economic System | 281

Socialistic Capitalism or Capitalistic Socialism | 284

Fixing the US Economy | 289

Rebuilding the US manufacturing capacity | 290

A Plan to Rebuild the US Economy—Phase 1 | 292

A Plan to Rebuild the US Economy—Phase 2 | 297

Economic Checks and Balances | 300

Re-balancing Wealth, Income and Private Property | 308

Re-Americanizing American Businesses | 315

Part III: The Solution

Who Can Solve This Crisis | 319

The People | 328

Students | 332

Unions | 334

A New Political Party | 338

Organized Religions | 343

The Military, the CIA, the FBI and the Police | 346

Blind Obedience and Blind Patriotism—Virtues or Vices? | 350

Power tends to corrupt | 353

The Role of the Leader | 355

Musicians, Artists and Celebrities | 357

Christian Family Economics | 358

The List of Critical Actions | 361

Conclusion | 364

Introduction

THE UNITED STATES IS in the midst of a continuing serious economic crisis affecting a very large percentage of the population. 9 million people are unemployed (U6 rate), over 30 million people are under-employed, approximately 9 million people have two jobs, 75% of those employed live from paycheck to paycheck, and 71% of US workers are in debt (of this 71%, over 55% say they are over their heads in debt). Millions of people have had their homes repossessed. Millions of homes are in foreclosure and the trend continues. Over 46 million Americans are living in poverty. Fifty percent of recent graduates cannot find full time employment. There are over 1 million homeless students in the United States living in gas stations, airports, cheap hotels, empty homes, church basements or sleeping at times at the houses of different friends. Food, healthcare, education, housing (especially rents), and transportation (car prices and insurance) continue to rise year after year and at higher rates than wages. The number of pay day loan stores, title loan stores, 'buy your gold and jewelry' stores have increased significantly in the last fifteen years indicating the desperate financial state of the millions of people who are forced to do business with these predatory organizations. Student loan debt has increased from $240 billion in 2003 to $1.3 trillion in 2017 with over 40 million individuals burdened with this debt. Students and their parents take out these loans with the expectation that sometime in the future their student will obtain a good paying job with which to pay off the student loans. But, unfortunately, for the majority of these students there are and will be no good paying jobs. A significant percentage of Americans are in a desperate and hopeless financial situation. This is a severe crisis and yet the above issues receive little to no attention by the news media. It is almost like the major news media is trying to hide these issues, but why?

The US national debt is over $21 trillion, continues to increase and virtually nothing is being done to stop and reverse this. The national debt has now exceeded the annual US GDP. It has increased over $17 trillion since 2000 and the interest on the national debt is over $475 billion every year and this figure continues to grow as the national debt grows. US national defense spending is now approximately $1 trillion dollars annually and depending on what new military action that the US engages in can be significantly higher. The United States Federal government spends over $1 trillion more than it receives in revenues every year and the President, his administration and Congress don't seem to be overly concerned. While they make some claims about the budget deficit and the national debt, they are really not concerned because they do almost nothing about this other than make statements. Government spending is out of control and this out of control spending by the Federal, state, county and local governments have a very serious negative impact on the US economy. And almost nothing is being done to control government spending.

In the last 17 years, the US government has spent $17 trillion more than its revenues. And what was this money spent on? Did the government spend that money on education, healthcare, or infrastructure? Was that $17 trillion dollars spent on the people of the United States, the 99% majority? The people of the United States were handed $17 trillion in additional debt and they have received nothing in return. Had that $17 trillion been used to pay off student debt, improve education, build schools, build hospitals, build roads, fix bridges, build a high-speed rail system, invest in renewable energy, reduce poverty, reduce homelessness, improve mental health, and reduce substance addiction, then the people of the US would at least know how the money was spent and recognize that there were benefits. But what or who did the US government spend $17 trillion on?

While the last fifteen years have been financially crippling for very many people, they have not been for all people. In fact, the last fifteen years have been the worst of times for tens of millions of people and the best of times for a few people. And this applies to corporations. While some corporations have gone bankrupt, some have seen significantly higher profits and some record setting profits. Wealthy individuals and corporations have been able to take advantage of these financial and economic crises to buy properties and businesses and encumber individuals, businesses and state, county and local governments with overwhelming debt. While the net worth of 250 million people and companies have decreased significantly over the last fifteen years, the net worth of a few million people and corporations have increased significantly. The losses of so many have been the gains of so few.

The United States is in a financial crisis with the majority of Americans suffering the effects. And yet, the government does not seem to care. The President, his administration and Congress do not seem to care. The President, his administration and Congress only seem to care about Big Banks, Big Corporations and Big Money. These politicians deceptively campaign with the promise of change and hope for the majority, but once elected these politicians only serve the rich minority. This is a crisis in itself. These crises, the political and economic crises, are so significant that there seems to be little hope for the future. Have pity on those who are between twenty and thirty years of age. Have even greater pity one those who are under twenty years of age. And pity the most, those who have not yet been born. The mistakes of this generation will impact multiple generations to come.

Has this all just happened by chance or has this happened by design? Has the transfer of wealth from the majority to a select minority occurred accidently or intentionally? What are the underlying causes of the current economic and political crises? Who is responsible for these crises? What can be done to fix the broken US economy? And what can be done to fix the broken political system?

The United States has a far greater threat to its security than terrorists or any foreign enemy and that is the imminent danger that the current economic crisis could result in a far more extreme, devastating and lengthy economic catastrophe than the Great Depression which started in 1929 and lasted for over twelve years. And yet, while sixty to seventy percent of the people realize the seriousness of the present situation, the top five percent have no grasp as to the severity of the current economic situation or what needs to be done in order to avoid what could potentially be the worst recession in US history. This is especially true for the members of the Federal government. The President, his administration and Congress seem to be totally incompetent to address and resolve the issues which threaten to wreak economic disaster on the majority of Americans. And that is because they are not impacted by this crisis. The President, his administration, Congress and the Washington-elite have not been personally impacted by the recession. Their lifestyles have not changed. They still live the good life. They go to parties, to the theater, to concerts, to the country club, to their summer homes, and on numerous vacations. They do not experience the difficulties associated with living from pay check to pay check, from not being able to find work, from having to work two jobs, from having bill collectors calling, from not being able to go to the doctor or dentist, from having debt that they may never be able to pay and from having lost hope of ever being able to retire. How can the President, his administration and Congress solve the economic problems facing the country when they do not understand what the problems are or how serious they are? Perhaps, they don't think that there is a problem? Perhaps, they don't really care?

There are two underlying causes to the situation that the United States is in; one economic, the other political. The economy of the United States is malfunctioning because it is broken, out of balance and out of control. It is not lethargic and needing stimulation—it is broken. On the political side, the government of the United States is also broken, out of order and out of control. The majority of those who have been elected to represent the people, in fact, do not represent the people nor do they pursue the people's best interests. Rather, these elected officials use the government to pursue their own selfish interests and benefits as well as the interests and benefits of a very small and select group of people. These two causes are related in that the malfunctioning of the government is one of the main causes of the malfunctioning of the economy.

Christian Economics

CHRISTIAN ECONOMICS, AS ANY other well-developed system, is an axiomatic system similar to Euclidean geometry in which all theorems or principles are based on first principles (axioms or postulates) and developed from these first principles. These first principles of Christian economics are based on Natural Law and the teachings of Jesus Christ. The principles of Natural Law are self-evident and are universally accepted by virtually all religions and people.

The first principle of Natural Law is that good is to be done and promoted, and evil is to be avoided. This principle applies to Christian economics. The second first principle of Christian economics is 'treat others in words and actions as you would have them treat you in words and actions' which is also expressed in Christianity as 'love your neighbor as yourself'. The third first principle of Christian economics is the absolute dignity and equality of each and every human being. Christianity teaches that human beings, all human beings, are made in the image and likeness of God. Jesus taught this principle through both his words and his actions. The absolute dignity of the human being applies to all human beings not just the rich, the powerful, the educated, men, older people, the healthy, the educated, the members of specific religions, specific nationalities, specific races or the beautiful. The absolute dignity of the human being applies to the rich and the poor, the powerful and the powerless, the educated and the uneducated, women and men, the old and the young, the healthy and the sick, the members of all religions, the members of all nationalities, all races and the beautiful and the ugly. The absolute dignity of each and every human being is the basis for the rights of each and every human being and the Christian imperative that every person is treated with dignity and respect in their social lives, their economic lives, their political lives and their private lives.

However, before continuing with a discussion of Christian economics it is both interesting and enlightening to apply these first principles to the US economy regarding prices, jobs, business practices, the minimum wage, wages in general, the outsourcing of jobs, pensions in private industry, home foreclosures, home repossessions, how employers treat their employees, how managers treat their subordinates, etc. Are prices, jobs, business practices, the minimum wage, wages in general, the outsourcing of jobs, pensions in private industry, home foreclosures, home repossessions, employer-employee relationships, and manager-subordinate relationships based on the principles 'that good is to be done and promoted, and evil is to be avoided', 'love your neighbor as yourself', the absolute dignity and equality of each and every human being and the imperative of treating every person with dignity and respect? Certainly not! It takes little reflection to realize that there is almost no influence of these basic principles of Christian economics within the US economy. The US economy for all practical purposes is pagan. In fact, the US economy is based, managed and directed by economic theories which disconnect morality and economic behavior and activities. And this is wrong, absolutely wrong. Every human action within business, between businesses, involving a contract, involving a transaction, the relations between employers and employees, the relations between managers and subordinates, the relations between businesses and customers; these are all subject to morality, that is, they are either right or wrong from an ethical point of view as well as from a Christian point of view. Current economic theories actually support the disparity between the rich and the working class and promote the economic dominance of the wealthy class.

How does God want people to act within their economic lives: their jobs, their businesses, their business transactions, how they treat employees, how they pay employees, how they treat business subordinates, how they deal with tenants, how they set prices, how they deal with other businesses, how they market their products and services, how they advertise, the quality of their products and services, etc. It is extremely unfortunate that the vast majority of Christians have totally disconnected their economic lives from their religious lives and their religious beliefs. Most Christians exclaim their belief, loyalty and love of God within church but totally deny Him within their economic lives acting as though God does not exist. Most Christians are pagans in their economic lives and this is totally inconsistent with Christianity.

How is the Christian mandate to love your neighbor as yourself to be applied in business, economics and politics?

And when the Son of man shall come in His majesty, and all the angels with Him, then shall He sit upon the seat of His majesty. And all nations shall be gathered together before Him, and He shall separate them one from another, as the shepherd separates the sheep from the goats. And He shall set the sheep on His right hand, but the goats on His left. Then shall the King say to them that shall be on His right hand: Come, you blessed of My Father, possess the kingdom prepared for you from the foundation of the world. For I was hungry, and you gave me to eat; I was thirsty, and you gave me to drink; I was a stranger, and you took me in; naked, and you clothed Me: sick, and you took care of Me; I was in prison, and you came to Me. Then the just will ask Him, saying: Lord, when did we see You hungry and fed You; thirsty, and gave You a drink? And when did we see You a stranger, and took You in; or naked and clothed You? Or when did we see You sick or in prison, and assisted You? And the king will answer them saying: Amen I say to you, as long as you did it to one of these My least brethren, you did it to Me.

Then He shall say to those on His left: Depart from Me, you cursed, into the everlasting fire which was prepared for the devil and his angels. For I was hungry, and you did not feed Me; I was thirsty, and you did not give me a drink. I was a stranger and you did not take Me not in; naked and you did not clothe Me; sick and in prison, and you did not care for Me. Then they will ask Him, saying: Lord, when did we see You hungry, or thirsty, or a stranger, or naked, or sick, or in prison, and did not minister to You? Then He shall answer them, saying: Amen I say to you, as long as you did not do so to one of these least, neither did you do it to Me.

Christians have heard this passage from the bible many times. And yet, so few Christians understand its true meaning and even less apply this passage to their economic, business and political lives. Who are the hungry, the thirsty, the naked, the strangers, the sick, and the imprisoned in modern society? Obviously, it is the homeless, the unemployed, those living in poverty, those who are underemployed, those who have had their homes repossessed, those who are physically, mentally and emotionally sick; and all those imprisoned physically, financially, and emotionally. Jesus identifies with these people and Christians are to see Jesus in these people. Do Christians see Jesus in the homeless, the unemployed, those living in poverty, those who are underemployed, those earning minimum wage, those who have had their homes repossessed, those who are physically, mentally and emotionally sick; and all those imprisoned physically, financially, and emotionally? The vast majority do not. What is worse is that many people who call themselves Christian actually deride these people. Christians claim to praise God in Church on Sunday but then they ignore and mistreat Him every day when they ignore and mistreat the homeless, the unemployed, those living in poverty, those who are underemployed, those who have had their homes repossessed, those who are physically, mentally and emotionally sick; and all those imprisoned physically, financially, and emotionally. The following is a more contemporary expression of Matthew chapter 25.

At the end of the world when God judges everyone, He will separate the good from the bad based on the commandment to 'love your neighbor as yourself'. He will say to the good, 'Come you blessed and inherit the kingdom prepared for you from the beginning of time. For I was poor and you helped Me out of poverty. I was unemployed and you helped Me to find a job or you gave Me a job or you created a job for Me. I did not have health insurance and you helped Me to obtain insurance. I was not making a living wage and you worked to have My employer pay a living wage. I was homeless and you helped me find a place to live. My house was in foreclosure and you helped prevent it from being repossessed. I was old and you helped Me with a socially-based income and health insurance. I was uneducated and you helped to educate Me. I was in prison and you helped change the system from retribution based to restorative based. I was discriminated against and you helped stop the discrimination.' And the righteous will ask Him, 'Lord, when did we see You in poverty or unemployed or without insurance or making less than a living wage or homeless? When did we see Your home in foreclosure or You uneducated or old and without an income or health insurance? When did we see you in prison or being discriminated against?' And God will answer, 'Whatever you did for any of my brothers or sisters, you did for me.' Then he will say to the others, 'Depart from me. For I was poor and you ignored Me. I was unemployed and you did nothing but say that is was My fault. I did not have health insurance and you resisted any means to provide Me with public health insurance. I was not making a living wage and you said that My employer should determine how much I was worth and that there should not be a minimum wage let alone a living wage. I was homeless and you crossed the street so that you would not have to walk by Me. My house was in foreclosure and you did nothing. My house was re-possessed and you helped with My eviction. I was old and you worked to take away my government mandated pension and health insurance that I paid for. I was uneducated and you said that only those that can afford an education should be educated. I was in prison and you threw away the key. I was discriminated against and you did nothing to stop the discrimination.' And the unrighteous will ask Him, 'Lord, when did we act this way to you?' And God will answer, 'What you did or did not do to your fellow human beings, you did to Me.'

Seventy-five percent of Americans identify themselves as Christians, so it would be logical to see a significant influence of Christianity within the US economy and political system. And yet, that is certainly not the case. With such a high percentage of Christians within the United States, there is obviously a very high percentage of so-called Christians within banking, the defense and weapons industry, the pharmaceutical industry, the chemical industry, the diversified manufacturing industry and within government (all levels and all branches). And yet the Christians in these industries and within government make no effort to apply Christian principles within their jobs. How could a Christian working within the banking industry support the foreclosure of over fifteen million homes and the repossession of over five million homes? How could a Christian person working for the banking industry personally apply and enforce policies that took people's homes away knowing that this affected women, children, and senior citizens? How could a Christian sheriff or police officer forcefully evict a family from their home removing their belongings and placing the family's belongings on the street while the family watched? How could a Christian help the corporation that they work for to outsource jobs to another country knowing that it results in the loss of employment for hundreds or thousands of employees and their families just to increase profits? How can a Christian work for a company that manufactures military weapons that helps promote military conflicts so that the company can sell its products and services? How can a Christian work for an employer who either directly or indirectly operate factories that employ young girls and even children paying them extremely low wages and making them work excessively long hours? How can a Christian employer pay adults with families at the minimum wage rate or less than the minimum wage? How can a Christian manager force employees to work without a break for ten or twelve hours at a time? How can a Christian manager lay off workers a day before a holiday so that the workers are not paid for the holiday? How can a Christian work for a company that intentionally reduces the hours of its employees so that it does not have to provide health insurance? How can a Christian work for a pay day loan company or a title loan company which has interest rates between 300 and 750 percent or higher? How can a Christian work for a company that pays male workers much higher than it pays female workers for the exact same work? How can a Christian work for a hospital or medical center which charges a person without insurance more than a person who has insurance because the insurance company gets a discount? (The person does not have insurance because they cannot afford insurance). How can a Christian work for a company that discriminates against older applicants? How can a Christian in government ignore the 9 million people who are unemployed, the 30 million people who are under-employed, the millions of people who have to work two jobs, the 90 million people who live from paycheck to paycheck, and the 46 million people living in poverty?

The current economic and political crises within the United States are the direct result of Christians not practicing their faith in their daily lives and this includes their business lives, their economic lives and their political lives. Unfortunately, the vast majority of Christians have closed their minds to the inconsistencies between their faith and the philosophies and practices of the business world which falsely claim that business is outside the realm of faith and morals as expressed in the statement 'it is neither right nor wrong, it is just business'. Good is to be done and promoted, and evil is to be avoided in all things including business and politics. The commandment to love your neighbor as yourself does not stop when it comes to business and politics; it applies to every facet of a Christian's life. If the failure of Christians to practice their faith in their economic lives is the cause of the current economic and political crises, then the solution is the application of Christian economics to the US economy and political system by Christians living their faith.

Human rights are based on the first principle of the absolute dignity of the human person. All humans have equal rights and every human being is obligated to respect the rights of others. Human rights are based on nature and because of this cannot be limited or taken away. They apply to all people without exception. Human rights, because they are derived by nature, cannot be applied to corporations or entities artificially created by the government; nor can human rights be applied to the government. A business does not have rights, only people have rights. A corporation does not have rights, only people have rights. A town, a city, a county, a state, or a country does not have rights; only people have rights.

Every human being needs freedom, safety, food, water, shelter, clothing, a livelihood, energy, transportation, communication, healthcare, disability care, old age care, education, privacy and rest/recreation (physical, emotional and psychological). Every human being needs care when they are very young, very old and very sick (physical, emotional or psychological). Corresponding to these human needs are human rights. People, all people have the right to be free; physical, emotional, psychological, financial, speech, thought, religion, movement, and political action. People have the right to safety; physical, emotional and psychological. This right applies to their person and their property. People have a right to food and water. Food and water cannot be so expensive that people cannot afford to buy them. Because the amount and sources of fresh water are limited, large sources of water such as lakes and ground water cannot be privatized since this would deny the basic human right to water. People have a right to clothing and clothing cannot be so expensive that people cannot afford clothing.

People have a right to housing; housing cannot be so expensive that people cannot afford housing nor can a person's home be taken away. If a person owes money or taxes on his or her home, then other ways must be pursued to obtain that money but the person should not be deprived of their home—it is their human right. People have a right to a livelihood; a person's livelihood cannot be taken away arbitrarily or because someone else wants to increase their profits. People have a right to education; education cannot be so expensive that people cannot afford education. People have a right to energy; energy cannot be so expensive that people cannot afford energy. People have a right to healthcare; healthcare cannot be so expensive that people cannot afford healthcare. When is food or water or clothing or shelter or energy or furniture or transportation or healthcare or education so expensive that people cannot afford these things? People need all of these things, not just one or a few of them. Obviously, there is an expense or price associated with each of these things. When the price of one of these necessities is so high that the person cannot afford to pay for the others, then that price is too high.

Pricing is best managed by businesses following the just price principle. A price for a service is just when it is fair to both the seller and buyer. It cannot be so high that a family's budget is impacted, nor so low that the business loses money. Businesses can set prices which are fair. They should not follow the false principle of maximization of prices. Nor does the pseudo principle of supply and demand dictate prices. Prices always need to be just and there is no moral basis for raising the price of a product or service because of scarcity. When businesses cannot manage prices justly, then the government needs to step in and make sure that pricing is fair and not extreme. Prices cannot be so high that the lower working class cannot afford the basic necessities in life: food, water, shelter, clothes, transportation, healthcare and education. Prices cannot be used by businesses to force other businesses to go bankrupt. Unfortunately, many businesses have used the immoral strategy of lowering prices to such an extent that smaller businesses cannot compete. This strategy is used to allow larger businesses to take over smaller businesses which reduces or eliminates competition, reduces service to customers and eliminates the livelihoods of people.

People have a right to rest and recreation: a person cannot be made to work so long in one day without a break for rest, nor for so many days in a week without a day break for rest, nor for so many weeks in a year without a week or weeks off for rest. Every person by nature has the right to movement, the right to communication, the right to work and the right to equal pay for equal work. Unequal pay for equal work is common for women and people of different ages. It often happens that within an organization two or more people do the same work but are paid unequally. Unfortunately, they do not know that they are paid differently. Every person has the right to privacy of their person, their possessions, their communication, their ideas, and their opinions. The government cannot deny this right, nor can employers deny this right.

Every human needs to own property, (clothing, furniture, housing, appliances, etc.) and every human being has the right to own property alone as well as jointly with others (co-own property within a corporation). One person's right to property is limited by every other person's right to property. One person or a group of persons cannot own so much property within a town or a county or a state or a country that others would be prevented from owning property, the amount of property required to live a safe and decent life. The right to own property is a human right which is derived by nature and therefore corporations or entities artificially created by the government cannot own property—the humans who constitute the corporation own the property of the corporations.

God created the universe and because of this everything belongs to God: the natural resources of earth (water, land, trees, elements, minerals, chemicals, petroleum, etc.) animals and other non-human living things. God created the universe for people, all people. God wants people, all people, and all people of every generation to share the natural resources of earth (water, land, trees, elements, minerals, chemicals, petroleum, natural gas, animals and other non-human living things. It is obvious that the natural resources of earth are finite. Since God wants people, all people, and all people of every generation to share the natural resources of earth, every generation of human beings must take care of these natural resources so that they may be available for future generations. Since God wants all people to share His goods, no person or groups of persons (corporations) should own or control so much of any natural resource as to prevent others from owning the natural resources that they need and have a right to.

God created the natural resources of the earth in order to satisfy people's needs for safety, food, water, shelter, clothing, energy, transportation, communication, health and rest/recreation. The use of these natural resources should not be based on first come first serve, a free for all type approach, a dog eat dog approach, the winner take all approach or a king of the hill approach. It should be clear that these things are to be shared by all people not necessarily equally but in a way that allows for everyone to have enough to satisfy their natural needs while differences are to be based on the individual's productivity. This means that there are both minimums and maximums with respect to the ownership of land and the other natural resources.

Natural resources are transformed by work (physical, design, organizational, managerial, etc.) into things that can be consumed or used for people's safety, food, shelter, clothing, energy, transportation, communication, and health. The economy is the corporation of people working together jointly to transform the natural resources from God into things that can be consumed or used by people. The purpose and objective of the US economy is to satisfy in the most efficient and effective way the natural needs and desires of all Americans for food, clothing, housing, a livelihood, education, healthcare, disability care, old age care, recreation/entertainment, social interaction, acceptance and respect. This statement which expresses the purpose and objective of the economy is a major tenet of Christian economics. The US economy needs to be organized and managed in order to achieve this objective. It needs to be organized and managed based on the principles of 'good is to be done and promoted, and evil is to be avoided', 'love your neighbor as yourself', the absolute dignity and equality of every person and the natural human rights of every human being.

The United States of America is a corporation of over 315 million people formally joined together for a common purpose: to satisfy the natural needs and desires of all Americans for safety, food, clothing, housing, a livelihood, education, healthcare, disability care, old age care, communication, recreation/entertainment, social interaction, acceptance and respect. The purpose of the United States can be divided into two areas; safety and economic. Safety involves physical, psychological and emotional security from domestic, foreign, environmental, and climate threat and attack. Safety extends to a person's body, thoughts and ideas, communication in all forms, property, association and actions. People's safety can be threatened either individually or collectively as a group or a corporation. The people of the United States are dedicated to maintaining the safety of all. The second and equally important purpose of the United States is economic. The economic purpose of the United States is the mutual satisfaction of the natural needs and desires of all Americans for food, clothing, housing, a livelihood, education, healthcare, disability care, old age care, recreation/entertainment, social interaction, acceptance and respect. Everyone has these needs and everyone has the right to have these needs satisfied. The people of the United States are joined together so that they can work together for the good of all. These two purposes and objectives of the United States are equally important.

The purpose of the government is to direct the corporation of the United States towards the attainment of its objective to satisfy the natural needs and desires of all Americans for safety, food, clothing, housing, a livelihood, education, healthcare, disability care, old age care, communication, recreation/entertainment, social interaction, acceptance and respect. Because the United States corporation is large and complex consisting of over 315 million people grouped into families, communities, social corporations and productive corporations working and interacting constantly and continuously, it is not possible for the United States to achieve its purpose and objectives without direction, management and regulation. Unfortunately, there is a fallacy that has been influenced millions of Americans and which holds that the role of government should be extremely limited. The fallacy sometimes referred to as the libertarian philosophy is very deceiving. Many people have espoused this philosophy because of certain inappropriate and in some cases immoral actions taken by the government. Unfortunately, the government today does not promote and support the true objectives of the United States, but instead promote and support the objectives of the wealthy elite. Because of this, the various branches and levels of government engage in policies and actions which are contrary to the true objectives of the United States which are the safety and economic welfare of all. As a result, people interpret these incorrect actions on the part of the government as the reason why there should be very limited government. So, while those who follow the libertarian political philosophy are correct in their position that many of the actions and policies of the government are wrong and even outrageous; they are incorrect in their conclusion that government needs to be limited in its abilities. A corporation with 315 million people cannot function efficiently and effectively without direction, management and regulation.

One of the main purposes of the government is to manage the economy so that the economy achieves its objective which is to satisfy in the most efficient and effective way the natural needs and desires of all Americans for food, clothing, housing, a livelihood, education, healthcare, disability care, old age care, communication, recreation/entertainment, social interaction, acceptance and respect. The management style of the government in managing the economy should be management by exception, that is, it should only get involved in the management of the economy when it is necessary. One case where the government needs to get involved in managing the economy is when there is unemployment. Central planning by the government should take place where and when private industry planning is lacking in order to promote full employment. It should do so by helping individuals create their own businesses. Maximum economic production for the economy, which is one of the purposes of the economy, can only be achieved through full employment. Another case where the government needs to get involved in managing the economy is when competition is out of control. The government needs to referee businesses to make sure that competition is fair.

The US economy is a social system consisting of millions of people working together, approximately 315 million people of which approximately 160 million people work to produce goods and services. Obviously, the vast majority of these people work together with the intention that all of them will be able to provide themselves and their families with safety, food, water, clothing, housing, education, healthcare, transportation, etc. It is just as obvious that these 160 million people do not work so that a small, select group of individuals can own or control most of the wealth and live lives of luxury while most other people live lives deprived of the basic necessities in life. Yet, in spite of the intentions of the majority of US workers, the US economy is far from realizing its objective. What is the problem? How can the US economy achieve its objective and why is the current US economy so far from achieving its objective?

From the premises that natural resources are limited and to be shared by all and from the purpose of the economy (to satisfy in the most efficient and effective way the natural needs and desires of all Americans for safety, food, clothing, housing, education, healthcare, disability care, old age care, communication, recreation, entertainment, social interaction, acceptance and respect), it follows that natural resources as property must be both privately owned and commonly owned. And this principle applies to all property; some property needs to be held by individuals (all individuals) and some property has to be held in common. There are over 315 million people in the United States. Everyone needs these things, at least a minimum amount of these things. The use and ownership of these things has to be done so that no one is deprived. That does not mean that everyone shares equally. What it means it that there has to be both minimums and maximums to the amount that one person or a group of persons can own or control, and that some things can only be shared in common. Parks, roads, bridges, large lakes and rivers, large underground water tables, scarce elements and minerals which are needed by the majority of people and underground sources of energy (coal, petroleum, and natural gas) have to be held in common. Again, these resources are limited and God gave these resources to all people, so they have to be shared by holding them in common. The kind and amount of natural resources that an individual or group of individuals can own or control as well as the kind and amount of natural resources that need to be held as common property can only be determined, managed and controlled through laws and oversight by the different branches of government and the different levels of government.

Again, the US economy is a social system consisting of millions of people, over 315 million people of which approximately 160 million people work to produce goods and services. Since the purpose of the economy is to satisfy in the most efficient and effective way the natural needs and desires of all 315 million Americans for safety, food, clothing, housing, education, healthcare, disability care, old age care, communication, recreation, entertainment, social interaction, acceptance and respect; it follows that all those people who are capable of working need to be employed and productive in supporting the economy. This concept is called full employment. There are 160 million workers who need to produce the goods and services required by the 315 million people. Obviously, it is best for the economy that all those who want to work are employed. The more people that are working, the more productive and efficient the economy is. Unemployed people do not support their own personal goals or the goals of the economy. How can current economic theories argue that it is good that 9 million people are out of work (the number of workers who are underemployed is over three times that)? How is it good for the economy that 9 million people have no income? How do these people pay their bills? How do these people pay for food? How do these people pay for housing? What do these people do when they get sick? How can these people provide for their children? 9 million unemployed people do not pay income taxes, do not pay Social Security taxes, and do not pay Medicare taxes.

Unemployment is a bad thing; bad for the unemployed and their families and bad for everyone in the economy. And yet, current economic theories actually hold that a certain rate of unemployment is a good thing. They argue that there needs to be a pool of unemployed workers so that businesses can draw from that pool of individuals when they need more workers. According to this theory, if there wasn't a pool of unemployed workers, then businesses would have to entice employed workers with better compensation to quit their current jobs and come and work for the new employer. When this happens, then employers pay more for labor and they have to raise prices causing inflation. Current non-Christian economic theories hold that an unemployment rate of between four to six percent is best. From a numbers perspective, this means that 6.4 to 9.6 million people should be unemployed. According to these economic theories, it is better to have 150.4 million workers supporting 315 million people rather than 160 million workers supporting 315 million people. Of course, this does not make sense. 315 million people need food, clothing, shelter, healthcare, disability care, old age care, transportation, furniture, education, etc. It obviously makes more sense to have 160 million workers providing these things for the 315 million rather than 150 million workers.

The arguments of current economic theory regarding full employment and unemployment rates are both false and deceiving. These arguments are based on the perspective of what is best for profit-based organizations and not what is best for the economy and not what is best for workers. For-profit organizations (not all organizations are for-profit) have as their primary objective the maximization of profit. Because of this they want to be able to minimize what they pay to workers both for new hires and existing employees. With a large number of people who are unemployed, there is more competition for jobs and people are often willing to accept less money than they feel that they are worth (good for the for-profit organization and bad for the worker and also the economy). Within a full employment economy (zero unemployment), there are always people looking for new jobs. There are young people entering the job market for the first time. There are people who want to relocate. And there are people looking for new opportunities. Christian economics holds that full employment is best for the economy and it is best for all workers. Full employment leads to full production and full consumption. Full employment provides more tax revenue for the various levels of government. It avoids the economic inefficiency of having to support those who are unemployed. And, it allows people to maintain their dignity as contributing to their own support as well as the support of the entire economy.

The very wealthy actually want high unemployment rates and they love the current real unemployment rate of 10 percent because it gives their businesses a cheap labor pool. Businesses can pay new employees considerably less than what they are worth and they can refrain from providing pay increases by telling employees that 'they are lucky to have a job'. While the very wealthy favor unemployment, they look with contempt on those who are unemployed. They hold that the unemployed are out of work through their own fault when, in fact, the vast majority of people who are unemployed (as well as those who are underemployed), are in their predicament because of policies and economic theories developed and promoted by the very wealthy as radical capitalist economics. People who have dedicated decades of their work lives to one company have been laid off because their jobs have been outsourced outside the United States. Were they bad employees? No! The company wanted to increase profits by using lower-wage workers in other countries where there are virtually no laws concerning labor protection. The company does not care about employees; it only cares about its profits. The company does not care about employee's children; it only cares about its profits. The company does not care whether the laid-off worker eventually has to file for bankruptcy or lose his or her home; it only cares about its profits. "It is neither right nor wrong, it is just business" replies the radical capitalist.

People have been laid off for the simple reason that the CEO and the executive team will not make their bonus objectives unless they reduce costs by laying-off workers. If a company is generating a ten percent net profit and the CEO's bonus is based on generating a net profit of twelve percent, how can the CEO make his or her bonus objective of twelve percent net profit? The solution is simple and is applied very often: lay off enough employees to hit the goal. The CEO and his or her management team do not care about the employees; they only care about their bonuses. The CEO and his or her management team do not care about the employee's children; they only care about their bonuses. The CEO and his or her management team do not care whether the laid-off worker has to file for bankruptcy or lose his or her home; they only care about their bonuses. "It is neither right nor wrong, it is just business" replies the radical capitalist.

Unemployment is bad, even terrible for the worker, but it is good for the radical capitalist. Most often unemployed workers take on increased debt by using credit cards or resorting to usurious personal loans. That is good for the radical capitalist. Unemployed workers are often forced to sell their homes or possessions at far less than market value. That is good for the radical capitalist.

Zero unemployment (and zero under-employment) is a wonderful thing for workers. Consider the lifetime career of a worker who never experiences any long period of unemployment or multiple periods of unemployment. Consider the benefits to college graduates who are able to find employment shortly after graduation. With zero unemployment, the net worth of workers over their careers would be higher. The stress, worry and anxiety of being laid off for tens of millions of workers have a heavy price on healthcare costs. With zero unemployment (and zero under-employment), these healthcare costs would be significantly reduced. Businesses actually benefit from a policy of not laying off workers in the long run. Workers who do not fear a lay-off are more dedicated and less likely to look for another job. The workers are happier and happier workers are more productive workers.

Would zero unemployment lead to price increases and inflation? No! Assuming that the radical capitalist theory on zero unemployment is correct with respect to the claim that wages will increase, does that imply that prices will rise? Within the context of maximum profitability, the corporation would want to increase prices. However, within the context of moderate and stable profitability, the corporation does not have to raise prices. And within the context of a democratic government that oversees and manages the economy and oversees and manages price increases, the corporation has no basis for raising prices as long as it is making a reasonable and fair profit. Balance and equity are the bases for a stable economy that benefits virtually everyone. Unfortunately, radical capitalist economics has as one of its main principles the maximization of profits for the capitalist and at the same time it denies the principle of economic balance and equity between capital and labor, between capitalists and workers.

Radical capitalism is a concept promoted by most current economic theories, though these theories do not use the adjective 'radical'. At the heart of these theories is the position that economics and economic activities are amoral, that is, neither moral nor immoral expressed in the expression 'it is neither right nor wrong, it is just business'. This principle frees people engaged in business from moral constraints and allows these people to pursue business objectives without any concern regarding basic morality and certainly not Christian moral principles. It is this principle of current capitalistic economic theories which allows businesses to put profits before people without any guilt and which is the main cause of the current economic and political crises within the United States and throughout the world. Is it possible for capitalism to be moral? Yes, it certainly is—but currently it is not. This is where it is the responsibility of Christians to make capitalism compatible with Christianity.

Another pseudo-theory of radical capitalist economics which illustrates the bias in favor of the capitalist and the bias against the worker involves 'the minimum wage'. Radical capitalist economics hold that there should not be a minimum wage. The government should not regulate wages whatsoever and should allow businesses to determine wages. These theories hold that since the main objective of a corporation is to maximize profits, and profit maximization is accomplished by minimizing costs and maximizing prices; it follows that companies have to minimize wages. The company does not care if the wages it pays its employees are insufficient to live on and to support a family; it only wants to maximize profits. The company does not care that the employee will never be able to afford a home, buy a car, or someday to retire, it only wants to maximize profits. The company does not care that the employee receiving such low wages has to work sixty, seventy, or eighty hours a week preventing him or her from getting an education or training to better themselves, it only wants to maximize profits.

The purpose and objective of the US economy is to satisfy in the most efficient and effective way the natural needs and desires of all US citizens for food, clothing, housing, a livelihood, education, healthcare, disability care, old age care, communication, recreation/entertainment, social interaction, acceptance and respect. Approximately 160 million workers (assuming that all people are working) have to support 315 million people. The goods and services that people need and want are provided through the labor of the workers. It is true that capital is required to help generate these goods and services, but the actual production and delivery of these goods and services is through the labor of the 160 million people. Workers work to provide an income for themselves and their families. It is unjust, contrary to Christian economics and counter to the purpose of the economy to pay an employee less than a living wage, a wage adequate for the worker and his or her family for food, clothing, housing, education, healthcare, disability care, old age care, transportation and recreation/entertainment.

Does a minimum wage or even a living wage lead to price increases and inflation? No! Within the context of moderate and stable profitability, the corporation does not have to raise prices if it pays its workers a living wage. Companies were making reasonable profits decades ago before they began outsourcing from Asia where workers are paid sub-human wages. Within the context of a democratic government that oversees and manages the economy and oversees and manages price increases, the corporation has no basis for raising prices as long as it is making a reasonable and fair profit

Raising the minimum wage to a living wage is actually good for the economy. Workers receiving more pay will turn around and spend that money, increasing demand which drives the economy. Balance and equity are the bases for a stable economy that benefits virtually everyone. Balance and equity imply moderation and the lack of extremes. Obviously, the concept and objective of maximization of profits is incompatible with a balanced economy. Christian economics theory supports and promotes the economic good of all, while radical capitalist economic theory supports and promotes the economic dominance of a select minority over the majority.

The US is one large corporation. It is a body of people working together for a common cause; the good of all people within the United States. The US economy is also a corporation. The states are corporations as well as cities and towns. Both public and private schools are corporations. Hospitals are corporations and businesses are corporations. States, cities, towns, schools, hospitals, and businesses are part of the US economic corporation and because of this need to be subordinate to the US economy as a corporation. What that means is that all corporations must support the US economic objective of satisfying in the most efficient and effective way the natural needs and desires of all 315 million Americans for safety, food, clothing, housing, a livelihood, education, healthcare, disability care, old age care, communication, recreation, entertainment, social interaction, acceptance and respect. Each corporation has as its indirect object the same objective of the US economic corporation. Each corporation has as its patriotic duty to support the objectives of the US economy. Since there are millions of corporations within the United States, it is necessary to coordinate these corporations by laws, regulations and government oversight to make sure that the overall objective of the US economic corporation is pursued and achieved.

Who owns the US economy or the US economic corporation? Who owns the United States? Who owns the state of California, the state of New York or the state of Texas? Who owns the city of Chicago? Who owns the Mayo clinic? Who owns the University of Georgia? Who owns Notre Dame University? Who owns Exxon-Mobil? Who owns Wal-Mart? Unfortunately, for hundreds if not thousands of years, there has been a social, political and economic fallacy that social organizations can be and are owned by one individual or a small group of individuals. Kings, emperors, tyrants, dictators, oligarchies, oligopolies, and politburos have denied the human rights of the equality of people and the right of people to govern themselves and have taken and take the position that societies belong to them and that the purpose of societies is to maximize the benefits to them. Kings, emperors, tyrants, dictators, oligarchies, oligopolies, and politburos have and do exploit people for their own selfish purposes. They hold that they are smarter and superior to everyone else and that either they have superior rights or that others have no rights at all. Kingdoms, empires, oligarchies, and plutocracies are morally wrong. They are morally wrong in spite of what history and literature has to say about them.

A common word used today is "exceptionalism". US politicians refer to the United States as exceptional, implying that the US is better than other countries. This idea is behind the foreign policies that see the US dominating virtually the world, because the US is exceptional and the rest of the world is not. Unfortunately, this is just another example of the wealthy elite, the power elite, acting to exploit others (not just individuals but whole countries) for their own selfish purposes and to maximize their wealth and power.

Up until the last few hundred years, the most prevalent political structures have been kingdoms, empires and oligopolies and there are still such structures today. Within kingdoms, empires and oligopolies; judges, academics and church leaders justified the politics, policies and actions of the ruling elite. They in turn taught everyone that what was done in the name of the king or emperor or ruling class was right and the military and police enforced a blind obedience to the commands, laws and philosophies of the ruling class. The people were not to question only to obey. This lasted for thousands of years and most history books and books of literature glorify the ruling class and the members of the ruling class. The same is true today. The news media glorifies the rich. Also, Christianity starting with the reign of Constantine took a more compromising position with the ruling class in order to avoid persecution. This cozy relationship with the ruling class by Christian leaders (leaders of Christian churches and organizations) generally led to Christian leaders remaining silent regarding the immorality of the ruling class in most cases. While kings and emperors attacked other countries in order to expand their kingdoms or empires and in the process tortured, raped, enslaved and killed even women and children; Christian leaders said nothing. While kings, emperors and oligopolies subjugated the people, ignored their rights, and totally ignored the principles of 'do good and avoid evil' and' love your neighbor as yourself'; Christian leaders said nothing. And the people, academics and historians naively took this silence to mean acceptance and endorsement of the exploits of the ruling class. How sad and how unfortunate! When will people start thinking for themselves and not blindly believing and following those who exploit them and those who support the exploiters?

The US economy, the United States, the state of California, the state of New York, the state of Texas, the city of Chicago, the Mayo clinic, the University of Georgia, Notre Dame University, Exxon-Mobil, and Wal-Mart are social organisms, that is, they are groups of people working and functioning together as a living body. Each person is like a cell within a body that functions both for its own good as well as for the entire body. As living bodies of people, each corporation is owned by the people comprising the corporation. Who owns the US economy? The people of the United States own the US economy. Who owns the United States? The people of the United States own the United States. Who owns the state of California, the state of New York or the state of Texas? The people of California own the state of California, the people of New York own the state of New York, and the people of Texas own the state of Texas. Who owns the city of Chicago? The people of the city of Chicago own the city of Chicago. Who owns the Mayo clinic? All of the people involved in the operation of the Mayo clinic own the Mayo clinic. Who owns the University of Georgia? All of the people involved in the operation of the University of Georgia own the University of Georgia as well as the people of Georgia. Who owns Notre Dame University? All of the people involved in the operation of Notre Dame University own Notre Dame University. Who owns Exxon-Mobil? All of the people involved in the operation of Exxon-Mobil own Exxon-Mobil. Who owns Wal-Mart? All of the people involved in the operation of the Wal-Mart own Wal-Mart.

Ownership involves rights, responsibilities, liabilities and benefits. Every person owns their self; their bodies, their thoughts, their speech, and their actions. Every person has rights, responsibilities, liabilities and benefits with respect to their bodies, their thoughts, their speech, and their actions. No one else and no other group of people can own the body, the thoughts, the speech and the actions of another person. A group of people joined together by a mutually agreed social contract can co-own the group's common ideas, communication and actions. In such a case, the group as a group has the rights, responsibilities, liabilities and benefits of the commonly owned ideas, communication and actions of the group. No one else and no other group of people can own the common ideas, communication or actions of another group.

This concept of ownership forms the basis of the United States, the US economy, the various states, cities, towns, non-profit organizations and for-profit organizations because they are all social organisms. Unfortunately, this concept of ownership is different from the concept of ownership that has continued from kingdoms, empires and oligopolies. This concept holds that one individual or a group of individuals can own a social organization or a social organism, even though this violates the rights of the individuals comprising or constituting the social organism. Of course this is the same fallacy that has existed for thousands of years and was used by kings, emperors and the ruling class to exploit the majority. And today there are academics, lawyers, judges, and others who support this fallacy despite the absurdity of this principle.

How could a king or emperor own an entire country; its economy, its land, its resources and its people? Certainly, the concept is absurd, yet this has existed for thousands of years. How can a few people own or control an entire country; its economy, its land, its resources and all or most of its people? From the very beginning of the United States, the US economy and government have been dominated and controlled by small group of people. Ignoring the true objective of the economy which is to satisfy in the most efficient and effective way the natural needs and desires of all Americans for safety, food, clothing, housing, a livelihood, education, healthcare, disability care, old age care, communication, recreation, entertainment, social interaction, acceptance and respect; this small group of people have manipulated the government (all branches and all levels), laws, the news media, and academics to enable themselves to amass great fortunes at the expense of the working majority. And yet most Americans are blind to all of this. People work hard thinking that someday they will get ahead financially but the vast majority of people never do. They live their entire lives struggling financially, living from pay check to pay check. And now these super-rich people who dominate and control the government and economy want to take away the few social safety nets that allow the majority of people to avoid abject poverty: social security, Medicare, and unemployment insurance.

One of the greatest fallacies and errors of modern economic and political times is the concept of a corporation. This concept has been developed and promoted by the ruling elite of the United States: those very rich individuals who dominate and control the US economy and government. This concept defines a corporation as an artificial person (an oxymoron) with legal rights and privileges and whose owners are immune from liabilities associated with the corporation. This concept is wrong for many reasons some of which show the concept to actually be absurd. One might challenge the claim that the above notion of a corporation is absurd given that the government, academia, the media, and almost everyone accept this notion as true. A response to such a challenge involves the moral tale by Hans Christian Andersen called the "Emperor's New Clothing." In this tale, two tailors run a scam on the emperor where they promise to make the emperor a splendid new set of clothing but instead steal the expensive yarn which they were given to sew the clothing. These tailors did not make any new clothing for the emperor but made the claim that the clothing was invisible to anyone who was stupid or incompetent. The emperor, his royal court, and almost all of the people dared not to claim that he the emperor was walking around in his underwear because none of them wanted to be considered stupid or incompetent based on the marketing of the two scam artist tailors. This tale parallels the development and promotion of the modern concept of a corporation as an artificial person with rights and privileges and whose owners are immune from liabilities associated with the corporation. The people who have developed and promoted this concept are like the tailors in the story. The US economy and the government are like the emperor. And the academics, the media, the judiciary, and the vast majority of Americans are like the royal court and people in the story. While the concept of an artificial person is absurd, no one dares to say so lest they be called stupid, incompetent and uneducated.

Another absurd aspect of this notion of corporation has to do with the corporation owner's immunity from liabilities associated with the corporation. The so-called owners of the corporation manage and direct the corporation. Because the owners want to maximize the profits of the corporations and because the corporation itself is amoral, the owners can and do often perform actions which impact the health and welfare of workers and consumers knowing that they are immune from the liabilities associated with such actions. Even though it is the deliberate actions of the owners which are the cause of the harm to the people affected, the laws hold them blameless. Unethical business practices, harmful drugs, dangerous or unsafe products and environmental pollution are some of the harmful actions which the owners of the corporation are immune from. Even though it is the action of the owner which causes the harm, the law considers the corporation not the owner as responsible. It is like a person with a glove who strikes another person and claims that it is the glove and not he who is responsible for the blow. The owner of the corporation is like the person wearing the glove and the glove is the corporation. It is truly absurd to consider the corporation defined as an artificial person to be responsible and liable rather than the owner even though the corporation cannot act on its own since it is inanimate and the actions of the corporation are in fact the actions of the owners. This safeguard from liability is the reason why the very rich developed and promoted this false notion of a corporation. These owners want the rights, privileges, and benefits of the corporation without the liabilities and responsibilities of the corporation. That is wrong. To purposely hide one's actions behind the corporation to prevent liability for the consequences of those actions is wrong.

The definition of a corporation needs to be changed and the laws surrounding corporations need to be changed as well. A corporation needs to be defined as a social organism, an organization of people (real people, living human beings) working together for personal, common and US economic objectives. The owners of the corporation are all those who enliven the organism, that is, those actively involved in managing, directing and operating the corporation. Owners can only be human beings. The owners of the corporation, as owners, must bear the responsibilities and liabilities of the corporation. The corporation needs to be chartered by the government in which it will operate and the charter needs to specify its purpose, its constitution, and how it elects its directors and managers. Changing the definition of a corporation and changing the laws affecting corporations is a critical component of restructuring and rebalancing the US economy and political system.

The Great Depression which started in approximately 1929 lasted twelve years and had devastating effects on the majority of Americans. The working class experienced extremely high levels of unemployment, homelessness, depression, suicide, high school dropout rates, divorce, malnutrition, and illness. The Great Depression—why did it happen? People wanted to consume, businesses wanted to sell, and companies wanted to produce. People wanted and needed to buy goods and services: food, clothing, housing, furniture, appliances, healthcare, transportation, etc. But they did not have the money to buy these things. They did not have the money to buy because they had either no income or a greatly reduced income. Companies wanted to manufacture. People wanted to work. There was no lack of natural resources. So, why did factories close? Why did stores close? Why did banks close? Why were people laid off from work? Why couldn't people find work? Why did so many people have to suffer, especially children and older people?

The primary cause of the Great Depression which started in 1929 and lasted for twelve years was the imbalanced distribution of wealth and income between the working class and the capitalist class. This imbalance was caused by the low tax rate for the upper income group, big corporations realizing enormous profits because of high prices and not sharing those profits with workers in terms of higher pay, unregulated lending, high interest rates, unregulated speculation in the stock and exchange markets, and the intentional and contrived movement of income and wealth away from the working class to a very select capitalist class. These same factors are the causes underlying the current economic environment?

One of the main principles of any national economy is the correct relationship between labor and capital. Labor and capital are partners in an efficient and effective economy, and their mutual respect and collaboration are critical to the proper functioning of the economy. Because labor and capital are equal and essential elements of an economy, they must share power equally, both economically and politically.

In order not to appear vague, perhaps it would be best to think of capitalists as the individuals comprising the top 1% of the income/asset hierarchy and labor as those individuals comprising the lower 99% of the income/asset hierarchy. Capitalists use capital to generate an income, while workers use their labor (physical, intellectual or both) to generate an income.

The basic dynamic of an economy is the continuous cycle of demand, production, sale, consumption. The economy is driven by consumption and jobs are created because of consumption. When consumption is down, jobs are lost. When consumption is up, jobs are created. Businesses only create jobs in response to demand or consumption, both forecasted and actual.

A production or productive system is any system that produces goods or services. There are obviously a wide range of such systems. Some of the more common productive systems are manufacturing organizations, distribution and sales organizations, banking organizations, construction organizations, entertainment organizations, educational organizations, consulting organizations, software organizations, telecommunication organizations and health care organizations.

There are two basic components to a productive system: capital and labor. Capital can either be land (and the natural resources on the land), buildings, equipment, material, intellectual property, technology or cash/funds which can be used to buy the necessary assets and materials required by the productive system. Labor provides the ideas, designs, philosophy, direction, management, physical work, etc. that is required to generate the goods and services which will be sold by the organization. Labor can be either intellectual or physical. By intellectual labor is meant creative activities such as designing, developing, planning, organizing, managing, writing, etc. Physical work covers a wide range of activities from those involved in manufacturing and construction to playing sports to singing and acting to speaking to teaching to nursing. In the initial or start up stages of the production system, the capital is provided by individuals or capitalists. After the production system is operating in a profitable mode, the capital is no longer provided by capitalists but rather is generated by the system or organization itself. This is a very important point to understand. After an organization is generating a profit on its own, the organization itself generates its own capital. For a corporation that has been in existence for a few years, virtually all of the land, equipment, materials, assets, and cash that it owns has been generated by the organization itself and the workers who were responsible for producing the goods and services which were sold to generate the capital used to either buy or pay off the loans on the property, equipment, materials and other assets. After the corporation has begun to generate capital, the initial capital provided by the capitalists is no longer relevant and the capitalist provides absolutely no contribution to the enterprise. Virtually all of the assets or capital of the vast majority of corporations is capital that was generated by the organization itself through the labor or the workers.

Production provides the goods and services that satisfy the demand of consumers. Production always seeks to match demand. Every planning function within an organization is continuously working to forecast demand and match capacity, production, procurement and inventory to forecasted demand. Increased consumption (which increases forecast) increases production; decreased consumption (which lowers forecast) lowers production. Production of goods and services comes essentially through the labor of the working class (the lower ninety-nine percent of the population) facilitated by capital from the capitalist class (the top one percent of the population) assuming the organization has not reached the point where the capital of the organization belongs to the organization itself. In this case the profits from this joint venture of labor and capital must be equitably shared between labor and capital, that is, between the capitalists and the workers.

The working class constitutes the majority percentage of the consumptive part of an economy. Given that consumption drives the economic cycle and that the working class is the major part of consumption, it follows that the economy is driven by the working class's consumption. However, the working class can only consume to the extent to which it is capable of buying goods and services. Since the working class is the main factor in both the production and consumption phases of the economic cycle, it must be given its fair share of the profits so that it can purchase and consume.

Unfortunately, what has happened and is happening is that the capitalist class has been taking far more than its fair share within the national production system. And because the total is limited, the more that the capitalist class has taken, the less there is for the working class. This has caused the great imbalance between capitalists and workers; the imbalance that is severely affecting the economy in a negative way as is seen in the high percentage of unemployed, under-employed, those living in poverty, homeless, and those living from paycheck to paycheck.

Over the past forty years, the wealth, financial stability and earning ability of the working class has significantly declined. Most working class families' assets have shrunk. Twenty-five percent of the US population have zero to negative net worth. Over a hundred million people in the United States live from pay check to pay check. Tens of millions of families have had to resort to excessive debt to operate financially and millions of these will suffer from the burden of their debt which will never allow them to retire. There are over 48 million people living in poverty within the United States.

Because of the great amount of income spent on debt and interest, because of the lag in wages behind real inflation, and because of out-of-control costs, especially energy, food and health care; consumption by the working class has been and continues to be reduced drastically. As consumption by the working class decreases, production which is driven by and is correlated to consumption proportionately decreases. When production is down, businesses react by laying-off workers to reduce operating expenses. Of course, when people are unemployed, they have even less money to spend. This in turn leads to even less spending by the working class which businesses respond to by laying off more workers. This downward trend will continue without end except for the total collapse of the economy unless something is done to stop it. The United States is now is this downward trend with nothing to stop it because those who can stop it are politically powerless to act and those with political power are in fact responsible for the imbalance between capital and labor that has created this broken economy.

The vast majority of elected officials represent primarily the capitalist class. This means that their primary focus with respect to administering, legislating, and adjudicating is to promote the welfare and goals of the capitalist class. It has been and is this biased representation that has led to the gross imbalance between capital and labor which is the cause of this continuing economic crisis. These elected officials ignore the fact that they have been elected by the people and are obligated to promote the welfare of the general public, not a very small, select and elite group within the population.

These elected officials, who represent the capitalist class, have allowed and facilitated a virtual attack by the capitalist class on the working class. While it would be more appropriate to consider this assault on the working class by the capitalist class as a war, it is a one-sided war in that the working class has done nothing to defend itself. And, it is a pre-emptive war.

Within the domestic area, the United States government has eliminated the proper controls which seek to maintain the appropriate balance between capital and labor. Within the foreign area, the United States government has promoted and is promoting a global empire for the capitalists.

At the heart of the capitalist campaign is the fallacy of free market economics. The fallacy hides behind the misleading term 'free'. Because everyone believes in and desires freedom, people blindly accept almost any concept that uses the word "free." While people want freedom, they do understand that there is no such thing as absolute freedom; freedom without any limits whatsoever. A person's freedom is limited by the freedom of every other person. In the United States, a person is free to drive down a highway. In its general sense, everyone will agree with that statement. At the same time, everyone understands and agrees that the freedom to drive down the highway is limited. Only people who have the ability and a license are free to drive down the highway. A person's freedom to drive down the highway is also limited by the other people using the highway. The government passes laws and enforces those laws in such a way as to maximize the freedom of everyone. Speed limits, stop signs, and traffic signals provide the necessary order to a free society of drivers.

The fallacy of free market economics lies in the assumption that there should be no restrictions, no regulations, and no oversight by government. It is similar to the idea that there should no speed limits, no traffic signals; everyone will naturally respect everyone else. While this would work for most people, it definitely would not work for everyone. There would be a small group of people who would not respect the rights and privileges of the rest of society but instead would take advantage of the lack of appropriate and agreed upon controls in order to capitalize on the situation for their own personal and selfish purposes. A free market with no rules, regulations or management is not a fair market, but a fair market is always a free market. A fair market is based on rules, regulations and management. To achieve a free market, it is first necessary to achieve a fair market.

There has to be government controls and government oversight within the economy in order to maximize the freedom and opportunity of all. There cannot be a free market in the sense promoted by the capitalists; a market without any regulations and controls. It is like a football game without any rules or referees. Rules bring order; without them there is chaos. The natural constraints on the economy come from a free and representative government: a government that represents the people; serves the will of the people and acts to regulate the economy so as to maximize the wealth and prosperity of all of the people. It is the role of the government to maintain the balance between capital and labor through regulations, supervision, and adjudication. If there is some aspect of the economy that is out of balance, the government must do what is necessary to restore balance. There is no other means of achieving and maintaining a balanced, efficient and effective economy than the government; the Federal, state, county and local governments.

The US economy consists of 315 million people, millions of goods and services, and hundreds of thousands of businesses all interacting constantly and continuously. There are billions of transactions and interactions between these economic entities occurring daily. The aggregation of all of these entities, interactions, and transactions constitute the economy of the United States. Can such a gigantic and complex system function efficiently and effectively without oversight, management, and regulation?

Imagine what would happen if one million people were gathered together for one year in a very small area without any direction, without any rules, without any laws, without any kind of supervision and without any management. What would happen? Would there be order or chaos? Would there be harmony or conflict? Would all of the interactions and transactions between the one million people be fair and balanced? Would everyone treat everyone else as equals? Would the vast majority of the one million people be happy? Order, harmony, equity, balance, respect, and happiness cannot come about without rules, laws, and supervision. These rules and laws and this supervision must come from an impartial third-party which the majority agrees to or selects through a fair election process. And this is what is called government.

An economic system cannot function efficiently and effectively without rules, laws, supervision and management. At the same time, there cannot be too many rules and laws or too much supervision and management. Micro-managing people and their activities are almost as bad as no management whatsoever. Rules, laws, supervision and management must be moderate not excessive—but rules, laws, supervision and management have to exist to achieve and maintain order, equity, efficiency and effectiveness. In addition, government should only manage by exception. Management by exception implies that action is only taken by management when there is an imbalance or something is not working. Applied to the government and the economy, the government should only take action when there is an imbalance or problem in the economy, otherwise it should allow the economy to function on its own.

Many of the factors that caused the Great Depression exist today, especially the unbalanced distribution of wealth and the lack of regulation of the financial industry. However, currently there are also many other factors undermining the efficient and effective functioning of the US economy that did not exist at the time of the Great Depression. The US economy is burdened by an enormous trade deficit caused by the imbalance between imports and exports and excessive government spending on foreign policy; military bases, military engagements, foreign aid, and intelligence operations. There are more and larger multi-national corporations today than at the time of the Great Depression and they exert a far greater influence on the US government than the corporations that existed at the time of the Great Depression. The aggregate effect of all of these factors have the potential to cause a much more severe and lengthy depression that the one that started in 1929 and severely impacted the majority of the population. In fact, these factors have the ability to totally ruin the United States economy.

Consider what would happen if the US economy was totally ruined? Most local and county governments would go bankrupt, and it is probable that the Federal government would also go bankrupt. As these governments go bankrupt, public and social services would be greatly reduced. Social security, Medicare, Medicaid, unemployment insurance and social services would either cease or be drastically reduced. Many if not most public institutions such as schools, hospitals, libraries, and parks would close. Those employed by the various levels of government would be laid off. Basic services such as police and fire protection, and sanitation services would be severely reduced. Private companies would take over these services and charge whatever prices that they want. The Federal government would have to significantly reduce the military.

The thousands of businesses whose major customer is the government would probably close. In a domino fashion, thousands of businesses would close and tens of millions of people would be out of work with no income whatsoever. Imagine unemployment at seventy percent. That would mean over 100 million people out of work. Imagine senior citizens who no longer receive social security payments every month (there are 65 million people on Social Security). Imagine people not having money to buy food, to pay their utilities, or to pay for their housing? Imagine students not being able to attend public schools because they were closed (there are 70 million students attending public schools). Could this happen? These things certainly could happen for the underlying factors that could bring about the collapse of the US economy exist, are operating today, and are increasing in their effect on the economy?

All economic systems involve consumption and production. Production generates goods and services which are consumed and or utilized through consumption. The economic cycle consists of continuous production and continuous consumption. The major economic systems within history have been capitalism, socialism, and communism. At the same time, the type of government that exists and operates along with the economic system (capitalism, socialism or communism) needs to be considered since the government and the economy are intimately related within a nation. The primary difference between capitalism, socialism, and communism as economic systems has to do with the ownership or control of property: land, natural resources, artificial resources (buildings, machinery, equipment, materials, energy, furniture, etc.) and intellectual concepts (theories, models, designs, formulations, recipes, music, artistic expressions, and literary expressions), human labor, human activities, and communication. All of these things are property.

In a purely communistic economy, the government owns and controls all property. The government owns and controls all of the land, all of the natural resources, all buildings, all machinery, all equipment, all materials, all energy, all furniture, all theories, all models, all formulations, all recipes, all music, all art, all literature—the state owns and controls everything even people. Because of the extreme nature of communism, the government that promotes and supports communism must be virtually totalitarian, that is, it must control every facet and activity of society. Communism is wrong because it denies the natural and personal rights of life, liberty and private ownership of property. Communism also denies the principle that the benefits of society received by a person should be proportionate to the contribution made by the person.

Radical capitalism or pure and total capitalism is completely opposite to communism. In a purely and totally capitalistic economy, all property is privately owned or controlled. All land is privately owned or controlled. There are no public forests, public forest preserves or public parks. All roads and streets are privately owned or controlled. There are no public highways whatsoever. All natural resources are privately owned or controlled. All trees, water, coal, ore, natural gas, petroleum, and chemical deposits are privately owned or controlled. There are no public lakes or rivers. Theoretically, even space and the air could be privately owned or controlled. All buildings, all machinery, all equipment, all materials, all energy, and all furniture are privately owned or controlled. There are no public buildings. There are no public schools. There are no public museums. All theories, models, designs, formulations, recipes, music, artistic expressions, literary expressions, manual labor and communication are privately owned or controlled. From a theoretical point of view, even human beings could be privately owned or controlled in a purely capitalistic economy. The government in a purely capitalistic economy provides virtually no public services. The military is privatized, law enforcement is privatized. There is no Social Security, no Medicare, no Medicaid, no unemployment security program.

Radical capitalism minimizes the role of government and makes governments virtually powerless. It is based on the false principle of 'survival of the fittest' and allows individuals to accumulate property without any limit or constraint. If further denies the universality of the human right to own private property and it denies the equality of human beings. Radical capitalism holds that private property should only be held by the most elite members of society and not by everyone.

Imagine a society in which everything was privately owned and controlled. There would be no public roads, no public services, no public education, no public fire protection, no public emergency services, and no public law enforcement. The person or persons who owned the water supplies, or the roads, or the schools or the police, or the fire services, etc. could choose to sell or not to sell water or access to roads, or access to schools, or access to police and fire protection services. That is because private property is considered an absolute in a purely capitalistic society. In a purely capitalistic society, private property is superior to all other rights. It should be obvious to everyone that natural resources (land, trees, water, coal, ore, natural gas, petroleum, chemical deposits, etc.) are limited—there is not an infinite supply. If one person or a small group of people own or control all or even the vast majority of natural resources, then the majority of people are subject to and dependent on the plutocratic minority for the necessities of life. The government in a purely and totally capitalistic society is controlled by the minority which owns the majority of property. Democracy and pure capitalism are completely incompatible for pure capitalism is based on inequality. The rights of those who own or control more property are greater than the rights of those who own little or no property. Uncontrolled capitalism as it moves towards absolute capitalism tends towards plutocracy as a government and plutonomy as an economic system with extreme economic disparity, very low social mobility (great difficulty in moving from the working class to the capitalist class), and economic slavery of the working class to the rich class. Like communist governments, plutocratic governments based on radical capitalism are also totalitarian.

The United States is not capitalistic. It is in fact partially socialistic and partly capitalistic. Public roads, public services, public buildings, public schools, libraries, veterans' services, Social Security, Medicare, unemployment insurance, workers compensation, police protection, fire protection, etc are all examples of socialism within the United States. However, there has been a movement in the United States over the last forty years which is trying to transform the economy from a hybrid socialistic-capitalistic one into a purely and totally capitalistic one. Most people in the United States have been led to believe that capitalism is good and both socialism and communism are bad. The only real way of measuring or evaluating an economic system is to look at the standard of living for the majority of people living within the system. Are public roads, public services, public buildings and public schools bad? The vast majority of Americans enjoy these services. Are public libraries a bad thing? Are healthcare for veterans, education and training benefits for veterans, home loan programs for veterans, and burial benefits for veterans bad things? Is social security which is government mandated old-age and disability insurance and which provides benefits to 63 million Americans a bad thing? Are Medicare, unemployment insurance or workers compensation bad things?

If the essence of a capitalist system is the private ownership and or control of the production system, then kingdoms and empires were capitalist systems since the production systems were owned and controlled by the king and his noblemen. Unfortunately, the economic life of the majority working class within kingdoms and empires was terrible. The king and his noblemen owned virtually everything including the lives of the people. The economy of the United States has always been based on capitalism. Yet, there have many periods in US history that show a complete failure of capitalism as measured by the majority working class; the age of the Robber barons and the Great Depression being the most infamous. The Great Recession of 2008 is another example. There have been 47 recessions since the founding of the United States. Recessions always have a significant impact on the working class. Recessions have been and are bad for the majority of people, but they are very good for a select minority. Many wealthy families owe their wealth to a recession.

Capitalism as an economic system in which the production system is owned and or controlled by private individuals does not necessarily bring about an economy which benefits the majority of the members of the nation. At least this is true when a relative minority of the population (perhaps one or two percent) own or control virtually the entire production system of the economy. It would be different if it was ninety-nine percent or more of the population which owned the production system. Within kingdoms and empires and throughout the history of the United States the production systems were owned and or controlled and are owned or controlled by a small and elite minority. The vast majority of the people have little to no ownership share whatsoever in the US production system and virtually no control over the US production system. While people do in fact comprise the production system and generate as output all of the goods and services that are available for consumption, the capitalists claim ownership of virtually everything. They look down on the working class and do not consider the worker as a partner or equal in the production system. As a result, the capitalists within kingdoms, empires, during the period of the Robber Barons and during the Great Depression took far more than their fair share of the profits of the production system and deprived the working class (which represented the majority of the population) of what was their fair share preventing them from being able to buy the goods and services which they needed and wanted and which was necessary to drive the economy. In order for capitalism to be effective, the private ownership of the production system needs to be as widespread as possible throughout the members of the nation. Capitalism, or private ownership of the production system, needs to be distributed throughout the entire population and not concentrated in the hands of a few.

This means that the ownership and control of the United States production system, the complex network of farms, factories, distribution centers, transportation carriers, stores, banks, hospitals, schools, etc, should not be concentrated in the hands of a small minority of individuals. No, instead the ownership of the United States production system needs to be distributed as much as possible throughout the entire population.

What is better for the economy ; one mega $400 billion corporation, with over 6100 stores or 6100 different corporations with average revenues of $66 million? ($400 billion divided by 6100)? What is better for the economy, one mega $370 billion corporation, Exxon-Mobil, with 22,000 stations or 22,000 corporations with average revenues of $17 million? What is better for the economy, one mega Bank of $140 billion, Citigroup, with over 5000 branches or 5000 independent, separate banks with an average of $28 million in annual revenue?

Giant corporations are financially more powerful than most countries. Virtually all large corporations dominate the marketplace, dominate consumers and dominate suppliers (and they also dominate the government). They have few competitors and through common goals and purpose, they form oligopolies that dictate price to both customers and suppliers and policies and laws to the government.

Things are tending towards the feudal situations of the Middle Ages and the coal mining towns in the 1800's where the corporation owned the mines and owned and ran the entire town. The company paid the employees in company money, which could only be used in company stores. The only homes that could be bought or rented were company homes. The only bank was the company bank. The police were company police. Employees and their families were vassals to the company. The United States is actually moving in the direction of pure and total capitalism : bridges, roads, schools, and services are being privatized. A significant percentage of the efforts in Iraq and Afghanistan have been privatized. There were more mercenaries in Iraq than US military. This privatization is not only extremely expensive, but it also reduces or eliminates public control and accountability to the people. Privatization of what rightly and naturally belongs to the people results in deprivation and injustice. For certain things must be shared by all of the people and not hoarded by a few. This movement towards total and absolute capitalism is the primary cause of the current economic crisis.

The current US economy is significantly out of balance and there are six main factors which reflect this imbalance that if not rectified soon will cause the current crisis to exceed the Great Depression in length and severity.

1. Unrestrained prices; primarily but not limited to energy, health care, education, and food
2. The ever-widening economic disparity between the top one percent of the population and the lower ninety-nine percent of the population that constitutes the working class
3. The increasing instability of the working class' ability to work and produce and the increasing rate at which workers are prevented from working at their full potential
4. The financial rape of the working class by an uncontrolled and out-of-control financial industry.
5. The continued failure of the US government to balance its budget and to cease borrowing money.
6. The enormous flow of money out of the US economy caused by the fantastic trade deficit, the excessive expenditures of the US government on foreign aid, military operations (the wars in Iraq, Afghanistan, and the maintenance of over eight hundred military bases/ located outside the United States) and the extensive operations of various governmental departments outside the United States. No economy can survive when such a large percentage of its GDP flows out of its system.

What needs to be done to reverse the current economic crisis and restore the proper balance to the United States economy? What needs to be done to restore the proper subordination within this nation, that is, the subordination of the government to the Will of the People? What follows are more details of the causes of the current economic crisis and the actions required to restore balance to the US economy and subordinate the government to the Will of the People and these actions are based on Christian economics. The application of Christian economics to the US economy is the solution to this current crisis that is affecting over 100 million people in the United States.

Origin of the Current Economic Crisis

THE MEDIAN HOUSEHOLD INCOME is approximately $57,000 a year. That means that half the families within the United States have gross incomes of less than $57,000 a year and net incomes of less than $42,500 a year after paying Federal tax, employment taxes, etc. This is $3,540 a month. Since there are approximately 126 million households, that means there are about 63 million families or between 150 million to 200 million individuals who fall into this income class. Most families who have a net income of less than $3,540 a month live from pay check to pay check. They have little to no money left over after paying their bills. If prices increase on the average by 3 percent a year and their incomes increase by a similar 3 percent, there is no problem. But if prices increase significantly more than their incomes, they are in trouble. There are also many families whose net incomes are greater than $42,500 a year who also live from pay check to pay check because of medical expenses related to unexpected medical reasons or because the families were spending money on education for their children.

Since 2000 the prices of basic necessities such food, clothing, electricity, heat, transportation, education and healthcare rose between 40 to 50 percent, while the average income rose about thirty percent. Food, electricity, heat, transportation and healthcare account for about 65 percent or more of the family budget for those whose net income is in the lower 50 percent of household incomes. Since these families were already living from pay check to pay check, they did not have any extra money or income to absorb these year over year increases in the prices of basic necessities. In order to survive financially and pay for these price increases, a significant number of these 58 million families used credit cards (and home equity loans if they were home owners) to bridge the difference between the higher expenses and their inadequate monthly net income.

Many families also refinanced their homes reducing their equity to pay for education and healthcare. This, of course, was only a temporary fix. Soon, their credit cards reached their limits, and they could not use credit to pay for basic necessities. Complicating their already desperate financial situation, once these families reached the limits on their credit cards, their interest rates increased as well as their monthly payments.

Since these families were already financially constrained, they now had to play the 'who should I pay' game. This was and is a strategy used by families (tens of millions of families) who do not have enough money to pay all of their monthly expenses. Because there was not enough money, these families were forced to pay their bills late and pay irregularly. Paying credit cards, auto loans, mortgages, utility bills, water bills, and phone bills late incur late fees. Late fees are a scheme used by businesses and municipalities to increase revenues and profits. Late fees can be significant (ranging from 5 to 10 percent) and when almost every expense involves a late fee, the family's monthly obligations, which already exceeded their income, increased significantly. And, now on top of the additional monthly expenditures because of the increases in the prices of basic necessities and increased credit card and home equity payments they suffered with higher interest rates and late fees which further worsened their financial situation. Besides the burden of continuing price increases which exceeded income increases, millions of people lost their jobs due to outsourcing from 2000 to 2008.

For millions of families in these situations (prices growing faster than income, loss of employment and reduction in income due to outsourcing), they reached a breaking point. What did these people do? They only way to financially survive, at least for a short period of time, was to stop paying their mortgage—their largest monthly expenditure. While these families could make partial payments on their mortgages, the mortgage companies did not allow partial payments preferring instead to foreclose and re-possess people's homes. And there was no one there to help these people.

Such is the origin of and main reason for the recession (now called the Great Recession) which started in 2008 and lasted for five years. And, what is most troubling is that this situation (though not as extreme as ten years ago) is continuing and expanding to more families due to job loss, continued price increases, and the vulturous policies of the credit card, finance and banking corporations. Student debt has tripled in the last ten years and is now over $1.4 trillion. Auto loan debt has doubled in the last ten years and is now $1.3 trillion. Home ownership is down 9 percent in the last ten years and rents are up twenty to twenty-five percent.

However, the news media has claimed that the cause of this 2008 Great Recession was sub-prime mortgages, mortgages given to families who could not afford to pay them. Obviously, the families who were given the so-called sub-prime mortgages were able to make the monthly payments at first. But then something happened so that they could not make their monthly mortgage payments. If families could not make their monthly payments, then that meant that they did not have enough money to make their mortgage payments! They did not have enough money to make their payments, because they either lost their jobs or prices on other essential items such as food, electricity, heat, gasoline and healthcare increased so significantly that they could not afford to make their mortgage payments. A family will always place food, electricity, heat and healthcare before their mortgage payment when spending money. And yet, the situation where these families were not making their mortgage payments was not the cause of the recession, but rather how the banks, mortgage companies and the government reacted to this situation (actually it was the lack of action on the part of the government which was the major contributing cause). The banks and mortgage companies did what they usually do and what is in their best financial interest and not what is in the best interest of the mortgagee or the economy. They foreclosed on these loans, millions upon millions of them. And the government; Federal, state, county and local did nothing. The table below shows the number of foreclosures in the United States from 2000 to 2011. The yearly increases from 2000 to 2006, especially the number of foreclosures in 2006 (1,200,000), should have been a gigantic red flag for George Bush, his administration and Congress; but yet they did nothing. And the number of foreclosures in 2009, 2010 and 2011 should have been a gigantic red flag for Barack Obama, his administration and Congress; but they also did nothing. What is even more amazing is the total number of foreclosures between 2000 and 2011, over 21 million. This should be considered within the context that there are approximately 45 million residential mortgages in the US. While some homes may have been foreclosed twice in that period, the numbers still show that over 45 percent of all residential mortgages received a foreclosure notice between 2000 and 2011. While some of the 21 million mortgages were sub-prime mortgages, the majority of them were not. These 21 million foreclosures resulted in 4.7 million home repossessions, approximately 10 percent of all residential mortgages.

Year	Foreclosures	Percent Increase
2011	3,900,000	3%
2010	3,800,000	9%
2009	3,500,000	17%
2008	3,000,000	36%
2007	2,200,000	83%
2006	1,200,000	50%
2005	800,000	25%
2004	640,000	-3%
2003	660,000	-6%
2002	700,000	30%
2001	540,000	15%
2000	470,000	
Total	21,410,000	

While George Bush did not notice the red flag of foreclosures in 2006, or at least he did not do anything about it, the banks certainly took notice. Banks had been bundling mortgages together to sell them to investors instead of holding on to these mortgages themselves. The money the banks received was used for other mortgages, which in turn were bundled and sold to other investors. These bundles of mortgages took on the aspect of investment products which were bought and sold and whose values were based on the risk associated with the mortgages themselves. As the number of foreclosures increased the value of these investment products decreased significantly and the banks were not able to continue to sell these bundles of mortgages because investors considered them poor investments since they assumed that the banks would have to repossess many of these foreclosed properties. These foreclosed mortgages were then revalued by the banks and were given the name of toxic assets. These so-called toxic assets made it appear as though the bank had lost a significant amount of money based on the assumption that the banks would lose money when they had to repossess the properties. When the shareholders in the banks saw these toxic assets on the banks' financial statements, they began to sell their shares of the bank stock because of lack of confidence in the banks. This caused a significant sell off of bank stocks driving down the price of shares of the banks. This led to the banks going to Henry Paulson, the Secretary of the Treasury under George Bush, who orchestrated the so-called bail out of the banks. Before and in spite of the bail out of the banks by the Federal government, banks restricted the money that they made available for business loans. Businesses were already impacted by a significant reduction in sales caused by all those people whose homes were in foreclosure or whose homes were repossessed not spending money on things other than necessities. With sales down and no money for expansions, businesses resorted to layoffs with over 8 million people losing their jobs between 2008 and 2010.

What happened to all of the people who lost their homes, that is, whose homes were repossessed? Some families became homeless. Some families became squatters in abandoned buildings. Many families had to move in to slum housing. Many families had to move in with relatives. Because their credit ratings were ruined, these families found it extremely difficult or impossible to move into an apartment because most landlords require a credit check and will not rent to someone with a low credit score. Did the mortgage companies care that people became homeless or squatters or were denied a lease? Not at all! The mortgage companies didn't care; all they are concerned about is maximizing their profits. They don't care about people or morals or anything else, they are only concerned about money.

What is amazing is that the mortgage companies are so blinded by their greed that they ended up losing significant amounts of money when in fact they did not have to. The mortgage companies could have changed the interest rates back to what they were when the families were able to make payments. The mortgage companies also could have worked out temporary payment plans with these families. Reducing the adjustable interest rates back to the original amount or working out special payment plans would have allowed the mortgage companies to continue to make money. Remember that the mortgage companies borrow money at one to two percent and loan it to borrowers at five to nine percent; their gross profit margins are between four and five hundred percent. If the mortgage companies were to charge three or four percent interest, they would still make a very good profit. Yet, the mortgage companies did not do either of these things. Instead, the mortgage companies forced foreclosures and repossessions and then had to sell the homes at significant losses. For those poor families who had variable rate mortgages and who could make payments at the original rate of interest before the reset or who could make partial payments were forced out of their homes. And the mortgage companies lost money by having to sell the home for less than they had invested in it. It was a lose-lose situation for the mortgage companies and the families who lost their homes—all because of the greed of the mortgage companies. The only winners are and have been those people and businesses that have been able to buy foreclosed homes for pennies on the dollar. It should be clear that the greed of the mortgage companies precipitated the Great Recession of 2008 and continues to undermine its long-term recovery.

What could have prevented the recession that started in 2008? When the first red flag appeared in 2006, George Bush could have and should have placed a moratorium on foreclosures and required the mortgage companies to provide five year loan modifications based on what the families could afford. If foreclosures ceased and therefore repossessions as well, there would have not been a financial crisis for the banks, there would not have been a sell-off of bank shares, there would not have been a bail out by the US government, 4.7 million families would not have lost their homes, 8 million people would not have lost their jobs and there would not have been a recession.

There are two results to the situations explained above; one is the housing crisis and the other is the general reduction in consumption by 150 to 200 million people. 150 to 200 million people represent one half to two-thirds of the US population. The continuing recession is being caused by 50 to 60 million families (between 150 and 200 million people) who are extremely constrained financially. These people would like to buy cars, appliances, clothes, entertainment, healthcare, education, etc. but cannot because they cannot afford to. Toxic assets, poor investments, and the other vague euphemisms cited by Bush and Obama as the causes of this economic crisis were and are totally wrong. And, the American public was led to believe that the money that was given as bailouts to the banks, insurance companies, auto companies, etc. somehow would trickle down to these 150 to 200 million financially desperate people. Trickle-down economics and corporate welfare does not work. And that is why the recession/stagnant economy continues ten years later.

The economy will not turn around until these 50 to 60 million families are helped out of their financial slavery and enabled to consume the goods and services which they need and desire. Positive and sustainable economic growth will not occur until this situation is corrected. For the economy is driven by the work and consumption of the people and not by the stock market. All of the investment in the world will not and cannot rebuild the economy unless that investment is in these people who are the basis and backbone of America.

PART I

Causes of the Current Economic Crisis

Pricing

AT THE BEGINNING OF 2000, the US national average for a gallon of gasoline was $1.25. Eight and a half years later, the national average was over $4.00 a gallon. That represents a 320% increase or an average of 38% per year. During this same period, food prices increased 40%, an average of almost 5% per year, while healthcare costs rose by approximately 35%, an average of 4% a year. In similar manners the prices of transportation, clothing, furniture, appliances, education, etc, rose far in excess of the 13% increase in household income during that same time period. Virtually every commodity traded on the various commodity exchanges experienced very significant price increases during that time. And while the price of gasoline dropped to an average of $3.60 a gallon in 2013 and $3.00 a gallon in 2018, the prices of most other things have continued to rise.

Because the economy is integrated, that is, the various elements are inter-connected with each other either directly or indirectly; an increase in one item such as petroleum causes corresponding price increases in most other goods and services. While minor increases are typically occurring and do not cause the economy to fall out of balance, significant increases as illustrated above cause severe disorder in the economy. The economy cannot absorb such extreme price increases because with every increase in prices there has to be a corresponding increase in wages to keep the economy in balance. These significant price increases which occurred between 2000 and 2008 were one of the causes of the Great Recession starting in 2008. It is obvious that such significant price increases are neither desirable nor beneficial to the economy. And yet they occurred. Why? They occurred because there are no controls on price increases. Corporations and markets can raise prices without warning, without limit, and without regard for the effect on the economy. Clearly, these elements of the economy, petroleum, food and healthcare, were out 'out of control' up to the Great Recession.

Christian economics holds that prices must be fair, both to buyer and to seller. Prices cannot be raised so high that it significantly impacts a person's or a family's ability to pay its other primary expenses. Sellers must sell goods and services at a reasonable price, that is, a price that covers operating expenses and allows for a modest profit. Unfortunately, most current economic theories focus on maximization of profits. The purpose and objective of the US economy is to satisfy in the most efficient and effective way the natural needs and desires of all Americans (all Americans and not just a privileged few) for food, clothing, housing, a livelihood, education, healthcare, disability care, old age care, communication, recreation/entertainment, social interaction, acceptance and respect. This objective can only be achieved within a balanced economic system. This balance needs to occur between suppliers and producers, and producers and consumers. In a complex economy, an attempt to maximize profits for one or a few organizations, causes an imbalance which if not corrected can have a domino effect. Maximizing profits for an organization by maximizing prices causes a minimization of buying potential for the consumer. This minimization of buying potential for the consumer results in the consumer not being able to buy other things or pay other expenses which impacts those organizations which provide those other goods and services.

Unfortunately, those current economic theories which promote the maximization of profits also promote the principal that corporations are artificial, and that morals do not apply to corporations 'it is neither right nor wrong, it is just business'. This principal is the basis for placing profits before employees, profits before suppliers, profits before consumers, profits before the good of the economy and profits before the good, health and safety of people.

Everyone needs to understand the implications of excessive price changes, either increases or decreases, on the economy. This should be discussed in schools, at business conferences, by the media, and within the various branches and levels of government. Price management within the context of a balanced economy is first of all the responsibility of businesses themselves. Businesses can and must control prices. However, like driving on a highway where there are speed limits, there needs to be guidelines and regulations regarding price changes.

One of the primary purposes of government is to maintain the appropriate balance between the various elements in society. There needs to be equity and balance between people: the different age groups, the different ethnic groups, and the different economic groups. Individuals, groups, the interactions between individuals and groups, and the interactions between groups all need to be kept in balance. There needs to be balance between individuals, between individuals and businesses, between businesses, and between industries. Balance implies equilibrium, parity and harmony; it does not imply subordination or domination. Balance does not imply equality but rather the absence of extremes and excesses.

Price management is a necessary tactic which must be used by the government to maintain balance and stability within an economy. The government must oversee and limit prices when necessary, for there are no natural limits to prices. Supply-demand theory does not apply to food, energy, healthcare, education and the other basic necessities in life. The dynamics and focus of the modern corporation is to maximize prices and eliminate anything and everything that would attempt to constrain pricing. The modern corporation, which is a construct and instrument of the capitalist class, has as its sole objective the maximization of profits. Maximization of profits comes from maximizing prices while at the same time minimizing costs and expenses (especially material, labor and taxes). In addition, the corporation considers itself to be absolutely amoral. It considers all of its actions as being neither right nor wrong, neither moral nor immoral. Corporations are totally indifferent to the reality that their products may result in injury or even death. They are only concerned regarding the potential expense that they may incur through lawsuits resulting from the deaths that have occurred. Corporations are also indifferent to working conditions that may result in loss of life, limb or health of their employees. They are only concerned about the potential liability resulting from lawsuits involving employee damages. Corporations are indifferent to the facts of people losing their homes, people declaring bankruptcy, or people losing their jobs through their direct actions. And the owners of the corporations hide behind these amoral corporations and calm their consciences by rationalizing that they are not responsible for the wrong-doings of the corporation. They look upon the corporation like a robot, guiltless because it has no conscience and because it is not a moral being. The modern corporation is like the Trojan horse. Outwardly, it appears to be a gift to society. But inwardly, it is filled with people intent on economic conquer and domination.

Corporations constantly seek to increase profits by raising prices or reducing costs (primarily labor, materials and taxes) or both. The CEO and the executive team all have significant monetary incentives to raise prices and reduce costs without limit. When the company achieves record profits, the CEO's next bonus is based on exceeding the record profits of the year before. The owners want more and more without limit—they want it all. Between 2000 and 2010 the oil oligopoly raised prices without any regard to the effect those price increases would have on the entire economy. They know that people need energy to drive to work and to heat or cool their homes. But they didn't care. For their sole aim was to maximize profits. Because they hide behind the amoral person of the 'corporation', they are indifferent concerning the economic hardships (and in some cases economic ruin) resulting from their extreme prices increases. Over the past forty years, US corporations have been reducing costs by outsourcing jobs to lower wage countries and countries which have poor safeguards for workers. First it was manufacturing jobs and then office jobs: customer service, call centers, helpdesks, accounts payables, accounts receivable, human resources, payroll, and engineering,

Significant price increases that wreak havoc on the economy can only be prevented by government over-sight and management of price increases. Of course, the idea of government price increase management is considered heresy by the capitalist class and the champions of capitalist economics. But price controls have worked in the past (during World War II) and they are the only means of preventing the economic disorder that caused the 2008 Recession. The idea is for the government to prevent significant price increases that impact the entire economy as well as monitor and regulate the basis for price increases. Besides preventing price increases which significantly impact the economy (national, state, and local), the various governments (Federal, state, county and local) must control the outsourcing of jobs. American corporations and American CEO's have a moral responsibility towards the people of the United States, all people.

Everything within an economy is related and inter-connected. For most goods and services, there is a series of suppliers, each connected to each other, most of which add value to the good or service as it is transformed from raw material to finished good or finished service. This series of suppliers is often referred to as the supply chain of the finished good or finished service. Obviously, the efficiency of the various supply chains is essential to the proper functioning and balance within the national, state and local economies. Supply chain efficiency results from collaboration among the various elements of the supply chain, the lack of domination of the supply chain by one or a few corporations and the prevention and elimination of any link that adds no value to the final product or service.

Over the past one hundred and fifty years there has developed a network of nodes within many supply chains that add absolutely no value whatsoever. They do however add price. These businesses function within commodity markets and trade commodities adding no value whatsoever to the commodities that they are trading. These so-called investors will buy commodities, yet never physically receive the commodity, nor store it, nor transport it, nor transform it in any way. Nor are these so-called investors even capable of physically receiving, storing, transporting or transforming the commodity that they buy. These so-called investors merely buy the commodity with the intention of selling it a short time later at a higher price and yielding a profit for themselves. From a supply chain efficiency point of view, from an economics point of view, and from the final consumer's point of view, these investors represent a gross inefficiency since they add no value yet increase price.

Commodity market trading is a major factor in the present economic situation that the United States is in. Commodity market traders are adding significant price to commodities and yet there are no controls whatsoever on their activities. Consider the various commodities which are traded and whose supply chains are impacted by non-value added activities and whose prices are higher than they should be because of these non-value added activities: corn, oats, rice, soybeans, rapeseed, wheat, milk, cocoa, coffee, cotton, sugar, frozen concentrated orange juice, hogs, cattle, sheep, chickens, electricity, crude oil, natural gas, heating oil, gasoline, propane, iron ore, aluminum, copper, lead, nickel, tin, zinc, scrap steel, lumber, gold, platinum, silver, rubber, wool, and others. How much is added to the price of food, the price of energy, the price of furniture, the price of appliances, and the price of cars because of the price manipulation caused by buying and selling these commodities without adding any value whatsoever to the commodity.

Again, the role of the government (Federal, state and local) is to manage, direct and regulate the economy so that the economy can most efficiently and effectively satisfy the needs and desires of all people for food, water, clothing, shelter, furniture, appliances, energy, transportation, education, healthcare, disability care, old age care, etc. The government is failing in its responsibility to supervise and manage the economy by failing to regulate the commodity markets and eliminate these non-value-added actions by investors. The government must regulate the marketplace for commodities. The government must require and enforce that any person, persons or business that wants to engage in buying and selling commodities of any kind whatsoever (crude oil, metals, grains, farm animals, etc.) must be capable of physically storing, handling and transporting the commodities that they will buy and sell in the quantities that they intend to buy and sell. Furthermore, every purchase must result in the physical possession of the commodity before it can be sold. The practice of individuals and businesses who buy and sell commodities without ever taking physical possession of the commodity is a serious problem within any economy. These individuals who engage in buying commodities with the only intention of selling those commodities at a higher price without adding any value constitute a serious economic disorder that needs to be corrected immediately. It has been claimed that forty to fifty percent of the price of crude oil is due entirely to so-called investors who add no value to the crude oil supply chain and are not even capable of adding value to the crude oil supply chain. And this is true for other commodities as well. There has been a global food crisis for the ten several years with high prices for rice, wheat and corn and the non-value-added activities of commodity investors is one of the main causes of this crisis.

The government; Federal, state and local, regulate who can engage in a business or profession. The government regulates who can practice medicine or dentistry, who can sell drugs, and who can practice law. Even electrical contracting, plumbing contracting, and the various building contracting professions are regulated by the government. The government will only allow a qualified person, persons or business that can perform the work according to industry standards, to engage in a particular enterprise. The government is fully within its power to regulate the commodities trading industry and require those people engaging in the buying and selling of commodities to be qualified, that is, capable of handling, storing, transforming or transporting the particular commodity, or adding some value to the commodity.

While commodity speculators were partly responsible for the significant rise in the price of oil from 2000 to 2008, the major oil companies themselves are mainly responsible for the extreme and disordered rise in oil that precipitated the recession. In the same period that oil prices saw significant increases, oil company profits saw corresponding significant increases. Profits represent the difference between sales and costs. Oil companies either produce petroleum from their own fields, produce petroleum from non-owned fields for which they have contracts, or they buy petroleum on long-term contracts. It is important to note that the oil companies, like any fiscally conscious company, seek to control their costs. To control their costs, oil companies will enter into long-term contracts with their suppliers to stabilize the costs of petroleum. Unfortunately, most people naively think that the oil companies are paying commodity market price for the oil that they use to produce gasoline. That is absolutely incorrect. The cost of crude oil for the major oil companies has remained relatively stable from 2000 to 2008. This should be clear from the fact that during that time they realized record profits. The extremely high profits that the oil companies realized were the result of extremely high prices, artificially manipulated by Big Oil, with relatively stable costs. Profit equals price less cost. Profits increased dramatically because prices increased dramatically while costs remained the same.

The price of gasoline in the United States is primarily the result of manipulation by Big Oil. Through a long-term campaign by capitalist economists in which people have been brainwashed to think that all prices are the result of 'supply and demand', through propaganda associated with commodity market trading, and through the subordination of the Federal government through its lobbying efforts; Big Oil is seeking to maximize its profits by maximizing the selling price of gasoline, diesel fuel, heating fuel, natural gas, propane, chemicals and all of the other derivatives of petroleum. And there is no one and nothing to control them. Big Oil has significant influence on the government (Federal, state, county and local). National energy policies, environmental policies and even foreign policies are dominated by Big Oil to the detriment of most of the US population.

What can be done to manage the price of gasoline, diesel fuel, heating fuel, natural gas, propane, chemicals and all the other various derivatives of petroleum which have a major and critical influence on the entire US economy?

First, gasoline, diesel fuel, heating fuel, natural gas, propane, chemicals and all the other various derivatives of petroleum need to be declared national strategic economic resources. National strategic economic resources have an extremely high influence on the entire economy. An increase in the price of a national strategic economic resource has a direct and immediate effect on the economy. Because of this, these resources must be carefully monitored by the government and price increases outside of defined limits must be reviewed and approved by the government. Next, the financial records for the last ten years of every US based oil company (as well as every oil company that does business in the US) need to be made public. What needs to be disclosed to the public is the cost that each oil company pays for a barrel of crude oil, the total amount of revenue generated by a barrel of oil and the amount of profit that the company makes on each barrel—all on a quarterly basis for the last ten years. It will be clear when the oil companies began to manipulate prices and deceive the public, it will be clear as to the extent of the profits that the oil companies have been making, and it will be clear that prices need to be managed.

Price management should not be limited to oil and its derivatives. While excessive and inordinate gasoline, diesel, heating fuel and natural gas prices have had perhaps a severe impact on the economy and the lives of most Americans, the prices of food, electricity and healthcare have also risen dramatically and inordinately within the past ten years. Like petroleum, these items are controlled by oligopolies that have manipulated their respective markets. Like petroleum, these industries are currently out of control and need immediate government intervention.

Was the price of gasoline at over $4.00 a gallon fair? In 2000 the price of gasoline was $1.25 a gallon and the oil companies were making a decent profit at this price? From 2000 to 2008 the price of gasoline increased about 18.5% per year and the profits for the oil companies increased proportionately. If the price of gasoline was subject to government oversight and could increase by only five percent a year during that time instead of 18.5%, then the current price of gas would have only risen to about $2.40 a gallon in 2008 and it would never have exceeded $4.00 a gallon. If the government limited the price increase of gasoline to five percent per year, the oil companies would still have seen their profits increasing considerably.

The Oil Companies do not want to sell gasoline at a fair price even though a fair price would generate a reasonable profit. The intent and focus of the oil companies is to maximize profits, which they can do primarily by maximizing price and minimizing costs and expenses. The owners and executives of the oil companies hide behind the cloak of the corporation, an amoral yet legal person. Whatever the owners and executives do, as long as it is in the name of the corporation, is neither right nor wrong as the common phrase 'it is neither right nor wrong, it is just business '. So, the oil companies are intent on maximizing profits and they are not constrained by morals. From the corporation's point of view, anything and everything is justified in seeking maximum profits. Wars have been started for the sole purpose of maximizing profits.

Will a corporation deceive consumers by presenting false and misleading information? Absolutely! Will a corporation manipulate the market? Absolutely! Will a corporation engage in unfair business practices in order to eliminate its competition ? Absolutely! The owners and executives of corporations deceive, manipulate and compete unfairly because they hold that it is not they, who deceive, manipulate and compete unfairly—it is the corporation that does so and what the corporation does is neither right nor wrong. Of course, this is wrong and immoral. Yet where is the Christian majority within the United States? Why are Christians silent to these things? Why in many cases are Christians actually engaging in these immoral actions? And why do so many Christians actually espouse the philosophy and principles of radical capitalist economics when it is at variance with Christian principles and the philosophy and principles of Christian economics?

Doesn't supply and demand control prices? Doesn't supply and demand drive all economics? Can't consumers reduce prices by lowering demand? No, no, no! Supply and demand without government oversight and management will not control prices. Supply and demand without government oversight and management does not drive all economics. And consumers do not have the ability to control prices in markets dominated by oligopolies and virtually all markets are controlled today by oligopolies.

What can consumers do to reduce the price of food? What can consumers do to reduce interest rates on mortgage loans, auto loans, or credit card loans? What can consumers do to reduce the amount that a doctor charges for a normal office visit? What can consumers do to reduce the costs of operations and other medical procedures? What can consumers do to reduce the cost of health insurance, auto insurance, or life insurance? What can consumers do to reduce the price of a college education ? What can consumers do to reduce the fees charged by lawyers? What can consumers do to reduce prices on goods or services that they require? Obviously, the answer to every one of these questions is 'nothing'. A person cannot stop eating. A person cannot stop going to the doctor. A person cannot avoid getting an education.

Capitalism is not a bad thing. In fact, capitalism is a good thing and necessary for the economy. It is the uncontrolled, inordinate, exaggerated, and radical form of capitalism that is bad and unfortunately, it is this variant of capitalism that controls the economy and the government today. It is this uncontrolled or 'out of control' capitalism that is the root of the severe problems affecting both the US economy and government today. And it is the modification of capitalism by Christian economic principles that is the solution to these problems.

The theory of supply and demand is the basis for the economics system of this radical form of capitalism. This economic system is a set of theories developed by capitalists for the exclusive benefit of capitalists. The main objective of this system is the domination of the working class by the capitalist class, the domination of the majority by the select few, and the perpetuation of this imbalance on to the end of time. Radical capitalist economics hold that the capitalist is superior to the worker, and the worker is subordinate to the capitalist. In fact, the worker is looked upon as somewhat less than human. This is clear based on how workers are classified within an organization. Workers are no longer considered as personnel (persons), but as resources (human resources) and capital (human capital)—things that are used and things that are owned.

The key theory of radical capitalist economics involves price, supply and demand. While economics is a social science, the theory attempts to establish the relationship between supply, demand and price as a scientific fact. It is amazing how extensive mathematical models have been used to try to demonstrate and prove this theory. The complexity of these models overwhelms students of economics who merely acquiesce and accept these theories out of a kind of religious faith rather than on the strength of their arguments. Underlying the capitalist theory on price, supply and demand; is the theory of maximization of profits. The capitalist theory on supply and demand promotes and supports the maximization of profits for businesses, companies and corporations and ignores the concept of maximizing the wealth of virtually everyone through economic balance and equity

Does price have to increase as demand increases? Does price have to increase in a captive market? The following example provides the answers.

The ABC bakery makes and sells bread. It operates successfully and generates an after tax net profit of fifteen percent. Because of good economic conditions, the bakery experiences an increase in customer demand. Because of this increase in demand, the bakery hires additional workers and buys new equipment. Because of increased demand, the bakery's sales have increased significantly. The increased sales have resulted in increased profits, yet its percent profit is still fifteen percent. Given the strong demand for bread, the bakery could increase prices in order to increase profits further, but, does it have to raise prices? The customers are happy. They are buying enough bread to satisfy their needs at a fair price. And the bakery is operating near capacity and making a good profit. What good to the customers would come from the bakery increasing the price of bread? Since the customers' income is limited, an increase in the price of bread will lead to either the customer buying less bread or having to buy less of some other items that they also need. If the customer buys less bread, then how is that good for the bakery and how is that good for the customer? Does price have to increase as demand increases? Certainly not! It is a deceit of radical capitalist economics to make people think that price has to increase as demand increases. Unfortunately, people accept this and end up being manipulated by radical capitalists into buying things at unfairly high prices—all because the radical capitalist wants to maximize profits.

The ABC bakery above is located in a rural area. Due to a family situation, the only other bakery in the area has closed and now there is no competition for ABC. The consumers in the area are within a captive market; they have no other choice but to buy bread from ABC bakery. ABC bakery makes a reasonable profit on the sale of bread. Since it is the only bakery in the area, it could charge significantly higher prices—but does it? Does ABC bakery have to charge higher prices for bread? Is there some economic principle that forces it to raise prices? Does price have to increase in a captive market? The answer to these questions is 'no'

Of course, it is true that businesses raise prices when demand increases and within captive markets. But they don't have to. Businesses see opportunities to increase their profit margins in these cases and they ignore what is fair and just. Is it fair to charge a person a higher price because there is high demand? Is it fair to charge a higher price when there is no other place to buy the item? Why are the prices for food so high at theme parks, sports stadiums and vacation towns? Why are rental property prices so high in college towns and vacation towns? Fair and just prices are prices which are fair to both company and consumer. The theory of supply and demand totally ignores what is just and actually helps businesses take advantage of consumers. Businesses hide behind this theory and consumers blindly accept unjust prices because of this theory.

Consumers and even some businesses (primarily small businesses) are powerless when it comes to unjust prices. There are three types of unjust prices: unfairly high prices, unfairly low prices, and extreme changes in prices.

The price of a good or service is unfairly high when it is grossly out of line with prices for comparable goods or services within the same market, and when it is out of line relative to the economy. Unfortunately, there are many markets which are now dominated by a few corporations. In some local markets there may only be one supplier. In these markets prices can be unjustly high because of collusion by these few dominant corporations to set high prices. While price fixing is illegal in the United States, the government virtually ignores the practice even though it is the responsibility of the government to prevent and eliminate unfairly high prices not only because such prices are unjust and harms the consumer or business which is forced to pay the unfair price but also because these unfair prices affect the economy.

It is estimated that there are over 140,000 convenience stores in the United States and the number is growing. Most gasoline stations and most pharmacy store chains such as CVS and Walgreens are also convenient stores. It is a known fact that prices at convenience stores are higher than the prices of comparable items at supermarkets. While it is not unjust to have a slightly higher price at a convenient store, it is unjust to have a significantly higher price. Consider as an example the price of a gallon of milk. If the average price at local supermarkets is $2.00 a gallon, what would a fair price be and what would an unfair price be at a convenience store? If a milk product that is comparable to the milk product that is sold at local supermarkets is sold at a convenient store for $2.20 a gallon, a 10 percent higher price, then that would not be considered unjust. But if that gallon of milk sold for $2.50 a gallon, a 25 percent higher price, then that would be considered unjust.

Besides convenience stores, vending machines are another instrument where businesses engage in unjust pricing. There are tens of millions of vending machines in the United States selling food, beverages, toys, toiletries and even cash (ATM machines). It is common knowledge that the prices for the products sold through these machines are extremely high compared to comparable products sold at local stores. Similar to convenient stores, it is not unjust if the prices for the items sold from vending machines are perhaps 10 percent higher than the average price for the comparable items sold at a local store. But it is unjust when these prices are more than 25 percent higher, and many prices in vending machines are actually 100 to 200 percent higher.

How many convenient stores and vending machines are owned and operated by Christians? With 75 percent of Americans claiming to be Christians, there has to be a significant number. Of course, these Christians are not bothered by the prices that they charge. Objectively, they would have to admit that their prices are significantly higher than the prices for comparable items at local stores. Yet, they don't want to admit that their prices are unjust and what they are doing is wrong. Why is that? They have allowed themselves to be misled and deceived by the philosophy and principles of amoral capitalist theories. These theories establish the corporation as an amoral intermediary between the business owner and the customer. Based on these theories, owners are immune legally and morally from actions that they engage in through the corporation. Christian business owners have blindly and naively accepted these theories and feel no guilt in what they do in the name of business even though it is objectively wrong.

The price of a good or service is unfairly low when the intent is to drive competition out of business and when it is grossly out of line with prices for comparable goods or services within the same market. Wal-Mart is notorious for pursuing a strategy of unfairly low pricing to eliminate the competition within the local, rural market. In small towns prior to the arrival of Wal-Mart, local businesses were primarily family-owned and operated and relatively small in size. In these towns there were a few pharmacies, clothing stores, furniture stores, hardware stores, and grocery stores. All of these businesses employed a few hundred people. Because these establishments were locally owned and operated, customers dealt with the business owners themselves and the profits from these locally owned businesses were mostly re-invested locally. Upon the arrival of Wal-Mart with their ruthlessly low, subsidized pricing strategy, customers naturally went to Wal-Mart instead of the local businesses. Because Wal-Mart was often selling at a loss which it could handle because of its financial reserves, the small businesses could not compete and eventually had to close. Once the majority of small, local businesses were eliminated, Walmart would increase prices because there was virtually no competition. The local economy and customers actually suffered from all of this. The pay and benefits of the average worker was less than that of the workers of the local, family-owned businesses. Customers coming in could not ask to talk to the owner, and the profits were not re-invested locally.

A similar strategy was used within the trucking industry in the 1980's after Ronald Reagan deregulated the trucking industry. Large carriers with significant cash reserves lowered prices to a point where they were not making money. Small carriers with little to no cash reserves could not lower their prices to compete with the large carriers. Their revenues suffered to the point where they could not continue operating and the large carriers bought them. After the industry was consolidated into a few large carriers who dominated the market, they raised their prices. There were many independent, small trucking companies that were family run. This strategy that was employed by the large trucking companies enabled by the deregulation of the industry destroyed tens of thousands of these small independent trucking companies and most of them want bankrupt. This was not good for these family-run businesses and it was not good for the economy. Today, forty years later the transportation industry is dominated by a few large carriers who maintain high prices and exploit the drivers who work for them.

It is another common practice by large corporations which want to grow through acquisitions of suppliers to increases their purchases from a supplier until they represent a very significant percentage of the supplier's business. Once that happens, the large corporation forces the supplier to reduce their prices often to a point where the supplier can no longer operate profitability. When this happens, the supplier is positioned for an easy take-over by the large corporation. Is such a practice fair? Certainly not!

A captive market is a situation in which a consumer is constrained by one or a few suppliers. Captive markets almost always involve unfair, unjust prices. Food and beverage prices within captive markets such as stadiums are unfairly high. While a hotdog at a small restaurant one block from a baseball stadium sells a hotdog for $1.50, the same hotdog costs $4.50 within the stadium. People are so captive within entertainment arenas, that private security guards check people's personal belongings for contraband food and drink. Food, beverages, and fuel at service facilities within tollway systems which are captive markets are unfairly high. Special events such as college football games, conventions, and special sporting events are also situations were temporary captive markets are artificially created where hotels, restaurants, transportation service providers and parking service providers raise prices to unjust and unfair levels. Once the event is over, the prices return to normal, fair levels.

Another example of a captive market that exists every day is last minute air travel. Many people are forced to make last minute plans to travel by air because of family emergencies or business necessities. The airlines know that they have a captive market with these people and charge unjustly high prices. Besides unjustly high prices for last minute travel, airlines charge change fees ($150 and up), luggage fees, standby fees and fees to get on the plane first. It is not the fees themselves which are unjust but the amount of the fees that are unjust. Airline now also charge a price difference between the original ticket price and the last-minute travel ticket price when a person wants to take an earlier flight on the same day as the original reservation even though there are open seats on the plane. The airline companies see an opportunity to literally get something for nothing (they are charging a fee and there is no cost on their part—it is 100% profit) and they feel no guilt in this. It is outrageous, but no one expresses outrage.

Gasoline stations raise prices before holidays knowing people are going to be travelling. They raise prices solely for the sake of profit, there is no other reason. Is that fair, is that just? It is not.

Businesses are also victims of unjust prices within captive markets. If there is only one supplier within an area from which the business has to purchase, the supplier usually sets unjustly high prices knowing that the business has no choice. Do businesses within captive markets have to charge unfairly high prices? Certainly not! Amoral capitalist economy theories support and encourage the practice of setting excessively high prices in captive markets. The owners of the corporations that do so don't care that these prices are unjust and counter to the objectives of the US economy.

Extreme changes in price (interest rates are prices) are very detrimental to a balanced economy and need to be prevented. Consumers and business customers cannot adjust to extreme price changes. From 2003 through 2008 the price of petroleum derivatives almost doubled. This extreme increase had a severe impact on the transportation industry, on virtually every industry relying on the transportation industry as well as on consumers. Consumers and businesses cannot adjust to such an extreme change in prices. The balance of the entire economy was altered because of the unjust, unfair, and sudden increase in the price of petroleum products. And this also has happened for steel, copper, rice, wheat and many other commodities. In order to be fair and have little to no impact on the economy, price changes need to be gradual and they need to correspond to the market's ability to adapt to such changes.

Stable and fair prices are certainly good for the economy, certainly good for consumers, and actually good for businesses. Price controls (upper and lower limits on price changes) are good for businesses in that they provide stability in planning and prevent ruthless competitors from trying to drive them out of business through unfair, subsidized prices. Unfortunately, fanatical capitalists will cry and scream about price oversight just like the school yard bully who is told that he can no longer bully people. They will employ propaganda campaigns and use tactics to scare people into thinking that price oversight is not good for consumers, not good for business and not good for the economy. But the opposite is true. Price oversight benefits 99 percent of the population. It is good for consumers, good for businesses and absolutely necessary for a stable, growing, efficient and effective economy.

It is clear that pricing can be unjust and unjust pricing as a business practice is widespread. Christian economics holds that pricing can be unjustly high, unjustly low, and that rapid changes in pricing can be unjust. And one of the most notorious practices of unjust pricing occurs within captive markets. Unfortunately, current amoral capitalistic economic theories support unjust prices (though these theories do not refer to them as unjust since everything done by a business is amoral, that is, it is neither right nor wrong, it is just business). Unjust prices violate two of the most basic principles of Christian economics: 'good is to be done and promoted, and evil is to be avoided' and 'love your neighbor as yourself'. When will Christians wake up and realize that the economic philosophy and principles that they are following are not Christian? Christians engaged in business must consider what they are doing in the context of Christian principles and not in the context of amoral capitalist principles. People in business actually cheat customers through unjust pricing but don't consider it cheating because capitalistic economic theories say that it is an acceptable business practice. It is not.

Is capitalism and Christianity compatible? Yes, they are—but not the form of capitalism prevalent today. Christians must be a light to the world, the business world, and help Christianize capitalism, its philosophy and its principles.

Interest, the Price of Money

MONEY, LIKE OTHER GOODS, is bought and sold. The price of money is called interest, though there are also other prices such as late fees, over-limit fees, special handling fees, etc. The price of money like all other goods and services can be unjust. There can be unfairly high interest rates and monetary fees, excessive interest rates and monetary fees within captive markets, and extreme shifts in interest rates and monetary fees—all of which negatively impact the economy.

Banks and other financial institutions borrow money from people, from other banks, and from other financial institutions. This price that the bank or other financial institution pays for money represents its cost, similar to the cost that a distributor pays for the goods that it sells. The bank or financial institution then sells the money that it has bought at a higher price generating a profit. The difference between the cost of money that the bank pays and the price that it sells the money for is called its gross profit. After subtracting its operating expenses, its marketing expenses, its general expenses and its administrative expenses; the remainder is called net profit. Subtracting taxes from net profit gives what is income for the bank or financial institution. Banks and financial institutions are corporations which currently have the sole goal of profit maximization within the context of current amoral capitalistic economic theories. Could banks and other corporations seek a maximum profit within the constraints of a Christian economics system where business actions are moral and subject to Christian principles? Certainly! Obviously, the profits would be maximized subject to moral and Christian constraints and would be less than the profits realized without any moral constraints whatsoever.

The price of money (interest) must be fair to both buyer and seller. The price of money (interest) must be the balance point between benefits to the buyer and benefits to the seller. In order for the price of money to be fair, it needs to be set within the context of all the costs and expenses within an individual's budget. Interest cannot be so high that it reduces an individual's ability to pay other necessary expenses. Nor can interest be extended out over such a long time that the individual is prevented from being able to retire.

The cost of money to a bank over the last 10 years, that is the price that a bank pays for money, has varied between zero and 2 percent, with the current price being approximately 1 percent. The current interest rates that consumers are paying for money that they are buying from banks and other financial institutions range from 4 to 600 percent. Mortgage rates range from 4 to 8 percent. Auto loans, furniture loans, and household goods loans range from 4 to 18 percent. Credit card loan rates range from 12 to 36 percent. Personal loan rates range from 20 to 600 hundred percent. All of these rates do not include the additional price of money associated with late fees, over-limit fees, loan origination fees, special handling fees, etc.

The financial institutions are paying 1 percent for money that they are buying and then turning around and selling that money for 6 percent, 12 percent, 24 percent, 36 percent, and even 600 percent. Since banks and financial institutions operate with little expenses and overhead, the profit margin that they are realizing is immense. Many consumers are being financially crushed by these exceedingly high and unfair interest rates and enslaved by the terms of the unjust contracts that they are coerced into. Consider the rapid growth and prevalence of payday loans stores, title loan stores and personal loan stores. 25% of the people in the US have negative or zero wealth, that is, their liabilities (what they owe) exceed their assets (what they own). 25% of the US population equals approximately 79 million people. These 79 million people struggle financially. And millions of these people are prey to the unjust interest rates of payday loans stores, title loan stores and personal loan stores. Many credit card interest rates are also unjust. In fact, it is doubtful whether any interest rate in excess of 12 percent can be justified as moral and certainly not in conformance with Christian principles. Many home owners are now trapped in mortgage contracts with high interest rates and are not able to refinance because of the restrictions by the banks. In fact, the vast majority of people who have had their homes repossessed lost their homes because the banks would not allow modifications to their loans?

Why are most interest rates and loan contracts unfair? Most interest rates and contracts are unfair because there is no balance between the benefits to the consumer and the benefits to the financial institutions. The economy thrives on consumption; the consumption of the 315 million people comprising the working class and not the consumption of the minority capitalist class. Anything that constrains or limits the ability of the working class to buy homes, buy cars, buy furniture, buy appliances, buy food, buy healthcare, buy an education, or buy any other goods and services constrains, limits and reduces the activity of and the growth of the economy. If the constraints on the working classes' ability to consume are great enough (as they are today), then there is minimal growth in the economy.

Most people think that inflation, an aggregation of price changes, can be controlled by the Federal Reserve System controlling the price of money to its member banks. That is not true. Only by government oversight and management can prices and inflation be controlled. Price management and interest rate management are first of all the responsibility of the owners of the businesses and banks. They have an obligation to the other members of the US economy not to set prices which are unjust and harmful to the economy. Of course, while most people will act responsibly, there are always people who will not. That is why the various levels of government through consumer protection agencies and the court systems need to oversee pricing and interest rates and correct unjustly high, unjustly low and extremely volatile prices and interest rates including the interest rates of the Federal Reserve Corporation. The various interest rates of the FED must have limits and sudden and extreme changes must be controlled.

Banks, mortgage companies and all other financial institutions also pursue a strategy of price maximization within virtually all markets through the deceptive practice of pseudo-risk. Banks, mortgage companies, and financial institutions use pseudo-risk to increase the interest rate or price of money both on new loans as well as existing loans? While there is a correct notion of risk which can be used as a basis for charging a slightly higher rate of interest, the current practice of assessing risk is unjust because it exaggerates risk for the sole purpose of charging a higher rate of interest, and in many cases a significantly higher rate of interest. Again, while objectively unjust, the individuals engaged in this practice or scam (for all practical purposes, it is a scam) do not consider it unjust since current economic theories hold that business practices and actions are amoral, that is, they are neither right nor wrong. But is should be clear that these practices are both unjust and un-Christian (contrary to Christian principles).

The current means of assessing risk is based on the credit ratings of the major credit bureaus and there are serious problems both with the scoring process and the credit bureaus themselves. There are four major national credit bureaus in the United States that allegedly measure a person's credit worthiness: Equifax, Experian, and Trans Union and Innovis. These organizations are for-profit businesses that have a most significant effect on the ability of a person to borrow money and the interest rate that a person will be charged. In fact, these organizations have an almost absolute authority in deciding who will and who will not receive financing and at what rate since virtually every financial institution will make their decision to lend money, at what rate and when to raise interest rates all based on a person's credit score from one of these credit bureaus. Clearly, these organizations are extremely powerful from a business point of view since they enable a financial organization to avoid potentially risky borrowers and also to increase profits by maximizing interest rates, loan fees and late fees.

These credit bureaus receive the vast majority of their revenues from financial institutions. Obviously, the biggest financial institutions are the largest customers for the credit bureaus. The credit bureaus want to make their customers happy. And the big financial institutions want to maximize profits. Financial institutions have been able to significantly increase profits by charging an excessively high rate of interest to a borrower because of the borrower's credit score and through the tactic of raising the interest rate on an existing loan simply because a person's credit score has changed.

While the process of evaluating a person's credit worthiness can be objective and statistical, it is not. The basis used by the credit bureaus for assessing and changing a person's credit score is mostly subjective heuristics or rules that they have developed to suit their goals. Of course, the primary goal of the credit bureaus is maximization of profits and since their profits come from financial institutions their strategy is to please the financial institutions by providing credit scores that maximize profits for the financial institutions. Credit scores can and should be based strictly on statistics. However, the credit bureaus do not want to rely on statistics to rate a person's ability to pay since that would reduce the interest rates that their customers, the big financial institutions, can charge. And they want to keep their customers happy.

Credit scores should be statistically based and calculated by organizations that have no profit motive. A credit bureau must be independent and objective, fair and impartial. For-profit credit bureaus are neither independent nor objective nor fair nor impartial since they are in business to make a profit and they make their money from the financial institutions. They are clearly biased in favor of Big Finance. The only way to achieve independent, objective, fair and impartial credit ratings is to have the government take over the task of determining a person's credit worthiness. For-profit organizations should not be allowed to provide credit ratings. These biased credit bureaus are also partially responsible for the current economic crisis since they have enabled Big Finance to raise interest rates and finance fees to the point where millions of people are severely constrained financially. Severely constrained consumers cannot consume.

Credit scores are meant to indicate a person's credit-worthiness or ability to pay off a current or a new loan. A person's ability to make payments on loans is based on both controllable and uncontrollable factors and these factors may be very temporary or extend for a longer period of time. A true credit score will estimate the risk to the finance company regarding the probability that a person will totally default on a loan. Total default means never, ever paying back the loan. If a person is unable to temporarily make payments on a loan because of unemployment, under-employment or illness that does not mean that they are in default. Unfortunately, finance companies are very quick to declare a person in default even though in fact they are not. Credit scores attempt to predict the future and there are many, many variables that need to be considered when estimating a person's ability to pay. However, the credit bureaus do not take all variables into consideration.

If a person loses their job, it can take anywhere from four to nine months before they are able to gain comparable employment assuming a relatively stable economy. During this time the person is not able to pay all their bills. It should be clear that this period of unemployment and inability to pay bills is only temporary. However, finance companies do not care. They assume that the person's inability to pay their bills is permanent. This is also the case for the credit bureaus. While it would make most sense to allow the unemployed person a deferment in their financial obligations, finance companies have no mercy whatsoever; they are only concerned about profits. As soon as the person pays late, they assess a late fee. If a person pays late two or three times, the finance company will significantly increase the interest rate. If the person fails to make payments for three or four months, the finance company begins a harassment program where they call the person dozens of times a day from eight o'clock in the morning to nine o'clock at night seven days a week. And since the person is unemployed and not able to pay, there is nothing that they can do. The finance company will only pursue the person for a month or two before they consider them in default. By that time the amount that the person has borrowed has increased significantly into the debt owed to the finance company.

Consider a person who has a credit card with a $1000 limit who has temporarily lost their job. Because of late fees, over-limit fees and excessively high interest rates (32%), the $1000 that they borrowed has doubled into a debt of $2,111.32 within 11 months. And even after the finance company declares the debt in default and totally ruins the person's credit, they sell the debt to a collection company which ruthlessly and relentlessly pursues the individual even to court in order to collect the debt more than half of which is interest and fees. Even if the person obtains employment in month 11, it is too late. The wheels of Big Finance have moved and crushed the person. This must also be viewed within the context of multiple accounts all of which could double the person's debt obligations. And now the person who became unemployed through no fault of their own and has struggled financially through eleven months of unemployment is faced with almost insurmountable debt and a dismal credit score.

INTEREST, THE PRICE OF MONEY

Month	Late Fee	Over-Limit Fee	Interest	Total Price for Money	Total Price as Percent
1	$30.00	$30.00	$28.27	$88.27	105.9%
2	$30.00	$30.00	$30.62	$90.62	108.7%
3	$30.00	$30.00	$33.04	$93.04	111.6%
4	$30.00	$30.00	$35.52	$95.52	114.6%
5	$30.00	$30.00	$38.07	$98.07	117.7%
6	$30.00	$30.00	$40.68	$100.68	120.8%
7	$30.00	$30.00	$43.37	$103.37	124.0%
8	$30.00	$30.00	$46.12	$106.12	127.3%
9	$30.00	$30.00	$48.95	$108.95	130.7%
10	$30.00	$30.00	$51.86	$111.86	134.2%
11	$30.00	$30.00	$54.84	$114.84	137.8%

This unfortunate person is now severely constrained financially even though he or she is now employed. Once they begin to make payments, they still have to pay over-limit fees in addition to the excessively high interest rates and that situation will continue for years. Also, they are now labeled by the credit bureaus as unworthy of any credit, they cannot consolidate their debt and they struggle if they can to pay all their debt most of which is interest and fees. And this scarlet letter of 'unworthy of credit' remains with them for the next seven years. Unfortunately, the government does not step in to help these unfortunate individuals, tens of millions of them and their families. But these severely financially constrained families have a significant effect on the economy. They cannot buy the goods and services which they need and want because they do not have any money left over after paying all their debt. This situation applies to the majority of the unemployed, the under-employed, those without health insurance who have experienced a major illness and many of those who have gone through divorce—tens upon tens of millions of individuals and families. And the aggregate effect of their significantly constrained consumption undermines the stability of the economy.

Virtually all credit scores are affected adversely by late payments. However, late payments do not indicate a failure to pay or even the potential for default. In other words, there is no risk associated with late payments. People who pay late obviously have a problem with their cash flow, not with their ability or intention to pay. Credit scores must distinguish between default and late payments. It does happen that a person gets a few months behind in making his or her payments. The credit card company cancels the account and sells the loan to a collection agency. The person subsequently pays the loan in full but his or her credit report shows a default from the over-zealous credit company who pre-maturely declared the account uncollectible. Credit scores are also based on the number of times a credit check is run. There is no basis for lowering a person's credit score because of the number of credit checks done.

Credit bureaus also unjustly penalize spouses, children and others who have been given a secondary credit card on another person's account. For example, an individual has a credit card account and wants to allow his or her daughter or son to have a credit card on this account. This card is actually a convenience card since the parent would typically allow their daughter or son to use their card. The credit account is solely the responsibility of the parent and the credit was based entirely on the parent's creditworthiness. If the parent's credit score decreases, the credit agencies will also decrease the credit score for the daughter or son who has the convenience card even though the daughter or son has nothing to do with the account. This makes absolutely no sense other than to the financial institution from which the son or daughter may go to some day in order to take out a loan or credit card on their own creditworthiness. This is a most unjust practice.

Credit scores are also based on past bankruptcies, foreclosures (even though there is no repossession), collections, tax liens, and periods of unemployment. These supposedly negative factors can be considered for up to seven or more years. That means that a person who has recovered financially and has paid all of his or her debts, is treated like a financial convict even though they have not defaulted on their obligations and have only paid late. Is this just? No! Is this good for the individual? No! Is this good for economy? No, because the individual is constrained financially from buying the goods and services that he or she needs and which the economy needs for stability and growth. However, this is good for financial corporations, since they can charge much higher interest rates based on these incorrect credit scores.

Finance companies use these inaccurate credit scores to increase interest rates even in the case when the poor credit score was the result of late payments to another finance company. In the event that the poor credit score was the result of late payments, there is no risk to the lender and no basis for raising the interest rate. A person with poor cash flow, who is punished by the various finance companies with higher interest rates, will experience even greater cash flow problems. Many situations of loan defaults are the direct result of these policies of increasing interest rates to the point where the borrower is ruined financially. These unfair practices need to be immediately eliminated by the government. Again, the only way to achieve independent, objective, fair and impartial credit ratings is to have the government take over the task of determining a person's credit worthiness.

Late fees, over-limit fees, and over-draft fees represent other prices of money that are unjust and very detrimental to the economy. These are relatively recent schemes by Big Finance to maximize profits. If a person makes a payment late or after the due date, the interest is calculated up to the actual payment date. In other words, the finance company is already charging a person for paying late. Depending on the amount owed and interest rate, late fees can represent a doubling of the interest or price one is paying for borrowing money. While a late fee is a price one has to pay for the use of money just as interest is, financial institutions use the expression 'late fee' to avoid any possible legal restriction on the rate of interest. Over-limit fees are another price of money that is totally arbitrary. In general, a person should not be able to exceed their credit limit since the limit is monitored through electronic transactions. In the vast majority of cases a person who has reached their credit limit can exceed it when interest accrues or a late fee is assessed. Again, there is no just or moral reason to charge an over-limit fee. Often times a person is charged both a late fee and an over-limit fee. This is especially true when a person is unemployed, under-employed, not working due to health reasons or going through or having gone through a divorce. In such cases late fees, over-limit fees and interest can amount to over 100%.

The average household has over $16,000 in credit card debt. Besides bank credit cards, there are retail credit cards from clothing stores, retail credit cards from gasoline companies, credit cards from schools; almost every business wants to sell a person a credit card. The expression 'finance company' applies not just to corporations that engage in just finance but also to retail corporations, airlines corporations, academic institutions, and others. The basic strategy of these financial institutions is to create perpetual annuities. They want a steady, continuous stream of money coming in from debtors who will pay for the rest of their lives. From the borrower's point of view, this is financial slavery with no opportunity of ever escaping. What is most alarming about this is the fact that this applies to the majority of the population—over fifty percent of the population. And the impact on the economy is obvious. With more than fifty percent of the population enslaved by ruthless financial institutions, these people have little to no discretionary income. They cannot buy more goods and services which they want and need because they cannot afford to. And the economy is driven by this consumption.

INTEREST, THE PRICE OF MONEY

Amount Borrowed	Interest Rate	Term (years)	Total Amount Paid	Total Interest	Monthly Interest
$2,500	18%	10	$5,406	$2,906	$24.21
$2,500	22%	10	$6,201	$3,7011	$30.84
$2,500	24%	10	$6,614	$4,114	$34.29
$2,500	26%	10	$7,037	$4,537	$37.81
$2,500	30%	10	$7,909	$5,409	$45.07
$2,500	32%	10	$8,355	$5,855	$48.79
$5,000	18%	10	$10,811	$5,811	$48.43
$5,000	22%	10	$12,402	$7,402	$61.68
$5,000	24%	10	$13,229	$8,22	$68.57
$5,000	26%	10	$14,075	$9,075	$75.62
$5,000	30%	10	$15,817	$10,817	$90.14
$5,000	32%	10	$16,710	$11,710	$97.59
$10,000	18%	10	$21,622	$11,622	$96.85
$10,000	22%	10	$24,804	$14,804	$123.36
$10,000	24%	10	$26,458	$16,458	$137.15
$10,000	26%	10	$28,150	$18,150	$151.25
$10,000	30%	10	$31,634	$21,634	$180.28
$10,000	32%	10	$33,421	$23,421	$195.17
$12,500	18%	10	$27,028	$14,528	$121.06
$12,500	22%	10	$31,005	$18,505	$154.20
$12,500	24%	10	$33,072	$20,572	$171.43
$12,500	26%	10	$35,187	$22,687	$189.06
$12,500	30%	10	$39,543	$27,043	$225.36
$12,500	32%	10	$41,776	$29,276	$243.96
$15,000	18%	10	$32,433	$17,433	$145.28
$15,000	22%	10	$37,205	$22,205	$185.05
$15,000	24%	10	$39,687	$24,687	$205.72
$15,000	26%	10	$42,224	$27,224	$226.87
$15,000	30%	10	$47,451	$32,451	$270.43
$15,000	32%	10	$50,131	$35,131	$292.76

The prices of goods, services and money are totally out of control. Pricing needs to be fair. Radical capitalist economics ignores the principle that pricing should be fair and instead holds that prices (from the view point of the business) should be maximized. Common are the phrases 'let the buyer beware' and 'whatever the market will bear', both of which underscore the capitalist view on pricing. However, the economy consists of both buyers and sellers, and economic stability is based on the proper balance between buyer benefits and seller benefits. Fairness to both buyer and seller is essential and critical for an ordered and just economy.

There are no moral constraints on prices because people in business follow the current amoral economic theories. There are no market constraints on prices, because consumers have no influence on prices. There are virtually no controls on businesses especially big corporations. Even the laws and the courts favor the seller over the buyer. Businesses can charge whatever price they want and the consumer is forced to pay it. False is the proposition that the consumer does not have to buy. The consumer has to eat, the consumer has to have heat in the winter, the consumer has to have electricity, the consumer has to go to work, the consumer has to seek healthcare when they are sick or injured.

Consumers are at the mercy of Big Business and Big Finance, yet Big Business and Big Finance are merciless. The economy is out of order and out of balance because of these prices. Is there not someone or something that can bring prices back into control? Is there not someone or something that can bring fairness and justice to prices? Is there not someone or something that can save the majority of Americans from financial hardship and perhaps a hundred million Americans from financial ruin because of these prices?

If Christians applied Christian principles to their business lives and helped modify the strategies and policies of the businesses that they own or work for in such a way that justice and morality is factored into every business decision and action, then most of the prices of goods, services and money would become just and fair. Unfortunately, not all people will accept the principle of just and moral business practices. So, besides Christians bringing Christian principles to business, it is necessary for the government to oversee prices. The government needs to help the economy realize it's objective of satisfying the needs and desires of all people for the basic necessities in life through price oversight and price management. The majority of people have no problem with police officers. The majority of people have no problem with traffic signals or traffic laws. The majority of people have no problems with laws which regulate people's extreme and unsafe behavior. The majority of people have no problem with government oversight of the practice of medicine, law, electrical work, plumbing, etc. The government controls how fast a person can drive, how much alcohol a person can consume, and how much a truck can weigh. The vast majority of people, the 315 million working class people, would have no problem with government oversight and management of prices. Obviously, the wealthy minority would do all in their power to prevent this from happening. In spite of the denial by the wealthy minority, government oversight and management of prices is good and essential for a balanced, equitable, and growing economy which benefits all Americans.

Balance and justice need to be restored to the economy, and Christians are probably the only ones capable of bringing this about through the practice of Christian economics. Christians should no longer compromise their principles and follow the current amoral economic theories which are the causes of the current economic and political crises. Christians need to be Christians in their public lives; their economic, business and political lives.

The Distribution of Wealth

THE UNITED STATES ECONOMY is a corporation of over 318 million people. This corporation has as its purpose and objective to satisfy in the most efficient and effective way the natural needs and desires of all Americans for food, clothing, housing, a livelihood, education, healthcare, disability care, old age care, recreation, entertainment, social interaction, acceptance and respect. Happiness for the majority of people is simple. A person who has enough food and water, has clothing, has shelter, has furniture, has appliances, has energy, has transportation, has the means of communicating, is educated, has healthcare, has disability insurance, has unemployment insurance, has old age insurance, has the opportunity to rest and recreate, has the ability to interact socially, and has respect from others for their rights and dignity—he or she is happy.

Unfortunately, the US economy is failing to achieve its objective. There are tens of millions of people who in spite of working very hard are lacking basic necessities. They lack these necessities because they do not have sufficient income and wealth for them. Most working people have seen their effective income decrease and their wealth decrease as well. Over 79 million people in the US have negative or zero wealth. The purpose of the government of the United States is to coordinate and regulate the activities of its citizens with the goal of supporting and facilitating life, liberty and the pursuit of happiness for all people. The government's role in coordinating and regulating the activities of its citizens certainly extends to economics.

The economic system of the United States is a complex network of people, activities and interactions. People have basic needs to support life. People need food and those things necessary for hygiene. People need a place to live which includes furniture, appliances, electricity, heat and air conditioning. People need clothing and footwear. People need healthcare. People need disability care. People need help when they are unemployed.

People need help when they are old. People need transportation. People need things to communicate with other people. People need things and services for their leisure. People need to be educated. People need to be entertained. In isolation, a person would have to provide all of the above on his or her own. Within a society of over 318 million people, different people perform different functions to provide for the goods and services needed and desired by all. This is called specialization of labor. Both the good of the individual and the good of the economy are based on the specialization of labor.

In general, all people are consumers and suppliers. Suppliers produce the goods and services demanded by consumers. Goods and services are produced by workers supported by capital provided either from investors, from financial institutions through loans, or through the retained earnings of the business itself. (For existing companies, all capital has been provided through either loans or retained earnings.) Investors, or capitalists, are partners with the workers in providing the goods and services to be consumed or utilized by the consumer or end-user. The sale-purchase transaction involves an exchange between the supplier and the consumer or end-user. Originally, the exchange involved goods being exchanged for goods, services being exchanged for services or a mix of the two. This kind of business transaction still exists today but is not very prevalent. The prevailing kind of business transaction involves the exchange of a good or service for money, which is a medium of exchange, that is, it makes transactions more convenient.

Demand, which is the desire and intention of the consumer to purchase a good or service, drives production, that is, production is dependent on demand. Suppliers or businesses are continuously trying to identify and estimate demand so that they can produce enough goods and services to satisfy demand. They do not want to produce more than what will be demanded, nor less than what is demanded.

The economy is based on the continuously repeating cycle of demand, production, sale, and consumption (or utilization). Everyone is both a consumer and a producer. And producers are either workers or investors. In order for this cycle to work efficiently and effectively prices for goods and services need to be fair to both consumer and producer and the income generated by producers needs to be fairly distributed to both workers and investors. Unfairly high prices severely affect the economy because they greatly reduce demand and consumption by consumers. An unfair distribution of producer's income which gives an inequitable greater share to investors thereby reducing the fair, appropriate, and economically necessary share to workers also severely affects the economy because that also greatly reduces demand and consumption by consumers. The majority working class' ability to buy those goods and services which it needs and desires has been significantly diminished due to the imbalance in the economy caused by the inequitable distribution of producer's income.

The ratio between the working class and the capitalist class is 99 to 1. That means that there are approximately 99 working class people to 1 capitalist person. The cumulative needs of the working majority, which represents ninety-nine percent of the population and number approximately 315 million people, far surpasses the needs of the top 1 percent capitalist class. The top one percent or 3 million people can only buy so much. They only need so much.

Assuming 2.6 people per household, the working class needs 120 million homes. Assuming the same 2.6 people per household and further assuming two homes for each family of the upper one percent, they only need 2.4 million homes. What is a greater driver for the economy, 120 million homes or 2.4 million homes? Which would generate more jobs, 120 million homes or 2.4 million homes? In fact, the greatest driver would be both 120 million homes for the working class (given that they have the income to afford those homes) and the 2.4 million homes for the capitalist class.

Assuming one car for every four people, the working class needs 78 million cars. Further assuming that the working class keeps a car for six years, the working class (given that they have the income to buy a car) will buy approximately 13 million cars a year. Using the same ratio of one car for every four people, the capitalist class needs 787 thousand cars. Further assuming that they buy a new car every two years (because they can afford to), they will purchase 394 thousand cars a year. What is better for the economy, the purchase of 13 million cars each year by the working class or the purchase of 394 thousand cars by the capitalist class? Which will sustain more jobs, the purchase of 13 million cars by the working class or the purchase of 394 thousand cars by the capitalist class? What would make the greater contribution to the gross domestic product, the production and sale of 13 million cars or the production and sale of 394 thousand cars? In fact, the greatest driver would be both 13 million cars for the working class (given that they have the income to afford those cars) and the 394 thousand cars for the capitalist class.

The working class outnumbers the capitalist class 99 to 1. Given that the working class can afford to, the working class will buy 99 times more furniture than the capitalist class. The working class will buy 99 times as many appliances as the capitalist class. They will buy 99 times as much food and 99 times as many clothes. The working class needs 99 times as much healthcare as the capitalist class and they require 99 times as many services as the capitalist class.

Which is the greater driver of the economy, the working class or the upper class? The stability and growth of the economy, in fact the entire economy itself depends on the consumption of the working class, and the working class can only consume to the extent that it can afford to.

The housing industry is suffering economically. Over a million construction workers, carpenters, electricians, plumbers, roofers, and painters are out of work. Why? Demand for new homes is down. Why is demand for new homes down? Because the working class cannot afford to buy the homes that they need and want. Why isn't the working class able to buy new homes that they want and need? Because they cannot afford to or they cannot get a mortgage loan!

The auto industry is suffering financially. Hundreds of thousands of workers have been laid off. Why? Car sales are down. Why are car sales down? Because the working class cannot afford to buy cars that they need and want. Why isn't the working class able to buy cars that they need and want? Because they cannot afford to or they cannot get a loan!

Virtually, the entire economy is suffering because workers cannot afford to buy the goods and services that they need and want for themselves and their families.

The total wealth of the US economy is limited—it is not infinite. The annual US gross domestic product (GDP) is limited—it is not infinite. The growth of the GDP year over year is limited—it is not infinite. The limited wealth generated by the economy, which is the result of both labor and investing, belongs to both workers and investors. And yet, the capitalist class, the top one percent of the population has been taking far more than its fair share of the limited newly generated wealth of the economy for the past forty years. In addition, the upper class has been taking money away from the working class. These two actions over the past forty years have caused a severe imbalance in the economy. The upper class has an enormous excess of wealth and income and the working class has a corresponding deficit of wealth and income. This has resulted in the working class, the main driver of the economy, not being able to consume the goods and services that it needs and desires. Of course, as consumption declines, so does production. And as production declines, so does worker income which leads to less consumption continuing the spiral of economic slowdown or recession. Besides being grossly unfair and unjust, this imbalance has caused a breakdown in the economy which continues to worsen.

The total wealth or the total income of the US economy can be compared to a pizza that is to be shared by 100 people. All 100 people are involved in some way in making the pizza. There are 100 pieces of pizza. If 1 person takes 40 pieces of pizza that leaves 60 pieces to be shared between the 99 other people. Now if another 4 people each take 5 pieces of pizza that leaves only 40 pieces to be shared among the other 95 people. Now, if another 10 people each take 2 pieces of pizza that leaves 20 pieces to be shared among the other 85 people. Lastly, if another 20 people each take 1 piece of pizza there is nothing left for the remaining 65 people. While initially one might think that each person should receive 1 piece of pizza that would only be fair if every person made the exact same contribution to the making of the pizza. Of course, that is never the case. Since people's contributions are different in overall value to the final product, the sharing of the final product should be equitable not equal. Fairness does not imply perfect equality. However, there are no circumstances where it would be fair for 35 people to take all the pieces leaving 65 people with nothing in spite of their contribution. Unfortunately, though, that is the situation that exists today. The top 1% of the population owns 40% of the total wealth. The top 10% owns 71% of the total wealth. What makes matters worse, the top 1 percent of the population would like to own and control 100% of the wealth of the economy to the deprivation of the 99%. Three million people want it all and don't care about the impact to hundreds of millions of other people. And it is amazing to think that some of these three million people claim to be Christians.

The greater the variance in the distribution of wealth between the capitalist class and the working class, the greater the negative impact on the economy. When the top 1% has more money, what do they do with it? They may buy a few more things, but they cannot buy enough to drive the entire economy. Capitalist theory holds that they will invest this additional money. But if the capitalist class has ownership and control of so much of the wealth of the economy to the corresponding deprivation of the working class, then investment will lead to nothing since the working-class majority cannot buy what they want and need.

The United States has over 540 billionaires, over 30,000 multi-millionaires (more than $30 million in net worth), and almost 10 million millionaires. These numbers have increased significantly in the last ten years and continue to increase. At the same time that the rich get richer, the working class has gotten poorer. Since the total net worth of the US economy is limited, the increase in the number of billionaires and millionaires implies a corresponding decrease in the net worth of individuals at the lower levels of wealth distribution. The number of homeless has increased, the number of people and families living in poverty has increased, the number of underemployed has increased, and the total net worth of the working class has decreased; all because the numbers of billionaires, multi-millionaires, and millionaires has increased. It is clear that the last forty years have seen a significant shift in wealth from the working majority to the already wealthy minority.

This shift has been the result of an active campaign by the capitalist class to take wealth away from the working majority and has been supported and facilitated by the government; every level of government and every branch of government. Unfortunately, the capitalist class has succeeded in taking control of the government by both direct participation and lobbying efforts. This shift in wealth and income has caused and is a major factor in the current economic crisis.

The current extreme variance in the distribution of wealth within the United States is actually unjust. The wealth of the extremely wealthy and very wealthy in the United States has not come about through productive labor, that is, work associated with the production of a good or service. No, their wealth has come about through either speculation (a business term for what is actually gambling) which is the trading of stocks, bonds, commodities, derivatives, etc. or through stock value appreciation. In both of these cases the individual makes no contribution to the US economy, adds no value to the US economy and does not promote the overall objective of the US economy which is to satisfy in the most efficient and effective way the natural needs and desires of all Americans for food, clothing, housing, a livelihood, education, healthcare, disability care, old age care, recreation, entertainment, social interaction, acceptance and respect. Yet, these people have been able to accumulate over three times more wealth then the lowest 80% of the population who work and do provide significant value to the economy. How can such a small minority who do not work and make no contribution to the economy have so much wealth while the majority who do work and make the major contribution to the economy have so little? That is a great injustice!

The great imbalance between the wealth and income of the top 1% of the population and the wealth and income of the lower 99% of the population needs to be corrected as soon as possible for the current economic stagnation cannot be reversed until this wealth and income imbalance is corrected. There has to be a minimum amount of wealth for every person within the economy and that minimum cannot be zero or less than zero. The minimum amount of wealth has to be sufficient for a person to have a home, furniture, appliances, a means of transportation, other things necessary to live; and savings for emergencies, potential disability, and retirement.

It is the responsibility of the government to oversee and regulate the economy, correcting imbalances and disorders. This imbalance in income and net worth that exists today between the 3 million capitalists and the 315 million workers can only be corrected by government oversight and management. But this will only happen if the Christian majority gets involved in the US political system and forces the government (all levels and all branches) to do so.

There are seven main actions that the government needs to take to correct this unjust imbalance. They are:

- refocusing the tax system
- redefining a corporation as a moral organism composed of and owned by all those involved in the operations of the corporation, that is, investors and workers
- raising the minimum wage to a living wage
- eliminating unemployment
- minimizing under-employment
- eliminating monopolies and oligopolies
- taking control of the supply of money away from the Federal Reserve, a private banking system, and restoring it to the Federal government

A Refocused Tax System

TAXES SERVE TWO PURPOSES. They fund the government and they correct economic imbalances. What is currently needed is to shift the tax burden away from the working class to the capitalist class until the appropriate balance between labor and capital is restored. The economy is stagnating because the working majority is not able to buy the goods and services that it needs and which the economy needs for stability and growth. The stability and growth of the economy is driven primarily from the consumption of the working majority. However, the working class is prevented from consuming because of reduced discretionary income, high prices, and too high a percentage of their income being used to service debt, debt that they were forced to take on in order to avoid financial disaster.

While there was an income tax during the Civil War and during the 1890's, there was not a continuous, annual Federal tax program until 1913. Besides generating funds for the United States government, the Federal income tax program has succeeded during certain periods of history in adjusting the imbalance in income distribution between the wealthy capitalist class and the working class. However, at other periods the Federal income tax program has grossly failed to adjust the income disparity between capital and labor. The Great Depression started in 1929 in the United States and lasted until the beginning of World War II. In the table below, it is seen that the Top Income Bracket tax rate was reduced by 67% from 1921 to 1929 (the period leading up to the Great Depression) dropping from 73% to 24%. It should be clear that this was a contributing factor in the Great Depression. It is interesting that in the last year in office of the Republican president Herbert Hoover whose term office coincided with the start of the Depression, the Top Income Bracket tax rate was raised from 25% to 63% representing a 252% increase. Unfortunately, the increase in the tax rate for the First Income Bracket rose from 0.4% to 4%

representing a 1000% increase. These income tax rate adjustments were an attempt to restore the distribution of tax burden to the same tax rates at the end of World War I. It was unfortunately too little, too late, and it significantly impacted the lower working class. These tax changes did nothing to correct the gross imbalance in income distribution between capital and labor. Raising the taxes of the very wealthy and lowering the taxes of the lower income classes in order to help improve the working class's financial position takes years before an improvement is seen.

U.S. Federal Income Tax Rates		
Applicable Year	**First Bracket**	**Top Bracket**
1913–1915	1.0%	7.0%
1916	2.0%	15.0%
1917	2.0%	67.0%
1918	6.0%	73.0%
1919–1920	4.0%	73.0%
1921	4.0%	73.0%
1922	4.0%	56.0%
1923	3.0%	56.0%
1924	1.5%	46.0%
1925–1928	1.5%	25.0%
1929	0.4%	24.0%
1930–1931	1.1%	25.0%
1932–1933	4.0%	63.0%
1934–1935	4.0%	63.0%
1936–1939	4.0%	79.0%
1940	4.4%	81.1%
1941	10.0%	81.0%
1942–1943	19.0%	88.0%
1944–1945	23.0%	94.0%
1946–1947	19.0%	86.5%
1948–1949	16.6%	82.1%
1950	17.4%	84.4%
1951	20.4%	91.0%
1952–1953	22.2%	92.0%

1954–1963	20.0%	91.0%
1964	16.0%	77.0%
1965–1967	14.0%	70.0%
1968	14.0%	75.3%
1969	14.0%	77.0%
1970	14.0%	71.8%
1971–1981	14.0%	70.0%
1982–1986	12.0%	50.0%
1987	11.0%	38.5%
1988–1990	15.0%	33.0%
1991	15.0%	31.0%
1993–2000	15.0%	39.6%
2001	15.0%	39.1%
2002	10.0%	38.6%
2003–2012	10.0%	35.0%
2013–2017	10%	39.6%
2018–	10%	37%

The table above also clearly shows the tax rates for the Top Income Bracket averaging in the 90% range from the beginning of World War II to 1963, the period of unprecedented economic growth in the United States. Unfortunately, history repeats itself. Starting in 1964 and continuing through today, the income tax rate for the Top Income Bracket has decreased by 62%, almost the same as the 67% decrease during the 1920's up to the start of the Great Depression. It is clear that this reduction in the tax rate for the Top Income Bracket has facilitated the great imbalance in income distribution which is at the heart of the current recession. It should also be clear that raising the Federal tax rate for the Top Income bracket is one of the solutions to the current economic crisis. Given that the US economy grew the most when the tax rate on the Top Income Bracket was the greatest, it follows that it is necessary to raise the tax rate for the Top Income Bracket back to 90% while lowering it for the First Income Bracket. Graduated income tax programs fund the government and balance the income disparity between capital and labor. The current economic crisis will only end when the working class, all 315 million people, has sufficient income to buy the goods and services which they need and which the US economy needs to regain stability and growth.

The so-called economic stimulus package of 2008, which was funded on borrowed money, did absolutely nothing to stimulate the economy. That is because it did nothing to improve the working class's ability to spend nor did it do anything to allow the working class to reduce its excessive debt burden. Significantly reducing the federal income tax for individuals whose adjusted gross income is less than $30,000 would give these individuals and their families thousands of dollars a year. What would these people do with $3000 or $4000 more a year? They would buy cars, furniture, and appliances. They would avoid foreclosure. They would reduce their excessive monthly payments, thereby increasing the amount of money that they would use to consume the goods and services that they need and want. They would buy clothes. They would take vacations. They would invest in education for themselves and their families. They might even start businesses. Their lives would improve. They would have financial freedom to pursue happiness. They would be able to achieve their share of the American dream.

The upper class should pay more in income tax. It should be clear that there is a positive correlation between the Top Income Bracket tax rate and economic growth and prosperity for the majority of Americans. That is, it is good for the economy to have a very high Top Income Bracket income tax rate. From 1964 to 2012, the upper limit tax rate has steadily declined and so has economic stability and growth.

In a similar manner there needs to be an immediate change in the corporate income tax structure. There needs to be a minimum such that any corporation with a net income of less than that minimum would not pay any income taxes. Above the minimum, there needs to be a graduated income tax rate similar to that for the Top Income Bracket. If corporations are legal persons, then they should have to pay income taxes like any other person. Federal income tax programs for corporations should generate funds for the government and balance the disparity between Small Business and Big Business. Competition is absolutely necessary for capitalism. The banking, manufacturing, energy, pharmaceutical, transportation, news media, insurance and other major industries are dominated by a few extremely large corporations. These corporations dominate the industry, the market, suppliers, customers and small businesses. These Big Businesses undermine competition and undermine capitalism. They prevent entry into their industries by small startup organizations. An aggressive Federal graduated income tax program for corporations can restore competition and true capitalism.

Continuing with the use of the Federal tax system to solve the current economic crisis, there should be an immediate termination of the tax-exempt status. No organization whatsoever should be exempt from income taxation. Tax-free foundations and so-called 'non-profit' organizations should no longer be exempt from paying taxes. If they are truly not making a profit, then they do not have to worry about income taxes. Foundations, hospitals, universities, and every other organization that currently is exempt from the income tax should be subject to income tax. Many major universities have endowments in excess of $1 billion. These endowments generate an enormous income for these universities and should be subject to income tax.

There should also be an immediate creation of an asset tax, with the first $1,000,000 in assets excluded from the asset tax. Every citizen, every person living within the United States, and every person owning property within the United States should be subject to this tax. Real estate, personal property, stocks, bonds, equities, businesses, and corporations are all assets and should be subject to this tax. Such a tax would be used to generate funds for the government as well as to balance the disparity in wealth between the capitalist class and the working class.

There also needs to be a graduated sales tax on the sale of stocks, bonds, and other monetary instruments as well as business acquisitions and mergers. True investors, who have a place in the economy and add value to the economy, must be distinguished from those that play the markets and who add no value to the economy. Those who play the markets buy and sell often; whereas true investors buy and either never sell or sell many years later. A graduated sales tax on business purchases would help prevent mergers and acquisitions which increase the size of Big Business at the expense of Small Business, competition and economic balance and stability.

Every US corporation and every US citizen must be made to pay income taxes on all income and income tax loopholes (for both corporations and individuals) must be eliminated. Many corporations and many very wealthy individuals avoid paying their fair share of income taxes, that is unjust and must be corrected.

Redefining the Corporation

CURRENTLY, A CORPORATION IS defined legally as an artificial person with legal rights and privileges and whose owners are immune from liabilities associated with the corporation. It further defines the owner or owners of a corporation in an artificial way as those who originally filed the paperwork to incorporate or those who were transferred ownership from the individual or individuals who originally file the paperwork. But these notions of a corporation, even though legal, are at odds with the essence of a corporation. For a corporation is a social organism composed of many people some of which are considered investors and most of which are workers. This social organism engages in activities which ultimately lead to the sale of a good or service. From a natural point of view, an organism owns the results of its actions since it is the efficient cause of the result. In terms of the corporation, the results of the corporation, the goods and services, are owned by the corporation. Since the corporation is in fact the social body of the individual workers and investors comprising the corporation, the goods and services produced by the corporation belong naturally to all the individuals of the corporation not equally but in proportion to the contribution of each individual.

The legal notion of ownership with respect to a corporation is incorrect and unjust because it is opposed to nature. This notion holds that the corporation itself as well as the goods and services produced by the corporation belong to the individual or individuals who filed the original incorporation paperwork or the individual or individuals to whom the original filers transferred the alleged ownership. The corporation, the goods and the services produced by the corporation and the profits of the corporation belong jointly though not equally to every investor and every worker of the corporation. It is most appropriate to refer to the investors as the capital shareholders of the corporation and the workers as the labor shareholders of the corporation.

The government needs to redefine the corporation and the definition of the owners of the corporation so that it corresponds to the natural and just meaning of a corporation and ownership. And all laws involving corporations need to be changed to correspond to this new and correct definition of corporation and ownership of a corporation.

If the definition of a corporation is changed and the definition of the ownership of a corporation is changed so that the capital shareholders and labor shareholders are considered joint owners, then the profits of the corporation will be justly shared by both capital shareholders and labor shareholders in an equitable way. Equitable does not mean equal. The profits should be distributed based on the contribution made to the generation of the profits. This will lead to an increase in income for workers which the workers will use to buy the goods and services which they want and need for themselves and their families which in turn will promote sustainable economic growth. The current unjust definition of a corporation and the unjust definition of the ownership of a corporation is the greatest reason for the unjust distribution of wealth among the population.

Unfortunately, many Christians accept this unjust notion of a corporation and the owners of the corporation. In fact, many of the so-called owners of corporations (based on this false and unjust definition of a corporation and its owners) are people who consider themselves Christian. Christians must seek justice in their lives; their social lives, their business lives, their economic lives and their political lives. And yet, these so-called Christian owners of corporations do not grasp the inconsistency in the current definition of a corporation and its owners and Christian principles.

Christians need to truly work to transform society (the economy and political system) into a society that is just and based on Christian economics: good is to be done and promoted, and evil is to be avoided, love your neighbor as yourself, and the absolute dignity and equality of each and every human being.

Raise the Minimum Wage to a Living Wage

The current Federal minimum wage is $7.25 an hour and has not changed since 2009. Since there are different ways to define minimum wage, Federal or state, and there are certain jobs that pay less than minimum wage; it is more appropriate to consider the number of people in the United States who make less than $10 an hour which equals $20,000 a year. There are 40 million people in the US who make less than $10 an hour or $20,000 a year. Many of these people have to support a family on this amount. These individuals and their families need food, clothing, shelter, furniture, appliances, heat, electricity, transportation, they need to wash their clothes, they need to get their hair cut, the need to go to the doctor, they need to go to the dentist, they need to get glasses, they need to pay for an education if they want to make more money, they need to save money in the event that they lose their job, they need to save money in the event that they become disabled, they need to save money for retirement, and they need to have some recreation for their mental, emotional and physical health. Can these 40 million people do all of this on less than $10 an hour? They can't!

Christian justice demands that every person working gets paid a living wage. A living wage is a wage sufficient for an individual and their family to pay for food, clothing, shelter, furniture, appliances, heat, electricity, transportation, clothes washing, personal grooming, healthcare (medical, dental and vision), education, savings in the event that they lose their job, savings in the event that they become disabled, savings for retirement, money to have some recreation for their mental, emotional and physical health and savings for an emergency. It is the duty of every Christian to promote a living wage for all workers and it is the duty of every Christian to pay a living wage.

The 40 million people in the United States that are paid less than $10 an hour are financial slaves to an unbalanced, inequitable, unjust economic system. What would these people do if they were paid a living wage? They would obviously spend it and they would save some. They would buy clothes. They would buy furniture. They would buy appliances. If they could, they would buy a car. If they could, they would buy a home. This extra money that they would receive if they were paid a living wage would go back into the economy as consumption and as savings, driving further production, increasing the Gross Domestic Product and providing more money for investment. Paying people a living wage is good for the economy. The minimum wage needs to be redefined as a "living wage" and calculated as a living wage by the Federal government, the state governments and local governments since the living wage needs to be based on the cost of living which can vary by state and by area within the state. And the living wage needs to apply to all workers: farm workers, workers who make tips, young workers, student workers, seasonal workers, recreational workers, home care workers, and disabled workers.

Eliminate Unemployment

THE REAL UNEMPLOYMENT RATE is difficult to estimate. It should be based on the number of people who are capable of work and who want to work if there was an opportunity. Unfortunately, there are not enough jobs for all of the people who want to work.

Outsourcing is to blame for a significant number of jobs lost within the United States over the past forty years. Through the 1970's, the United States was virtually self-reliant with respect to manufacturing Beginning in the early 1970's, corporations, intent on maximizing profits by reducing expenses (primarily labor), began to outsource from other countries. Prior to 1976 the US had a positive balance of trade, that is, it exported more that it imported. Since 1976 the US has had a negative balance of trade.

Initially outsourcing impacted manufacturing jobs in the United States. Then outsourcing impacted customer service jobs, then IT jobs, then accounts payable jobs, then accounts receivable jobs, then human resource jobs, then general accounting jobs, then engineering jobs. Unfortunately, corporations and those who run corporations do not care able people in the United States, their country, or their communities; they only care about profits and the compensation that they receive.

15 million people are unemployed in the United States. That means that there are 15 million people who would like to work but cannot find a job. Many of these people are so discouraged that they have given up looking for a job. These 15 million people (and potentially more people if they have family members who rely on them for support) are extremely constrained financially. They would like to buy things and they would like to spend money but they can't because they do not have the money. They do not have the money because they do not have a job.

Unfortunately, many people actually look down on the unemployed. They hold the position that those who are unemployed do not want to work and it is their fault that they do not have a job. 99.9% of those who are unemployed want to work. And most people who are unemployed do not have a job because of outsourcing. People do not want to lose their jobs, but it happens. Christians need to look with charity upon the unemployed and certainly not criticize them.

The purpose and objective of the US economy is to satisfy in the most efficient and effective way the natural needs and desires of all Americans for food, clothing, housing, a livelihood, education, healthcare, disability care, old age care, recreation, entertainment, social interaction, acceptance and respect. The US economy is failing with respect to these 15 million people. The government; Federal, state and local, is failing in its duty to supervise and manage the economy for the good of all people with respect to these 15 million people.

It is the responsibility of the government; Federal, state and local, to eliminate unemployment, not only by helping the unemployed find jobs, but also by helping the unemployed to start their own businesses through training, business education and start up loans. Unless and until these 15 million people find work with living wages, the economy will continue to stagnate and the government will continue to fail in its main responsibility which is to supervise and manage the economy for the good of all people in the United States.

Minimize Under-Employment

THE AMERICAN WORK ETHIC leads people to believe that if a person goes to college and works hard, then they will succeed in the business world. While true for some people, it does not apply to the approximately 30 million people who are under-employed. A person who is under-employed has education and or experience with which they should have a much higher level job than they have. There are people with college degrees who are working in the fast food industry making wages far less than they should receive. Their education provides them with skills that they cannot use because they cannot find a job that corresponds to those skills. There are millions of people with many years of experience who are working low-skill, low-wage jobs because they cannot find employment equal to their skills. Under-employed workers have been forced into jobs in order to avoid unemployment and to try to survive financially. What is also alarming is that the millions of college educated under-employed workers have excessive student loan debt. They invested in a college education and the US economy is not allowing them to realize a return on their investment. For the 30 million under-employed people, the American work ethic is a lie.

Most of the under-employed are the result of outsourcing. Businesses following the amoral economic theories of the last 40 years have placed profits over people. There is a moral obligation for every person in the United States and every business in the United States to promote the good of the US economy which means utilizing American workers. Family takes care of family, the community takes care of the community and a country takes of the country. This is just another expression of the Christian economic principle 'love your neighbor as yourself'.

75% of the people in the United States claim to be Christian and yet most seem to have no concern for the unemployed, the under-employed and those earning less than a living wage. The parable of the Good

Samaritan applies to the unemployed, the under-employed and those earning less than a living wage. Matthew chapter 25 verses 31 to 46 apply to the unemployed, the under-employed and those earning less than a minimum wage. The majority of people in the United States are Christian and as the majority Christians can change the economy so that Christian economic principles are followed and not the current amoral economic theories.

Because the total aggregate wealth of the US economy is finite and because working consumption drives the economy, it is essential that there be balance in the distribution of wealth and income between the capitalist class and the working class. Balance implies a lack of extremes. Currently, there is not balance in the distribution of wealth and income and there are significant extremes both on the high side and the low side. The capitalist class over the last forty years has acquired more than its share from the working class, severely limiting the working class's ability to purchase the goods and services that it needs and which the economy needs for stability and growth. The excess wealth that the capitalist class has acquired has been at the expense of millions of people. The top 3 wealthiest Americans have the same amount of wealth as the lowest 160 million Americans. Only the government through the above explained programs can restore the proper balance to the distribution of wealth and income in the United States which will benefit all and help reverse the current economic crisis. And only through the activism of Christians will the government begin to fulfill its responsibility to the people of the United States; all the people and not just the wealthy elite top 1%.

Eliminate monopolies and oligopolies

AN EFFICIENT AND EFFECTIVE economy is based on a balance between all the various elements comprising the economic system. No one element or no small collective can have a dominant position within a balanced economy. This means that the ownership and control of the United States production system, the complex network of farms, factories, distribution centers, transportation carriers, stores, banks, hospitals, schools, etc., should not be concentrated in the hands of a small minority of individuals. No, instead the ownership of the United States production system needs to be distributed as much as possible throughout the entire population.

What is better for the economy ; six banks that control 90 percent of the entire banking industry or thousands of banks; ten corporations that control 95 percent of the communications industry or thousands of communications corporations; a dozen corporations that control 85 percent of the energy industry (oil, natural gas, electricity) or thousands of energy corporations? The same logic applies to the food industry, the transportation industry, the healthcare industry, the insurance industry, the automobile industry and virtually every other industry.

Today large corporations dominate the marketplace, dominate consumers and dominate suppliers. They have few competitors and through common goals and purpose, they form oligopolies that dictate price to both customers and suppliers and policies and laws to the government.

Today there are multi-national, national and local monopolies and oligopolies which dominate their respective markets and ruthlessly pursue the elimination of all competition.

What is most detrimental about these monopolies and oligopolies is that they dominate the government; the Federal state, county and local governments. Through lobbying, the revolving door between government and private industry and campaign contributions, the major corporations within virtually every industry virtually control the government and dictate both domestic and foreign policies.

Blinded by greed, a thirst for power and extreme pride and arrogance (note the claim of exceptional used so often these days), these corporations seek to create modern day empires. Of course, from a Christian point of view greed, pride, and the desire to dominate and control others are vices not virtues.

Again, many people who claim to be Christians and who think that they are righteous in the eyes of God are the driving forces behind these monopolies and oligopolies. Monopolies and oligopolies are intrinsically selfish, and selfishness is contrary to Christian principles.

TAKE CONTROL OF THE SUPPLY OF MONEY AWAY FROM THE FEDERAL RESERVE, A PRIVATE BANKING SYSTEM

The Federal government handed over its responsibility of controlling the money supply in 1913 to a private system called the Federal Reserve. While the word 'federal' typically refers to a government, the Federal Reserve system is not part of the United States Federal government. It is rather strange that this private banking system assumed the name 'federal' and since most people think that the Federal Reserve system is part of the United States Federal government, it would almost seem that the use of the term 'federal' in Federal Reserve System was meant to deceive the public.

Control of the money supply is one of the main responsibilities of the Federal government. It is an extremely important task since the entire economy is directly influenced by the supply of money. The improper and incorrect management of the supply of money does in fact lead to economic recessions with the consequent impacts on the general public. And when the supply of money is increased, it needs to be supplied or created by the Federal government and distributed to the general public. With the Federal Reserve System (the private banking system), money is created by a private banking system and distributed to its own banks with the obvious benefits to these banks and not to the general public.

Money needs to be managed; the amount, the availability, the expansion and the contraction of the money supply. The management of money for the US economy is the responsibility of the Federal government. It is clearly not the responsibility of private or non-governmental businesses since government is chosen by and responsible to the people and private and non-governmental businesses are not. The government is meant to serve the people, while business is meant to serve a few people. Businesses are selfish and self-serving. The government, at least in principle, is meant to serve all the people.

The guiding principle for money management is balance. Money must be managed to maintain the balance and equity between consumers and producers, facilitate transactions between consumers and producers, and promote the maximization of wealth for the maximum number of people. Money management must not be, as it is today, a vehicle to maximize the wealth of a few at the expense of the majority. For these same reasons, the central banking function of the United States which is currently performed by the Federal Reserve System must be owned, controlled and managed by the Federal government. The Federal Reserve System is not a branch of the government and is in fact a private banking system. Again, the government is meant to serve the people, while private businesses (the Federal Reserve System) are meant to serve a few people. Private businesses (the Federal Reserve System) are selfish and self-serving, while the government is meant to serve all the people.

The determination of the amount of money required to facilitate the exchange of goods and services by producers and consumers needs to be made by specific formulas using very accurate statistics. Currently, the Federal Reserve System (the private banking system which controls the US money supply) uses rather arbitrary methods and their so-called expert judgement to determine when and how much to expand or contract the supply of money and their main supposed objective is the control of inflation. This methodology and this objective is wrong. First, the control of inflation, or rather prices, needs to be done by the Federal government overseeing and limiting price increases through fines and taxes. It is absurd to think that a private banking system, the Federal Reserve System, can control price increases and inflation through the expansion and contraction of money. In fact, the Federal Reserve System claims that it is its responsibility to control the growth of the US economy by its monetary policies. Yet, the Federal Reserve has failed miserably in the last 105 years since its creation. Cumulative inflation since 1913 is approximately 2400 percent and from 1974 to 1982 the average annual inflation rate was 8 percent. And supposedly the Federal Reserve system's objective is to control inflation!

While inflation is bad for most people, it is actually good for some people. When prices increase, people through their businesses and corporations are receiving more for their products and services than previously and in most cases, this is due to the desire for increased revenues and profits. Inflation represents the transfer of wealth from the middle and lower classes to the wealthy class. Since the Federal Reserve System is a private banking system and it has failed to control inflation (even though that is its purported objective), it may be that its real objective is to promote and support the increase in wealth for the upper 1 percent which also results in the decrease in wealth for the 99 percent.

Another fact that supports the feasibility of the claim that the real objective of the Federal Reserve System is to promote and support the increase in wealth of the upper 1 percent is the method in which they distribute newly created money. The Federal Reserve System distributes newly created money to its member banks (these banks are part of the Federal Reserve System) as loans. Can a consumer take out a loan from the Federal Reserve for a new home or a new car? No! The Federal Reserve only loans money to its member banks. In effect it gives money to itself. Obviously, there are significant benefits to its member banks especially when the interest rates on these loans are low. The member banks take the money loaned from the Federal Reserve and loan it to corporations and businesses at much higher interest rates allowing these member banks to assure stable revenues and profits. And, obviously, these member banks can decide what corporations to loan money to and at what interest rate.

The money created by the Federal Reserve System is distributed to its member banks who in turn lend it to corporations of their choosing. This process benefits the member banks and the corporations to which the member banks extend loans, but what about the average consumer, what about the members of the 99 percent—how do they benefit from this process?

The Federal government needs to retake control of the money supply, money creation and the distribution of newly created money away from the Federal Reserve System, a private banking system. The Federal government is responsible for managing the economy, promoting and supporting its growth. The Federal government is responsible for overseeing prices and limiting price increase, thereby controlling inflation.

The Federal government is responsible for seeking the maximum quality of life for every one of its citizens.

The Federal government needs to determine when to create money and add it to the economy and it needs to distribute this newly created money to the 99 percent through loans: mortgage loans on primary residences, auto loans, educational loans, etc. Imagine the good to society and majority of Americans if their mortgage rate was 2 percent. Imagine the good to society and majority of Americans if educational loan rates were 2 percent. Imagine the good to society if the Federal government through loans based on newly created money by the Federal government eliminated payday loan companies by providing personal loans at 4 percent.

The Federal government could significantly improve the economy and the lives of tens of millions of Americans if it would take back control of the creation and distribution of money from the Federal Reserve System.

The Relationship between Capital and Labor

HUMAN LABOR IS AN expression of the character of the laborer. Consider music. The musical composition is a product of the work of the musician. It is an expression of the musician and tells something of the character and personality of the musician. In a similar manner a work of art is an expression of the artist. It tells something about her or him. This relationship between the worker and the product of her or his work applies to all labor. It applies to the architect, the construction worker, the plumber, the mechanic, the teacher, the nurse, the farmer, the homemaker, the cook, etc. So true is the expression "by their fruits you shall know them." People most often answer the question, "Who are you?" with a reply involving what kind of work that they do. That is because a person's actions reflect who they are and what they are. A person can be evaluated by what they do or what they have accomplished. When a child is born, they are known or somewhat defined by their relationship to their parents, since they have not yet accomplished anything on their own. Once they begin doing things on their own, their actions reflect who they are.

Labor is natural to human beings and part of God's design. God intends humans to express themselves through their work; their work being a reflection of their personality and character. Hence, labor represents one of the most important activities of a human being. (It may be necessary to recall that by labor is meant productive human activity: creativity, design, organization, direction, as well as physical labor.) Because labor is natural to human beings, it is a necessary activity to human fulfillment. Humans have a natural tendency to act, to accomplish things. Humans that have desires or goals that do not pursue their goals by actions or work are incomplete as humans and unfulfilled. It should be understood, then, that labor is necessary for human beings. Labor should not be looked upon as a burden, but as a means of expressing oneself. Because of this, there is a natural dignity to human labor, as long as it is voluntary. For work makes humans more human.

Every production system is based on two essential elements: capital and labor. Capital is used to provide facilities, equipment, materials, funds, etc. in order to operate the system. Labor provides the ideas, designs, philosophy, direction, management, physical work, etc. that is required to generate the goods and services which will be sold by the organization. In the initial or start up stages of the production system, the capital is provided by individuals who are referred to as capitalists or it may be borrowed. After the production system is operating in a profitable mode, the capital is no longer provided by capitalists but rather is generated by the system or organization itself. If an evaluation is made of both capitalist and laborer at the time of startup, it is clear that both have an equal role and equal value. However, once the organization is functioning in a positive manner, it is obvious that the laborer is far more significant to the organization and plays an almost exclusive role in generating the profits. This is because the organization generates its own capital and is no longer dependent on capitalists. This is true for any organization that has endured beyond start up. It does happen at times that the organization decides to obtain additional capital through capitalists as opposed to loans and shares are sold to generate that capital.

Most organizations which have been in existence for quite some time have virtually no capitalists. Those individuals who provided the capital to help start these organizations are no longer living. There are, of course, individuals who have acquired either through inheritance or purchase the partial ownership of the organization associated with the original capitalists. These individuals are shareholders and should be defined as capital shareholders to distinguish them from the labor shareholders or workers. What role do these capital shareholders play within the production system? They do not provide capital; the capital is generated by the organization itself. They are not directly involved in the management of the organization, though they do play a role depending on the number of shares that they hold or control in the selection of the board of managers or directors. Capital shareholders do not provide ideas, develop strategies, or make decisions. They do not design, do not manage, do not create, do not sell, do not make, do not provide services, do not take orders, do not ship, do not repair, do not maintain legers, do not buy materials, etc. Capital shareholders or stockholders actually do nothing for the company and contribute nothing to the company regarding the production and delivery of goods and services. Yet, they claim ownership of the company, its assets and its profits based on capitalist theory.

While workers or laborer shareholders receive compensation on a regular basis, it is only by convention that the capital shareholders do not receive compensation in a similar manner. In fact, providing the capital shareholders with compensation on a regular basis (dividend distribution on a monthly or bi-weekly basis) would allow them to benefit immediately from their investment and not have to engage in the game of 'playing the stock market'. In addition, such an arrangement would underscore the equity between labor shareholders and capital shareholders. Furthermore, an arrangement of a constant dividend stream to capital stockholders would tend to motivate them to maintain their relationship with the organization rather than quickly selling their shares and buying capital shares in another organization through the stock market.

In the past year hundreds of thousands of workers have lost their jobs. Over the course of the last ten years including the period of the Great Recession, over 8 million people have lost their jobs. Why? Did these people do something wrong? No. Were they bad workers? No. The only thing that they were doing wrong from the company's point of view was they were earning a paycheck. Corporations are driven to maximize profits. Employees are considered an expense. In a few cases companies had lost money (their expenses had exceeded their revenues) and they laid-off employees in order to reduce expenses assuming that their revenues would remain the same. In the vast majority of cases companies just wanted to increase their profit margins or the CEO wanted to achieve his or her objectives in order to receive his or her big bonus. Getting rid of workers may be good for a CEO or for a company in the short term but it is not really good for them for the long term. However, laying-off workers is extremely bad for the workers and very bad for the economy. And what is bad for the economy is also bad for business.

From an economic point of view, 15 million laid off people are no longer productive members for the economy. Their means of earning money with which to buy the goods and services that they need for themselves and their families has been eliminated. Aggregate economic demand is lessened which leads to less production which in turn can lead to more layoffs.

What about the poor worker who has been laid off? The majority of Americans live from paycheck to paycheck and have virtually no savings. So, if and when most people are laid off from work, they have no funds to help them survive financially. While unemployment insurance keeps people from starving, it does little to prevent the drastic effects of unemployment. Unemployment is one of the leading causes of home foreclosures. People who have lost their jobs reduce if not totally deplete the equity in their homes. They are forced to move into an apartment, sell their furniture, sell their cars, sell their jewelry, stop going to college. The vast majority of the unemployed have no health insurance. Depression, divorce, alcohol abuse and drug abuse are extremely high among the unemployed. Many people who are unemployed resort to crime which can be seen by the high correlation between crime rates and unemployment rates. And why are these people unemployed? Why do they suffer financially, socially, and emotionally? These people suffer and will suffer for years because corporations want to increase their profits and because CEO's want to receive their bonuses.

Most workers are apprehensive and fearful of being laid off. If profits are down, people begin to fear that a layoff may be coming. Companies lay people off in many different ways, some are respectful of the employee and some are cruel and demeaning to the employee. Some companies lay people off by calling them into an office individually and notifying them of the layoff. Some companies will bring employees together as a group and make a general announcement that everyone in the group is being laid off. In some rare cases, people have been notified by email that they have been laid off or they have been prevented by security from entering the building where they work because they have been laid off. When a person finds out that they have been laid off, they immediately experience shock, confusion, anxiety, and depression. Dozens of questions cycle through their heads without answers. How will I tell my family? What about our family plans for a vacation? Will my son or daughter have to drop out of college? How long will it take me to find another job? What will we do about health insurance? Will we have to sell our home? Where would we go? Who will hire me? Will I be able to get the same pay? These questions cycle through a person's head within the first few moments of being notified that they have been laid off and they continue and worsen as time goes on and the person cannot find work. Why do these people have to suffer financially, socially, and emotionally? These people suffer and will suffer for years because corporations want to increase their profits and because CEO's want to receive their bonuses.

Are layoffs really necessary? Are they fair? Are they just? How should layoffs be viewed from a Christian economics point of view?

How is it fair to those people who have provided ideas for new products, who established new customers, who have built facilities, or who have built high quality products? How is it fair to those people who have dedicated their entire careers to the company and are responsible for making the company what is it? The vast majority of layoffs are neither necessary nor fair nor just from a Christian economics point of view. And this point needs to be repeated. The vast majority of layoffs are neither necessary nor fair nor just from a Christian economics point of view. They are the result of poor decisions, mismanagement, a false though legal ownership and management structure and greed.

While most people think that they understand what capitalism is, they are, unfortunately, very confused because they have been misled. The confusion results from the immense difference between what capitalism should be and the false and exaggerated practice of those who clothe their actions under the cloak of capitalism.

False capitalism is all about control. A capitalist is one who seeks to control an individual, a group of individuals, or a society of individuals with the objective of claiming total ownership of the results and products of the labor of those individuals. In complete opposition to true capitalism, this false capitalism desires to make no contribution whatsoever to the productive process, yet wants to claim the right and title to all the results of the production system. A true capitalist actively contributes capital to the production process and claims only a share of the results realizing and acknowledging that capital and labor are partners in the production process and partners of the results and profits.

The vast majority of corporations are controlled and from a legal point of view owned by individuals who have provided virtually no money of theirs to this enterprise. There are countless examples of people who have inherited control of a business. It may be true that those from whom they inherited control of the business may have invested some of their money at some time. However, that initial investment compared to the present worth or value of the business is usually insignificant. In many other cases, individuals have either borrowed or have used others' money to gain control of an enterprise. Of course, most people see nothing wrong with this. It is portrayed as the American dream to own a property or a business and have others pay rent or work for you, while you do nothing. While this is a dream for the landlord and business owner, it is not the dream for the worker. The true American dream is where everyone has enough money for food, a home, clothes, furniture, appliances, transportation, healthcare, disability care, unemployment insurance, old age care, rest and recreation. And this notion of the American dream is consistent with Christianity.

Unfortunately, it is the false notion of capitalism that is practiced today and which has the support of the law, the courts, and the government. The vast majority of capitalists have not contributed anything to the productive process of the company which they allegedly own. They have provided no capital. They do not contribute to the organizational management, the design of new products or services, the manufacture of products; they do not work. In effect, they contribute nothing and do nothing with respect to the productive process and system of the company. Yet, all profits and all assets belong to them. Any new designs, new ideas, any new intellectual property belongs solely to them even though they did nothing to create those new designs, ideas or intellectual property. By current law, the laborers of the company have no right whatsoever to the profits, assets and intellectual property of the company even though the profits, increase in assets and development of new intellectual property was solely the result of their labor. That is not right. That is not just. That has to change.

From a natural point of view there are two types of corporate shareholders: capital shareholders and labor shareholders. Capital shareholders provide or have provided the capital for the business and the labor shareholders provide the labor both intellectual and physical. True capital shareholders maintain an active role in the business and are committed to the long-term welfare of the company.

Unfortunately, stockholders today are not true capital shareholders. They temporarily hold stock in a company in order to realize a profit by selling their stock at a price greater than the price that they paid for it. They only perceive the value of the stock within the open market and give no real significance to the company except insofar as the perceived reputation of the company increases the perceived value of stock in the company. People who play the stock market, that is, they engage in almost continual buying and selling of stocks provide absolutely no value to the companies whose stock they hold and trade and they make absolutely no contribution to the economy. And yet most business practitioners within corporations have been lead to believe that the corporation exists for the ultimate and exclusive good of the stockholder. Virtually none of these stockholders have contributed to the organization and have acquired their stock by purchasing it from other stockholders. And, they do not hold the stock and take an active role in the management and direction of the company. No, they hold the stock waiting for an opportunity to sell it and make a profit. Because they provide virtually no value to the corporation itself, they should not be considered stockholders or shareholders. For the success of the organization is completely independent of them.

The management and direction of a corporation should be provided by both true capital shareholders and labor shareholders since both are responsible for the financial success of the corporation. Because of this, both capital shareholders and labor shareholders should form the board of directors and both should democratically select the management of the corporation. If both capital shareholders and labor shareholders ran the company, there would be few if any layoffs and the company would pursue stable growth over the long term rather than merely seeking to increase the perceived market value of the company and hence the value of a share of stock. This would also be very beneficial to the economy since it would minimize unemployment, stabilize long term economic growth and reduce random market fluctuations.

Making capital shareholders and labor shareholders equal owners of the corporation could easily be done by Congress passing a law and the benefits of capital shareholder and labor shareholder equality would be seen overnight. However, the pseudo shareholders who control corporations to exploit workers, exploit customers, exploit suppliers and exploit the corporation itself will resist any attempt to undermine their scam. And since these ruthless false capitalists control the government, there is no chance of changing the status quo until the people regain control of their government.

Stock Markets

MANY PEOPLE HAVE A very confused and incorrect view of the stock markets. Radio programs, television programs, and newspapers report on the stock markets as though they represented a barometer of the economy. They are not. In fact, the elimination of the stock markets would actually be a good thing for the economy

An investor, a true investor, is a person who contributes money to a business venture. That person shares in the risks of the business and is a partner with the workers (executives, directors, managers, and all other various workers within a corporation) in the production system that generates a good or service to be sold at a profit. The true investor is committed to the long-term good of the company and is entitled to share in the profits of the business.

The stock market is a marketplace where shares of corporations are bought and sold. Virtually all transactions involving the purchase and sale of stock do not directly involve the actual corporation whose shares are involved. On very rare occasions when a private corporation goes 'public', the corporation will sell shares within the stock market. This is referred to as an initial public offering (IPO). Also, on rare occasions, corporations will sell its own shares or even buy its own shares within the stock market. While not as convenient as using the stock markets, companies could actually sell and buy its shares without using a stock market.

The vast majority of stock transactions within the stock market involve the purchase of shares of stock from an existing stockholder and not from the company. The predominant purpose of buying and selling stock within the stock market is not long-term partnering with the company with which one buys stock. No, the predominant purpose of buying and selling stock within the stock market is short term gains or profits by playing the market. Playing the market, which is what the vast majority of individuals and so-called investment companies do, add absolutely no value whatsoever to the economy. In fact, playing the market has a negative impact on the businesses whose stock are being traded and on the economy as well.

If a person buys 1000 shares of stock from someone who is selling 1000 shares of stock, the company with which the 1000 shares are associated does not receive any money whatsoever. That is, there is no value or contribution to the company being made by this kind of transaction. There is actually an expense to the company with the trading of its stock in that the company has to issue certificates to the new shareholder and modify its database of stockholders. The millions of stock transactions that occur on a daily basis provide no value to the businesses whose stock is being bought and sold.

People and investment companies that play the stock market are focused on anything and everything that will increase the selling price of shares of stock that they own. And because they are only concerned with selling the stock at an opportune time, pressure is placed on corporations to do what is necessary to increase the market price of shares of their stock. The market price of stock is based on short term and short-sighted perceptions and not at all on the long-term growth or performance of the company. Stock holders do not care about customers, suppliers, or employees; they only care about financial ratios, reports, recommendations to buy, and other indicators that will lead the marketplace to perceive the stock as desirable and to be willing to pay the asking price and even more than the asking price for the stock.

So-called investment companies that buy and sell large numbers of shares (tens of thousands, hundreds of thousands, and millions) have the ability to place considerable pressure on the management teams of corporations to do what they can to raise the perceived price of their stock in the marketplace. This involves short term actions to improve the appearance of financial soundness. Very often the compensation plans of corporations' CEO's, CFO's and other executives are based on stock performance. As a result, the executive teams will undertake short term actions to raise stock prices by doing what is not best for long term growth and stability. Layoffs and drastic and dangerous reductions in inventory are often used to raise the financial ratios of a company to raise the price of its stock.

Investment companies and individuals who play the stock market are responsible for driving the corporation to maximize profits in the short term even if it harms customers, suppliers, employees and the economy. These same investment companies and individuals are responsible for the ruin of some companies through acquisitions.

These pseudo investors, who are supposedly the owners of the company, contribute nothing to the success of the business; yet they almost always gain. Workers who are responsible for making the company what it is are rewarded by being laid off to hit financial numbers for stock holders and they are treated worse than assets during mergers and acquisitions. And these same pseudo investors often only hold the stock in the corporation for a short period of time. They manipulate the corporation to raise the stock price and then sell the stock. They are short term owners who do not care about the mid-term or the long term good of the corporation. It is certainly not fair nor just that ownership, decision-making, and the ability to decide whether the corporation lives or dies lies with people who have not contributed anything whatsoever to the corporation and are only concerned with the stock price of the company and not the company itself. This is bad not only for the corporation, its workers, its customers, and its suppliers; it is very bad for the economy. A corporation must be managed for the good of its customers, its workers, its investors, its suppliers and the entire economy.

How can a Christian engage in these activities and totally disregard the rights of workers? Obviously, the majority of workers are Christians. How can a Christian stock holder look upon a worker as an expense that needs to be minimized? How can a Christian stock holder disregard the contribution that workers make to the corporation? If it were not for workers, there would be no corporation. Christian stock holders need to start acting like Christians in the business world and treat workers as human beings. Christian stock holders should love their neighbors (the workers of the corporation in which they hold stock) as themselves.

The stock market itself involves a zero-sum game, that is, the gains equal the losses. And because of the speed and magnitude of transactions taking place, those who are professional traders are the ones who gain and the majority of middle class individuals who buy stocks are the losers in the long run. Many financial institutions use computer systems to trade for them based on sophisticated strategies. Obviously, the middle-class person who has a fulltime job does not have the time to develop the knowledge and experience to engage in sophisticated trading. In addition, the professional traders and the large financial institutions trade large portfolios of stocks and derivatives, while the average person trades very small portfolios compared to the professions. Because stock trading is a zero-sum game and because the professionals (and there are few of them) have the time, the money and the expertise; they gain at the expense of the ordinary person of which there are millions of them. Unfortunately, the small investor is lead to believe that he or she can see the money that they play in the stock market grow over time, but that is really a fallacy. While a few average people will benefit from playing the stock market, the overwhelming majority actually lose in the long run. This is no different than gambling at a casino. While a very few people win gambling at a casino, the vast majority lose.

The real problem is that the stock market is not designed and managed to enable and promote long-term investing. Instead, it is designed to support very short-term trading specifically for the purpose of the professional trader and financial institution to gain at the expense of both the corporations whose stock is traded and the average person. And this is both unjust and detrimental to the purpose and objective of the economy which is to satisfy in the most efficient and effective way the natural needs and desires of all Americans for food, clothing, housing, a livelihood, education, healthcare, disability care, old age care, recreation, entertainment, social interaction, acceptance and respect.

Stock markets must be regulated to prevent the injustices explained above. A graduated sales tax on the sale of stocks which have been held for less than perhaps five years would help promote long-term investing and to prevent speculation and market manipulation. In order for stocks to be true investments and not speculative adventures or gambling instruments, they must remain with the individual or buying organization for a long period of time. Speculation involves the buying and selling of stocks with no objective of being involved with the company. A true investor gets involved in the activities of the company and is interested in the long-term welfare of the company. The stock market must be made to support the objective of the US economy and not allowed to undermine it.

Changing speculators into investors through a graduated sales tax on stocks or some other type of regulation could easily be accomplished by the Christians in Congress passing a law or laws. The solution is basically simple: Christians need to act like Christians in their public lives; their business lives and their political lives.

Imports, Outsourcing and the Economy

ONE OF THE BASIC principles of Christianity is the family. Even the relationship between the persons of the Trinity of God is expressed in terms of the family. Within the principle of the family is the corollary that family takes care of family. Each member of the family is responsible for taking care of the other members. Parents should take care of their children until they can take care of themselves. Brothers and sisters are responsible for helping their parents in caring for younger siblings. The children are responsible for taking care of their parents when their parents are old or infirm. Parents and adult children should help each other during times of illness, unemployment, financial difficulties, etc.

The principle of family takes care of family also extends to the extended family, the community and the country. Every Christian is required to do good to his or her family, extended family, community and country. Doing good to family, extended family, community and country is a positive activity and behavior. A Christian can be guilty of not being good to his or her neighbor, not only by doing harm to their neighbor but also by ignoring or neglecting his or her neighbor. The Christian obligation of doing good extends to economics; local, regional and national.

In the earliest days of civilization, the economy of the local society constituted a self-sufficient system. Composed of a limited number of families, this social unit was able to produce all the goods and services that it needed. Families and extended families worked together to satisfy the needs for human life: food, clothing, and shelter. Virtually everyone with the exception of very young children, the sick and the very old engaged in work in order for the entire extended family to eat, be clothed and be sheltered and safeguarded from the natural elements. Things functioned well within this mini-society and mini-economic system.

There are a few interesting principles involved in this first socio-economic system. First, there was the belief that everyone was required to work both for their own good but also for the common good. There was no thought of 'something for nothing', 'never having to work because others work for you', 'ownership of the fruits of someone else's labor ', 'control of others', or 'taking more than one's fair share'. Within the family, everyone who was capable of working was expected to work and did work. In fact, if a family member who was capable of working did not work, then they would not be entitled to eat and the other family members would resort to coercion in order to bring the inordinate individual back into order.

Another principle of these initial societies was respect for the very young, the sick and the very old; those who were incapable of working. Though these individuals could not work, yet they still required the basic necessities of life. In fact, because of their physical condition, their necessities for life were greater than normal. They required care and assistance from others which they could not provide for themselves because of their condition. It was understood by everyone that the economy and organization of this mini-society should account for and take care of these individuals. Work, then, was organized into those who generated food, clothing, tools and shelter; and those who provided care. All workers understood that they would benefit directly from and in proportion to their labors, but also that a percentage of the fruits of their labors would go towards those in the community who were not able to work. This principle was based partially on the fact that everyone in this society was related, but also on the realization by those who worked that someday because of age or health they would be in a position where they would have to rely on someone else for food and care. It was an initial and natural form of social security.

One of the greatest strengths of this initial mini-society was its structure. It was a community of families, all of which were related to each other by blood. Each family constituted a mini-society in itself consisting of workers (providers and care-givers) and those who required care. Each member was ordered not only to their own good but also to the common good of the family as a whole. In turn, the larger community was composed of families. These families were ordered not only to their own good but also to the common good of the community. For each family realized that their survival and the attainment of their own personal happiness could only come about through cooperation with the other families in the community. This society of families was based on personal work ethics, as well as individual and distributive justice.

Natural resources such as land, animals, plants, etc., were available to all. Ownership of personal property which was the direct result of one's labor was respected as a natural right. Ownership of land and natural resources was limited to the land and resources within the direct use and control of each family. There was also common ownership of land and resources by the larger community of extended families. This common ownership was based on the common good principle and involved resources which needed to be shared by all. In the event that an individual attempted to control and claim ownership of a natural resource which was needed by the entire community, then the community at large would do what was necessary to rectify this situation. Everyone seemed to have a natural understanding of personal rights and community rights and the proper relation between the two. These early societies were self-sufficient, sustainable, and adaptable.

The concepts and philosophies that animated the early societies and drove their economies apply to national societies and economies as well. One goal of a national economy is self-sufficiency. A nation must endeavor to produce all the goods and services that it needs and if there is an excess than the excess can be exported to other nations. So critical is the principle of self-sufficiency that an economy and a nation cannot survive if it does not pursue self-sufficiency. A country that does not manage its imports and allows its imports to exceed its exports is slowly destroying itself. For an economy must maintain its balance between production and consumption. Imports reduce production. When production is reduced so also is the generation of income and wealth for working class consumers. Working class consumption is the primary and major driver of the economy. As working-class consumers lose income due to reduced production because of excessive imports, their consumption is immediately reduced and there occurs a continued reduction of consumption through the reduction of assets and through an increase in debt. Working class consumers have limited assets and can only afford to manage a limited amount of debt before they experience catastrophic financial failure.

The people of the nation must work together to satisfy the needs for human life, and to provide those goods and services which people need and desire for their happiness. In an efficient and effective economy, each member is ordered not only to their own good but also to the common good of the nation. For each person must realize that their survival and the attainment of their own personal happiness can only come about through cooperation and collaboration with the other members of society.

In an economy based on Christian economics, virtually everyone with the exception of very young children, the sick and the very old engages in work both for their own good but also for the common good. An economy based on Christian economics has respect for the very young, the sick and the very old; those who were incapable of working. Though these individuals cannot work, yet they still require the basic necessities of life. In fact, because of their physical condition, their necessities for life are greater than normal. They require care and assistance from others which they cannot provide for themselves because of their condition. People in an economy based on Christian economics take care of those who cannot work because they know that someday because of age or health they will be in a position where they will have to rely on others for food and care. People understand that they should benefit directly from and in proportion to their labors, but also that a percentage of the fruits of their labors should go towards those in society who are in need as well as to the common good.

Every organization of whatever size needs to monitor its financial performance in order to determine whether or not the organization is on track to reach its goals. Individuals and families monitor their expenses against their budget as well as progress towards their savings goals. Businesses monitor expenses against budget, cash flow, income against plan, inventory levels against plan, etc. Businesses use a variety of metrics to gauge whether the various aspects of the business are on track or not. When an organization notes that its financial performance is not what it should be, actions are taken to rectify problems and get the organization back on track.

The US economy is an immense financial organization consisting of millions of individuals, families, businesses and institutions. Obviously, the financial performance of the entire economy needs to be monitored using various metrics and if some aspect of the economy is not on track towards goal, then actions must be taken. It should be clear that it is one of the main responsibilities of the government to monitor the economy and take corrective action when necessary. In fact, it is one of the primary responsibilities of the government to oversee and manage the entire economy.

It is ludicrous to think that the economy can function without any government oversight and management. Try to imagine the chaos that would occur in a football game where there were no rules and no referees. Try to imagine the chaos that would occur if all traffic laws were eliminated and there were no police officers to facilitate order. The order and success of football games is dependent on rules and referees. The order and successful flow of traffic is dependent on laws and police officers. In a similar manner, the order and success of the US economy can only be achieved through government oversight and management.

The principle of self-sufficiency with respect to the US economy implies that the United States should attempt to produce all the goods and services needed by its members. Imports and exports involve either the buying or the selling of goods and services with another economy. The principle of self-sufficiency dictates that the United States should minimize imports and maximize exports while at the same time satisfying the needs and wants of its members. It the responsibility of the government to monitor the economy and make sure that imports are minimized and exports are maximized while at the same time the needs and wants of the people of the United States are satisfied.

Unfortunately, virtually every administration of the US government over the last forty years has not only failed to manage imports to keep them within acceptable limits, but they have actually facilitated an enormous increase in them. These administrations, with total disregard for the economy and the majority of the people, have worked with businesses to eliminate all controls on imports whatsoever. Imports are now 'out of control', the imbalance between production and consumption is extreme, and the reduction in working class income and wealth is a major factor in the current recession.

Current corporations are defined and structured to be essentially selfish and self-serving. Their sole purpose is the maximization of wealth for the stockholder. Secondly, because corporations are amoral, they will do whatever is necessary to achieve their goal of wealth maximization for their stockholders. They lie, though they do not consider their false and deceitful statements as lies, it is just business. Current corporations defraud customers through deceptive contracts ; but they only consider it business. Banks and financial institutions enslave borrowers for life; but they only consider it business. Current corporations dismiss lifetime employees; but they only consider it business. Current corporations put people and families out of their homes without any concern for where they will live; but they only consider it business.

Corporations have no sense of obligation to their fellow citizens who are in need, they want more than their fair share, have no sense of the common good, and have no sense of patriotism. Corporations have no loyalty to employees, to customers, to suppliers, to citizens or to country. Corporations only care about the stockholders.

Corporations want to maximize profits by charging the highest price and minimizing costs. Starting with Richard Nixon, each president and his administration has worked with big corporations to outsource or offshore manufacturing jobs and now even services. It is estimated that 8 million factory jobs have been lost due to outsourcing and that number continues to grow. Over three million service jobs such as customer service representatives, pharmacy technicians, accounts payable personnel, computer operators, data entry personnel, word processors, tax preparers, medical transcriptionists, database administrators, software engineers, engineers, designers, architects, chemists, biologists, consultants, technical writers, paralegals, accounts, teachers, and radiologists have been outsourced and this number continues to grow. It is estimated that another 30 to 40 million more US jobs will be eliminated due to outsourcing in the next twenty years. What will be the impact of 30 to 40 million more US jobs being lost?

Corporations ignoring their responsibility to the people of the United States have closed their operations here, laying off millions of employees, and have started up operations in low-wage countries taking advantage of the workers there. The sole reason for doing so has been to increase their profits by reducing labor costs, reducing taxes and reducing liabilities. These corporations are comprised of many people who call themselves Christian and yet these corporations totally disregard Christian principles.

Is this business practice ethical and moral which intentionally lays off workers permanently in the United States and engages workers in countries where there are either no laws or very weak laws regarding child labor, minimum pay, working conditions, worker safety, worker benefits, and workers' hours for the sole purpose of increasing profit margins? Is it ethical and moral to lay off workers for the sole purpose of increasing profits? From a Christian point of view the answer is no! And yet millions of people who call themselves Christian do so.

This point needs to be repeated. It is morally wrong for a corporation to lay off a full-time worker simply for the sake of increasing profits. Workers make their livelihood from the work that they perform within the corporation. The corporation does not have the right (corporations do not have rights) to take away a person's livelihood. That is stealing from the person. The corporation cannot steal a person's livelihood. Corporations are cooperatives between workers and capital shareholders and while current laws have unjustly and incorrectly given capital shareholders control of the corporation, that is wrong. There exists a natural social contract between the worker and the corporation to which the worker belongs and is a part of. This social contract involves the relations between the worker and the corporation and prevents the corporation from laying off the worker for the sole purpose of increasing profits.

It is amazing that starting in the 1970's when corporations began laying off workers by the hundreds of thousands, closing facilities and outsourcing these jobs to low wage/poor labor law countries, Christian leaders said and did nothing about this. These laid off workers were unjustly deprived of their livelihood and they and their families suffered—and Christian leaders said and did nothing!

The United States is a family, a family of over 315 million people. Family takes care of family; this is the essence of patriotism. It is outrageous that so many US corporations have over the last forty years totally disregarded this principle and this responsibility to their family and have laid off over 20 million workers, all for the sake of a higher profit margin. And what is even more outrageous is that Christians have remained silent and have even helped in these unjust and un-Christian activities.

The good of the US economy is based on the principle of self-sufficiency. This means that imports need to be minimized and this implies that outsourcing needs to be minimized if not totally eliminated. Outsourcing undermines the objective of the economy which is to satisfy in the most efficient and effective way the natural needs and desires of all Americans for safety, food, clothing, housing, a livelihood, education, healthcare, disability care, old age care, communication, recreation, entertainment, social interaction, acceptance and respect.

Totally ignoring the necessity of controlling outsourcing and the impact on the economy, the executive branch of the US government over the last forty years has done all in its power to allow corporations to maximize imported goods and outsourced services so that they could maximize profits—all at the expense of US workers. These imported goods and outsourced services have benefitted corporations and provided absolutely no benefit to consumers. In fact, the inordinate and economically detrimental amount of imports and outsourced services has had a severe impact on virtually the entire working class (315 million people) as well as the entire economy. What makes matters worse; the current administration continues to decimate the working class by expanding the already economically damaging amount of imported goods and outsourced services. And the Congress of the United States supports this disastrous policy of the administration. Outsourcing is out of control. Imports are out of control. And there is no hope that the government will do anything to bring outsourcing and imports under control for the good of the entire country until Christians within the United States begin to practice Christian principles within their business lives, their economic lives and their political lives. The United States economy will continue to decline unless outsourcing is stopped and the manufacturing and service jobs that have been eliminated because of outsourcing are restored. Family takes care of family. Love your neighbor as yourself. Each and every human being needs to be treated with absolute dignity and equality! Do good and avoid evil. Outsourcing violates these principles of Christian economics.

Home Ownership and the Mortgage and the Rental Industries

OF THE MANY RIGHTS of human beings; life, liberty and the pursuit of happiness are explicitly enumerated in the constitution of the United States. Human rights are derived from nature and not bestowed by the government or society. For this reason, human rights can never be taken away. Human rights form the basis for society, government and the economy.

The human and inalienable right which is the basis for capitalism is the right to own property. This right is critical and essential to the preservation of life, the support of liberty and the pursuit of happiness. Among the most essential things that a person must own is a home, and this implies that every person should own a home. Home owner ship is intimately bound to being human. Home ownership brings freedom, independence, security and stability to the home owner. A person's right and ability to build or buy a home and live in it must be supported and protected by government. Home ownership is not only good for the individual and the family; it is good for the economy. The economy expands as home ownership increases and contracts as home ownership decreases. Because of this positive correlation between home ownership and economic growth, the government should foster the widespread distribution of home ownership throughout the entire population and prevent the concentration of residential property ownership in the hands of a select few.

A park bench is not a home. A cardboard box is not a home. A car is not a home. An apartment is not a home. A true home is a physical place which is owned by the person. For only through ownership can a person achieve the appropriate freedom, independence, security, stability and permanence which he or she needs and is entitled to by nature.

Home ownership increased significantly after World War II. It did so because the economy was growing due to moderate prices and an income tax structure where the highest tax rate was ninety-one percent through 1963. High tax rates at the upper income levels balance the distribution of income and wealth between the working-class majority and the wealthy minority. For about twenty years after World War II, there were no elaborate mortgage rate schemes and virtually all mortgage rates were fixed for thirty years. During this time mortgage interest rates were actually higher than they are today. Yet, foreclosure rates during this period were significantly lower than they have been for the last ten years. The foreclosure rates over the last ten years have averaged 1.8%, while the foreclosure rates during the 1950's and 1960's averaged about .2%. Today's foreclosure rates are nine times larger than they were in the 1950's and 1960's when the mortgage interest rates were actually higher. The difference between the US housing system in the post war period and the last ten years is the lack of fairness and balance in the relationship between the mortgage companies and the home owners. Mortgage companies today are ruthlessly intent on maximizing their profits and have almost total disregard for homeowners, for the residential construction industry, the building supply industry and the rest of the economy.

Mortgage companies have developed strategies (actually schemes) to dominate the relationship between themselves and people who are either taking out a mortgage or who have taken out a mortgage. Variable interest rates, balloon payment mortgages, reverse mortgages, forty and fifty year term mortgages, private mortgage insurance (PMI), non-interest bearing property tax escrows, late fees, loan origination interest points, yield spread premiums, and foreclosure policies designed to promote repossessions are among the more common strategies and tactics used by mortgage companies to maximize their profits at the expense of home owners and their families.

Mortgage companies borrow money at relatively low rates of interest with no collateral from individual investors, from corporate investors and from banks. They then lend out this borrowed money to individuals who are buying a single-family home or townhouse, or condominium. The mortgage company then 'services' the mortgage loan collecting monthly payments and maintaining all records associated with the loan. As the mortgage company collects monthly payments from its customers (the home owners), it makes payments on the loans that it has taken out from banks. The difference between the interest and fees collected by the mortgage company from the home owner and the interest that the mortgage company pays to the banks is income to the mortgage company.

In spite of the extreme profits that the mortgage companies make, they relentlessly pursue greater profits through various means. Variable interest rate mortgages are devices of the mortgage corporations to maximize profits and extract an unjust amount of interest from the borrower. If a person borrows $200,000 from a mortgage company to buy a home on a variable interest rate mortgage, the mortgage company has already borrowed the $200,000 at a fixed rate of interest from its lenders. Through their variable interest rate scheme, the interest rate adjusts and almost always upwards and never falls below the original rate. Since the mortgage company's cost is fixed, their profit margin increases—good for the mortgage company and bad for home owner. Imagine buying a bike for $200 and a year later the seller of the bike says that you owe him more money because the price of the bike is variable. That would be ridiculous. The price is fixed at the time of sale. It is ridiculous, unfair and unjust for the mortgage company to have a variable price (variable interest rate), yet they have gotten away with this unjust practice for years. And this variable interest rate scheme is the cause of many people not being able to make their mortgage payments. While they were able to make the original mortgage payment, they were not or are not able to make the new payment because it is significantly higher than the original payment.

Private mortgage insurance is another scheme of the mortgage corporations to maximize profits. Private mortgage insurance benefits the lender and not the borrower and represents an additional ten to thirteen percent interest added to a person's monthly payment. PMI is actually interest in that it is a cost for the use of money. A very high percentage of people whose homes have been foreclosed have paid an average of two to three thousand dollars a year for PMI. This translates into ten to fifteen thousand dollars in five years. Where did this money go? To whom was it paid? The mortgage company collects this money, but what do they do with it? If the money that was being paid to PMI was instead applied to the principal (the amount of money owed to the mortgage company), then the person would have ten to fifteen thousand dollars more in equity. If the money that was being paid to PMI was instead put into an interest-bearing escrow account, then if the person experienced financial difficulties they would be able to have their mortgage payments made for between six to nine months from this escrow account into which they have paid. A person that has become unemployed takes an average of four to six months to find a full-time job. If the money paid into PMI was put into this interest-bearing escrow account, it could be used to make the person's monthly payments during the time of his or her unemployment. How many foreclosures could have been and can be prevented if there was no PMI, but instead a person had to pay into an escrow account? Billions of dollars are collected every year from PMI. Mortgage companies love PMI. It represents free money that they do not have to pay for. They do not care about the home owner, they only care about profits.

It should be clear from the foreclosure and housing system crisis from 2007 to 2012 that PMI does not work according to its alleged purpose. PMI is meant to insure lenders from the potential inability of borrowers who have less than twenty percent equity in their home. This twenty percent equity metric is an attempt to measure people who are at risk of defaulting on their mortgages. People do not arbitrarily decide not to pay their mortgage. They are prevented from making their mortgage payments because of financial difficulties. PMI actually increases the likelihood of default and does nothing to prevent foreclosure. It would make much more sense for a person who has less than twenty percent equity in their home to be required to pay into an interest-bearing escrow account than have to pay PMI. If the person never has to use the money in their escrow account, it would be applied to their principal. Such a practice would be fair, just and beneficial to the economy. Such a practice could have certainly lessened the housing crisis of the Great Recession and prevented tens of thousands of families from losing their homes. PMI in its current form is unjust.

Another unjust practice of mortgage companies is the practice of requiring borrowers to make payments on their property taxes into a non-interest-bearing escrow account which the mortgage company manages. The supposed reason for such an escrow account is the potential risk associated with people not paying their property taxes. If people don't pay their property taxes, then the taxing government can take their home. Of course, people do not want to lose their homes. And the percentage of people who do lose their homes because of unpaid property taxes is so small as to be negligible. And in the case that a person was at risk of losing their home due to unpaid taxes, then the mortgage company could intervene in those extremely rare cases. Yet, in spite of the fact that the percentage of homes sold due to unpaid property taxes is extremely small, mortgage companies require the vast majority of borrowers to pay into property tax escrow accounts. There is no valid or just reason for property tax escrow accounts. The real reason why mortgage companies require the vast majority of borrowers to pay into these accounts is their ability to gain interest from the borrowers' money. Mortgage companies hold over forty billion dollars in these escrow accounts. Assuming that the mortgage companies receive five percent interest on these forty billion dollars of other people's money, they can gain over two billion dollars a year in interest from the borrower's money. It is free money for the mortgage companies. However, it is not fair; it is not just. But it happens and the government does nothing about this injustice. The money in these escrow accounts does not belong to the mortgage companies; it belongs to the home owners. Yet, the mortgage companies act as though it was their money.

Why do mortgage companies charge points (up-front interest) on mortgage loans? Why do mortgage companies charge lenders a higher interest rate than the market average and then pay mortgage brokers a substantial fee for locking in the lender at a higher interest rate? Why are mortgage interest rates so high? Why do mortgage corporations charge late fees on top of interest?

A mortgage loan should be a simple transaction. And because a mortgage loan involves a person's home which is intimately related to the person's right to life, liberty and the pursuit of happiness; it should involve minimal risk to the home owner as borrower. Yes, that is correct. A mortgage loan should involve minimal risk to the home owner as borrower. The mortgage loan transaction must be simple. It should involve a fixed rate of interest and a fixed reasonable term which will allow the home owner to pay off the mortgage loan in a reasonable amount of time. There should not be any extra interest up front at the time of closing the loan, nor any extra interest as late fees. Mortgage companies are in business to provide a service. The service that they provide is to help people become home owners.

The result of all the above discussed schemes, scams, and abuses by the mortgage industry and perhaps the greatest abuse and injustice perpetrated by the mortgage industry is foreclosure and re-possession. Foreclosure and re-possession is a terrible experience. A person who receives a foreclosure notice from the mortgage company is already in a depressed emotional state due to their financial situation. They have dreaded and anticipated the arrival of the foreclosure notice, usually delivered by a sheriff's deputy. They have received a foreclosure notice because he or she has not made their full regular mortgage payments for two months. While they may have been able to make partial payments, the mortgage company will not accept partial payments. The person who has received a foreclosure notice was not able to make their full monthly payments because they were not financially able to. Either their income has been significantly reduced due to loss of employment (99.99% of time through no fault of their own), medical disability, divorce (they cannot afford the mortgage payments on only one salary; or their mortgage payments have increased significantly because the interest rate on their mortgage is variable, or they are financially dying from the drastic increase in the price of gasoline, food, electricity, natural gas, propane, heating oil, health insurance, medical costs, medicine costs, dental costs, vision costs, etc.

The person that has received a foreclosure notice has already been harassed by the mortgage company, by credit card companies, by the telephone company, by the electric company, by the gas company, by the auto finance company, and by others. They have been threatened to have their phone shut off (or it already has been shut off), their electricity turned off (or it already has been turned off), their gas shut off (or it already has been shut off), and their car repossessed (or it has already been repossessed. These companies call seven days a week, multiple times a day, from 7:00 AM to 9:00 PM. They are relentless. Even the local government threatens to shut off the water and they will do it. The person who has received a foreclosure notice has already been 'beaten up' financially. They are depressed and they have lost confidence in themselves, in society and in government. They have problems sleeping at night and so does their whole family; husbands, wives and children.

After the person has received a foreclosure notice, they are besieged with correspondence from all sorts of lawyers and companies most of whose real purpose is to take advantage of a person in a financially unfortunate situation. And if this person does not get a job with a fantastic salary, they will lose their home. They will actually have to move out of their home; the home that they have lived in for many years, the home that they painted and decorated, the home where they had family parties, the home where their children took their first steps, and the home where they felt safe and secure. Where will they go? Will they ever be able to buy a home again?

From 2000 to 2011, there were 21 million foreclosures and 4.7 million home repossessions, approximately 10 percent of all residential mortgages. Assuming that three people live in the average home that means more than 14 million people were displaced from their homes between 2000 and 2011. Was these anyone there to help these people? What did the Federal government do to help these people? What did the state government do to help these people? What did the local governments do to help these people? What did the organized religions do to help these people? Nothing! Nothing! Nothing! Nothing! And there seems to be no end in sight to these foreclosures. How many more people will lose their homes before something is done?

Who really benefits from re-possessions? The people who have lost their homes and now suffer from the scarlet letter of poor credit certainly do not benefit from re-possessions? Are re-possessions good for the mortgage companies? Are re-possessions good for the government? Are re-possessions good for the economy ? Only people and companies (including the mortgage companies) who buy re-possessed properties and profit from the misfortune and financial abuse of others actually benefit from re-possessions. However, it is clear that the benefits to a few do not offset the harm to so many. And what is even more confusing is that so many so-called Christians have been involved in these foreclosures and re-possessions. It is hard to imagine Jesus foreclosing on people or having people evicted from their homes. If Jesus would not foreclose on people or re-possess people's houses or evict them from their homes, then how can Christians who are supposed to be the followers of Jesus Christ do so?

The right to shelter is derived from the right to life, for life cannot be supported without a home. Since rights are derived from nature, they cannot be taken away by the government, by the courts, by society, or by anyone or anything. In fact, the government, the courts, and society are obligated to respect and protect the right of an individual to a home.

If a person is living in a home or an apartment and they are temporarily unable to pay the full amount of their contracted mortgage or lease, it is against their rights to displace them from their home. As long as they are able to make some kind of payment, they should not be displaced from their home or apartment. This arrangement should continue until the cause or causes of their inability to make full payments are removed. Forbearance, yes! Foreclosure, no!

A person who has become unemployed will be unemployed for a short period of time. A 'rule of thumb' regarding the amount of time before an unemployed person finds employment is that it will take as many months as the person's previous income divided by $10,000. The median personal income is approximately $31,100. Using the above rule of thumb, it will take the average person about three to four months to find a new full-time job. For some people it will take a longer amount of time, for some people it will take a shorter amount of time. Once a person becomes unemployed, he or she files for unemployment compensation. Net unemployment compensation (unfortunately and ridiculously the Federal and state governments withhold income taxes) is a small fraction of the income that a person had when they were employed and it is totally insufficient to allow a person to meet his or her family's expenses.

Until workers are legally made equals with capital shareholders, unemployment is a fact of life for the majority of people. Gone forever are the days when a person could spend their whole working career with one company. Because of mergers, acquisitions, unfair competitive practices by big corporations, and outsourcing; most workers can expect to be laid off and unemployed multiple times during their working lifetime. During these times of temporary unemployment, these individuals need support by the government and forbearance from all the companies and organizations with which the person has financial obligations. Finding fulltime employment is more than enough for these people to worry about. They do not and should not have to worry about having to pay the mortgage, the rent, their car payment, their phone bill, their electric bill, their heating bill, their water bill, or any other bill or expense. Their main and only focus needs to be finding a job. The sooner that this person finds full-time employment, the better it will be for that person and the better it will be for the economy.

In order to allow the unemployed person to focus entirely on finding fulltime employment and making a positive contribution to the production side of the economy, all of the companies and organizations with which this person has financial obligations (mortgage company, landlord, finance company, phone company, electric company, heating energy company, etc.) must enter into government managed forbearance programs. The person is unemployed. It is not that they don't want to pay their bills, they can't pay their bills. Unfortunately, companies financially and emotionally abuse the unemployed person and his or her family. Companies charge late fees and over-limit fees, and most credit card companies will increase their interest rates dramatically. In addition, these companies begin their harassment campaigns of calling the unemployed person and hounding them for payment. These callers don't care that the person is unemployed because they are paid based on collections. From an allegorical point of view, the unemployed person is like a person who has fallen to the ground and the companies with which he or she has financial obligations come along and kick them and kick them refusing to allow them to get up. Financial abuse is actually worse than physical abuse. Physical abuse consists of either one event or periodic events. Financial abuse is continuous and prolonged.

At the time when the person files for unemployment compensation, he or she should bring a documented list of their financial obligations with account numbers, company names, addresses, and phone numbers. The government counselor should determine the various amounts that the person should pay on his or her financial obligations if anything at all. For example, if a person's total monthly expenses are $2000 and their total net income from all sources including unemployment compensation is $1000, then each financial obligation will be reduced fifty percent. The government counselor would contact each company and organization and notify them of the forbearance program and that it is effective immediately. In addition, all property taxes should cease during the forbearance program.

As soon as the person gains fulltime employment, unemployment compensation ends and the forbearance programs would also end. During the forbearance periods, the companies and organizations that are involved in the programs would accept the amounts determined by the government unemployment counselor and the difference between the normal payment and the forbearance payment would be ignored and forgiven. In other words, the difference should not accrue nor should the person be liable for this difference.

While unemployment is a major factor leading to people's inability to make their mortgage payments leading to foreclosure, it is certainly not the only factor. Seventy percent of full time workers live from paycheck to paycheck. Living from paycheck to paycheck means that a person's expenses equal or exceed his or her income. This concept, 'living from paycheck to paycheck', is incomprehensible to the wealthy. They either have never experienced such a situation or their experience has been erased from memory because of time. The vast majority of wealthy people and most upper middle-class people suffer from 'Marie Antoinette's syndrome'. When they are told that millions of people have no discretionary income and have expenses that equal or exceed their income, they respond that these people should take money from their savings, or sell some of their stocks or bonds, or sell one of their properties. The wealthy do not realize that the people who live from paycheck to paycheck have no savings, have no stocks, have no bonds, and have no extra property.

It is estimated that eighty percent of the US population live from paycheck to paycheck and this number has increased in the last fifteen years. In terms of numbers, eighty percent of the population equals approximately 250 million people. In the fifteen years a significant number of those people who live from paycheck to paycheck have gone from the state of their expenses equaling their income to the state of their expenses exceeding their income. This has happened because their income has not increased at the same rate as the rising prices. Gasoline prices have doubled. Food prices have risen forty percent. Electricity prices have risen over thirty percent. Natural gas, heating oil and propane prices have risen over fifty percent. Healthcare prices have risen thirty percent. Virtually every expense associated with basic living has increased. People must have food, heat, electricity, transportation and healthcare. In order to pay for expenses that exceed their income, these tens of millions of people have used their credit cards, taken out equity loans and or personal loans all of which have increased the shortfall between their income and their expenses. Thirty-four percent of people have taken out personal loans. Total credit card debt is over $1 trillion, the highest in history. And many of these people have reached their limit, they can borrow no more. These people are employed but are in extreme financial difficulties because of out of control and unregulated prices, rents, etc. They don't have enough money to pay all their expenses. What bill or expense don't they pay? They must have food. They must have heat. They must have electricity. They must have transportation to go to work. They must go to the doctor if they are sick. Because of their financial situation, many of these people begin to fall behind on their mortgage payments and other bills. The late fees make their financial situation worse and they get further behind. For many of these people, they reach the point where they are three months behind on their mortgage payments and the mortgage company forecloses on them. What makes matters worse is that this group of people whose income is insufficient to pay for their expenses because prices continues to grow faster than people's incomes and is the basis for continued foreclosures.

The last major group of individuals who either have had their homes foreclosed on or who will have their homes foreclosed on in the near future are those who are the victims of variable interest rate mortgages. While these people may have been able to make their payments before the interest rate increase, they are incapable of making their payments after the increase rate increase especially given the drastic increase in basic living expenses such as food, heat, electricity, transportation and healthcare over the last fifteen years. Why was it and is it necessary for the mortgage companies to kick people out of their homes when they are able make payments which were at one time acceptable? Are variable interest rate mortgages fair? Are they necessary? Are they good for the economy ? Are they consistent with Christian economics?

A person who enters into a mortgage contract with a financial institution is a partner with the financial institution. They are equals. This joint venture between the home buyer and the financial company has as its objective the successful acquisition of the home by the home buyer. All contracts must involve equal parties. There cannot be a superior-inferior relation or a dominant-submissive relation between the parties. It is the role of the government to act as an impartial third party to oversee contracts and assure equity and fairness between the parties. Consider the situation where an individual wishes to enter into a contract with a finance company or bank to purchase a car. The finance company or bank is comprised of hundreds or thousands of individuals and perhaps dozens or even hundreds of lawyers. A written contract has been prepared by the finance company's or bank's legal department or legal firm. This written contract contains thousands of words in a syntax referred to as 'legalize', a language intentionally cryptic in order not to be understood by a layman. Virtually, all contracts are biased in favor of the bank or finance company. Who is there to referee such a situation and make sure that the contract is fair? It must be the government, there isn't anyone else. It would be as simple as having all contracts pre-approved by the government and written in plain language to the average person. The individual should also have the ability to seek government council free of charge and in the event of a complaint, potential breach of contract, or what appears to be something done unfairly by the bank or finance company and the individual should have the ability to pursue litigation on their own without having to pay an attorney.

Currently, there is an unfair relationship between a person and a mortgage company. The financial institution has all the legal power while the home owner has virtually none. The person buying a home enters into a contract with the seller of the home. Since most people do not have sufficient funds to purchase a home because of the very high price relative to the buyer's income, the buyer enters into another contract with a financial institution to borrow the money needed for the purchase. Because of the dominant position of the financial institution and because the financial institution is intent on maximizing profits, the home buyer is forced into obligations which he or she would rather not incur such as the home being collateral, extra interest (points) at the time of the contract, private mortgage insurance, interest rate schemes, special fees, etc.

Foreclosures have had a significant negative impact on the housing market and on the entire economy. The foreclosures during the Great Recession of 2008 caused virtually all home values to decrease during that time because the market was flooded with foreclosed, re-possessed properties being sold for below market prices. Now ten years later, a high percentage of property values have not recovered, that is, their value today is less than is was ten or fifteen years ago.

Besides the financially crippling effect on the millions of people who lost their homes during the Great Recession which started in 2008, other people who were trying to sell their homes to avoid foreclosure could not do so because prices were down to such an extent that they owed more than the price that they could get if they could even sell their home. These people unfortunately end up being swallowed up by the spiral of foreclosures. The foreclosures during the period from 2006 to 2012 was the primary cause of the decrease in new home sales, the decrease in the construction of new homes, and the layoff of millions of carpenters, electricians, plumbers, and other people employed in the residential home construction industry. In addition, those foreclosures caused the significant reduction in the sale and manufacture of lumber, building materials and building supplies. Tens of millions of people were directly affected by these foreclosures. The financial damage that has been caused and continues to be caused by these foreclosures could have been prevented and can be stopped by ceasing and eliminating foreclosures and replacing foreclosures with forbearance programs.

Why did these foreclosures occur (and continue to occur) that have financially harmed and crippled tens of millions of people (and continue to do so today)? Was and is there a good reason for foreclosures? Foreclosures occur because the mortgage companies want to maximize profits. Blinded by greed, these mortgage companies do not care about the ten million people who have lost their homes because of foreclosures. Blinded by greed, these mortgage companies do not care about the hundred million people whose home values have decreased significantly because of foreclosures. Blinded by greed, these mortgage companies do not care about the millions of people who have lost their jobs because of foreclosures. The mortgage companies don't care about people, they only care about money. The stockholders who own the mortgage companies don't care about people, they only care about money. These mortgage companies have caused significant financial harm to tens of millions of people. And the Federal government has done nothing. And the state government has done nothing. And the leaders of the various organized religions have said nothing.

Millions of people have lost their homes through re-possession. Their credit has been ruined, they have lost the greatest investment in their lives, and they may never be able to buy another home again. Millions of other people have lost their jobs because of this out of control mortgage industry. The new home construction industry has been significantly impacted by these unnecessary foreclosures as well as the building supplies industry. And hundreds of millions of people have seen the value of their homes decrease because of this unregulated mortgage industry. What makes things worse is that there is nothing being done to rectify this situation. Because there is no effective government oversight and management of the excesses of the mortgage companies; foreclosures will continue, re-possessions will continue.

Something needs to be done. The mortgage companies are not going to change. Their ultimate goal is the maximization of profits. And they will use any tactics to achieve that goal, since they are amoral and have no ethics ("it is neither right nor wrong, it is just business "). Homeowners are powerless against the mortgage companies. Carpenters, electricians, and plumbers are powerless against the mortgage companies. The new residential construction industry is powerless against the mortgage companies. The building industry is powerless against the mortgage companies. Who is there to intervene to stop this economic crisis ? What can be done? How long will this continue? How much more harm will be done to the economy because the mortgage industry is out of control?

The only real agent that can effectively address the crisis of the mortgage industry is the government. The purpose of the government is to protect and defend people's rights and promote economic balance, equity, and stability. The government represents all the people and not just mortgage corporations.

While the recent trend and current practice is for the home to be collateral on the loan, this practice runs counter to the right to shelter. The home should not be collateral on the loan. When the government borrows money, there is no collateral. When banks borrow money (they borrow money every day), there is no collateral. When most corporations borrow money, there is no collateral. There does not and should not be collateral on home loans.

What would happen if a law was passed that made it illegal for a mortgage contract to have the home or anything else as collateral? What would happen if this took place immediately and applied to all existing mortgages as well as new mortgages? If a person fell behind on their mortgage payments and a mortgage company could not repossess their home, what would the mortgage company do? Obviously, they would work out some plan with the home owner. In fact, as soon as a person entered a financial situation where they could not pay the full amount of their monthly mortgage payment, they could contact the mortgage company to work out a temporary payment plan until they were financially able to make their regular payments again. If repossession and foreclosure was not an option for mortgage companies because the home was not collateral, then the mortgage company would obviously work with borrowers who were experiencing financial problems.

Imagine if all foreclosures ceased. Imagine if all those people whose homes have been repossessed and are currently unoccupied were able to move back into their homes and enter into a special payment arrangement with the mortgage company. If all foreclosures ceased and people could move back into their homes; property values would increase, new home sales would increase, new home construction would increase, unemployed carpenters would return to work, unemployed plumbers would return to work, unemployed builders would return to work, and the building materials industry would see an increase. Making foreclosures illegal would be good for those home owners facing foreclosure, good for the unemployed, good for all home owners (because home values would increase), and good for the economy.

Again, the only real agent that can effectively address the crisis of the mortgage industry is the government. The purpose of the government is to protect and defend people's rights and promote economic balance, equity, and stability. The government can make collateral mortgages illegal thus preventing foreclosures. The government can make PMI illegal and force mortgage companies to replace PMI with interest bearing escrow accounts owned by the borrower. The government can force mortgage companies to pay interest on property tax escrow accounts. The government can eliminate variable rate mortgages, balloon payment mortgages, loan origination fees, and yield spread premiums. Mortgage companies would like borrowers to make payments for the rest of their lives. The government can make forty and fifty year mortgages illegal. The long-term stability of working families is a critical responsibility of the government. For the economy depends on the stability of working families to produce the goods and services needed and desired by everyone. Interest fees and finance fees do not drive the economy; only purchases of goods and services. The less money that a person pays in interest on a home loan the more they can spend on things which drive the economy. The government can oversee and limit the profit margins of mortgage companies. The government represents all the people and not just mortgage corporations.

Yet, it should be clear that those who occupy the current positions within the government do not represent the people. No, they represent and promote the best interests of Big Business and in the case of the housing industry Big Mortgage. The Federal government has given hundreds of billion dollars to banks, investment companies, insurance companies, automobile companies and others. The government saved the investments of investors. What about the millions of poor home owners whose homes have been repossessed? What about the millions of poor homeowners whose homes are in foreclosure and may lose their homes? What about residential home construction companies? What about the millions of carpenters, plumbers, and other homes builders who are laid off? What about the building supply companies? The government is only concerned with Big Business. It is not concerned with small businesses or with families.

The government refused to help out home owners. Yet, it has spent between two to three trillion dollars helping banks and corporations. 9.3 million homeowners lost their homes from 2006 to 2013. Assume that these home owners had an average monthly payment of $1500. For 251 billion dollars the government could have gotten these people's homes out of foreclosure and paid their mortgages for one year giving them an opportunity to recover financially and put them into a position to make their mortgages again. The two to three trillion dollars that the government gave to investors (many of whom were not even American) did absolutely nothing to stop the US housing crisis between 2008 and 2013. The two to three trillion dollars that the government gave to investors (many of whom were not even American) did really nothing to help the economy. The two to three trillion dollars that the government gave to investors (many of whom were not even American) helped out merely thousands of people virtually all of whom were living good lives; they lived in nice homes, they had nice furniture, they had nice cars, and they had plenty of money. The two to three trillion dollars that the government gave to investors (many of whom were not even American) did absolutely nothing for the 9.3 million homeowners who lost their homes from 2006 to 2013. The two to three trillion dollars that the government gave to investors (many of whom were not even American) did absolutely nothing to increase the home values of the entire US housing market during that period. The two to three trillion dollars that the government gave to investors (many of whom were not even American) did absolutely nothing to help the new home construction industry, the unemployed carpenters, plumbers, new home construction workers, and the building supply industry.

With 251 billion dollars, the government could have prevented over twenty-four million people from losing their homes (9.3 million households times 2.58 people per household). With 251 billion dollars, the government could have maintained or increased the home values of virtually the entire US housing market. With 251 billion dollars, the government could have sustained the new home construction. With 251 billion dollars, the government could have helped continued employment for millions of carpenters, plumbers, and new home construction workers. With 251 billion dollars, the government could have sustained the building supply industry. With 251 billion dollars, the government could have helped virtually the entire economy. Unfortunately, those occupying the government do not care about millions of working class Americans; they only care about the wealthy minority. The US government has spent $8.5 trillion dollars on defense in the last 15 years and it could not spend $251 billion dollars on people whose homes were repossessed? Are the US government's priorities in line with Christian principles? Certainly not!

The mortgage industry is out of control and it engages in unjust practices. Variable interest rate contracts, balloon contracts, private mortgage insurance, non-interest-bearing property tax escrow accounts, late fees, extra interest at the time of loan closing, interest rate spread premiums, foreclosure and re-possession are all unfair and unjust tactics used by the mortgage industry to maximize its profits at the expense of the home owner. Because of the extreme and relentless use of these tactics, the mortgage industry has succeeded in negatively impacting the entire economy. This crisis cannot be solved by home owners. While the mortgage industry could solve this crisis, it will not because it is blinded by its own greed. The only real agent that can solve this crisis is the Federal government. But it won't! The Federal government is so influenced by the mortgage industry and Big Business that it does not understand what needs to be done. It too is blinded by the greed of Big Business. Instead of protecting home owners from the unfair and unjust tactics, schemes and scams of mortgage companies; instead of assisting home owners to avoid foreclosure and re-possession; the Federal government sides with mortgage investors and uses public funds to bail-out corporate investors. Christians should be outraged by the mortgage industry and what it has done to millions of families. Christians must begin to act like Christians and apply Christian principles to the mortgage industry.

Among the most essential things that a person must own is a home, and this implies that every person should own a home. Home owner ship is intimately bound to being human. Home ownership brings freedom, independence, security and stability to the home owner and is essential for a stable economy. While temporary housing is sometimes necessary, it is just that, temporary. People want and need a home which they own.

The practice of people having to rent from a landlord goes back thousands of years. It is based on the premise that the king or the emperor or the nobleman claimed to own all property. People's dwellings which they built were according to this premise: the property of the king, emperor or nobleman. Rents were originally taxes assigned by the king, emperor or nobleman to generate revenue. Of course, this notion that the king, emperor and noblemen owned all property was wrong and unjust. It denied the basic rights of people to own property and to own their own home. Yet, it continued for thousands of years and was supported by laws and the courts. As kingdoms and empires collapsed and were replaced by other forms of government, the notion of some person owning large expanses of land and the buildings on the land continued. The vast majority of people were forced to pay rent to the landlord for the use of the land that they farmed and the buildings that they lived in. And because of the political influence of these so-called landowners, the laws and the courts supported their unjust claim over the land and the buildings which people lived in. The legal systems of most countries have never recognized all human rights nor the Christian principles associated with human interactions and behavior. People who were forced to rent, and this was the majority of the people, paid rent during their entire lifetimes. This was clearly a type of slavery to the landlord.

Unfortunately, this unjust practiced of renting from a landlord continues to this day. The landlord is looking for a steady income from rents and wants those rents forever; for the rest of his or her life and for the lives of his or her heirs. Many people who pay rent will do so for the rest of their lives in spite of the desire to own their own home. Of course, with home ownership, the home owner only pays until the mortgage is paid off. People who rent and are never able to buy their own home will pay rent for their entire lifetimes. People can pay rent for 50 to 60 years. Considering their rent payments, they could have bought two homes in 50 to 60 years. And when they die, they have nothing.

The percentage of renters in the United States is thirty-seven percent and that is the highest rate in the last 50 years. The majority of the households who rent are in the lower-middle and lower income brackets. The number of families renting or forced to rent has been increasing over the last ten years because of the economic crisis and because of the unjust practices of the mortgage industry. Part of this increase in the percentage of families who have been displaced from their homes because of the unjust practices of the mortgage industry has been directly and intentionally caused by individuals who control both mortgage companies and rental companies because rentals can have a higher rate of return that mortgages.

Consider a young couple who does not have enough money for a down payment on a home. They would like to buy a $200,000 home but do not have the $20,000 needed for a down payment. So, they find a home to rent. The home happens to be owned by an investor who bought the $200,000 with a $20,000 down payment. The mortgage payment at a 5% interest rate for a 20-year term is about $1200 a month. The investor adds $250 for real estate taxes and maintenance and charges the young couple $1450 a month rent with a security deposit of $2175. In effect, the young couple is paying the investor's mortgage and real estate taxes and providing the investor with money for possible maintenance. If the young couple is never able to save $20,000 for a down payment and they rent for the next 20 years, they will have paid off the investor's mortgage. Most likely the investor will raise the rent every year over the 20-year term even though the mortgage rate is fixed and the property taxes do not go up every year. At the end of 20 years, the couple has nothing and the investor has a home probably worth more than $200,000. Once the mortgage is paid off, the $1200 of the monthly rent that was being used to pay for the investor's mortgage on the house now goes into his or her pocket. This is certainly not a fair or just arrangement, yet it occurs tens of millions of times and has occurred for hundreds of years. In arrangements like this, the landlord is unjustly taking advantage of the tenant.

If the landlord in the above example would consider a rate of return of 3 percent, which would amount to $6000 a year on a $200,000 home, and then add $250 for real estate taxes and maintenance; the monthly rent would be $750. A rent of $750 a month is just, a rent of $1450 a month is not. A monthly rent of $750 would allow the couple to save enough money for a down payment on their own home.

So-called investors not only rent out homes using this scheme, they rent out apartments, buildings, stores, land, streets, highways, bridges and many other things. Historically, renting has been the most common means of allowing a person to become wealthy, very wealthy and extremely wealthy—all at the expense of the renter. While it is not unjust to rent a home, an apartment, a building, a store, land, a street, a highway or a bridge; it is the rental price that is almost always unjust. Rent like any other price must be fair to both parties in other to be just. In the example of the couple renting the home above, the rent does not allow them to be able to save enough money for a down payment for their own home.

Landlords do not want to work. They want to earn an income and maximize that income by renting from others. They do not want people to stop renting from them. They would like people to continue to rent for their entire lives. This is contrary to the natural need and right of a person to own their home. Renting and home ownership are opposites. Christians must respect the right of others to own a home and not prevent or hinder a person from owning a home. Rents must be just. Rental contracts must be just. Home ownership, not renting, is good for the individual, for families, for society and for the economy. Stable family life is dependent on home ownership and a stable society and economy are dependent on stable families. At the end of the world when God judges everyone, He will separate the good from the bad based on the commandment to 'love your neighbor as yourself'. Christians who own mortgage companies and who are landlords must treat mortgagees and tenants as they would treat Jesus. They need to see Jesus in their mortgagees and tenants.

Corporations

THE HISTORY OF THE world is mainly the narrative of wealthy people using various means to increase their wealth and social power. The wealthy became the emperors, kings, queens and the so-called nobility. They dominated society. They claimed to own all land and all natural resources. They made everyone serve them, support them and fight their wars of aggression and aggrandizement. History is a record of what kingdoms did and what empires did and until recently very little regarding the common person. The history of kingdoms and empires is based on the actions of kings and emperors. The economies of these kingdoms and empires were driven by the work of the common people but the majority of the benefits of these economies went to the ruling class. The distribution of wealth was extreme with the ruling.01 percent of the population owning the vast majority of wealth. Because there was no middle class, almost the entire working class lived in poverty while the ruling class lived lives of outrageous extravagance. This state of society lasted for thousands of years.

About 800 years ago when manufacturing became an industry, there emerged a wealthy middle class. Over time this wealthy middle class became wealthier and more powerful than most kings, queens and the nobility. There were two factors which enabled this wealthy middle class to become so wealthy and so powerful: the claim that the business or businesses that they engaged in were owned by them, only them, and their claim that the relationship between them and those people who worked within the business was that of employer and employee and not joint business partners. These claims allowed these few individuals to maintain absolute control over the business organization that they were involved in, make all decisions regarding the business and claim absolute ownership of all revenues and profits. This position was not too different from that of kings, queens, and landlords who claimed to own all the land and the resources on the land. Workers in both cases were treated as a means of serving, supporting and facilitating the unlimited growth of the financial empires of the kings, queens, landlords and wealthy so-called business owners. The wealthy middle class used their financial power to gain political influence and with this political influence, they succeeded in having governments and courts support these two claims. These two claims have continued to this very day as well as the financial empires that have been created because of these claims. These two claims are at the basis of modern corporations. But are these two claims just? And are these two claims legitimate within the context of Christian Economics?

Were and are these two claims just; that the business or businesses that the wealthy person engaged in were and are owned by them and only them, and that the relationship between them and those people who worked or work within the business was and is that of employer and employee and not joint business partners.? And was the claim by emperors, kings, queens, and the nobility that they owned the land and all the resources on the land just? Absolutely and certainly not! These three unjust claims have allowed individuals to amass fortunes and in turn control economies and they were not and are not challenged by the Christian leaders. If only Christian leaders had taken a stand and declared these claims to be unjust, how different history and today's society would be!

What can make a discussion of these claims difficult is that the leaders of Christian organizations and the other various religious organizations have been virtually silent concerning these claims. Unfortunately, the vast majority of Christian leaders and the leaders of other organized religions have throughout history chosen a position of silence regarding the policies and activities of the ruling elite in matters of economics, politics and war. In spite of the physical, economic, psychological, and emotional sufferings of the working majority caused by the ruling minorities; Christian leaders have said and done virtually nothing to proclaim the injustices of the ruling minority.

And Jesus answering, said: A certain man went down from Jerusalem to Jericho, and fell among robbers, who also stripped him, and having wounded him went away, leaving him half dead. And it happened that a certain priest went down the same way and seeing him passed by—he said and did nothing. In like manner a Levite, when he was near the place and saw the man, passed by - he said and did nothing. For the last two thousand years, Christian leaders (popes, patriarchs, bishops, priests, ministers, etc.) have seen the injustices wrought on the working-class majority by emperors, kings, queens, the nobility, landlords and the wealthy middle class; and they have said and did nothing. For the last two thousand years, the robbers have been emperors, kings, queens, the nobility, landlords, and now the super-rich. The man who has been robbed and stripped represents the working class. And the priest and the Levite represent Christian leaders.

The claim by one person or a few people to own all the land and natural resources of a country is unjust and against the Natural Law. The claim by one or a few individuals to own a corporation comprised of dozens or hundreds or thousands of people is unjust and against the Natural Law. The claim by one or a few individuals that the workers within a corporation have no rights and are merely employees subservient to this one individual or these few individuals is unjust and against the Natural Law. These latter two claims have a stranglehold on modern corporations. Most corporations are owned and or controlled by a very few individuals and this is true for both private corporations and publically traded corporations.

Modern corporations are a construct and device of the capitalist class to allow them to engage in business while limiting both their liability and the business's liability both financially and socially. The owners of a corporation are not liable for the losses incurred by the corporation. If a corporation ceases to do business and is virtually bankrupt and if it still owes money to its suppliers, employees, customers and creditors; the owners are not liable whatsoever.

The owners, the board of directors, the officers of the corporation, the vice-presidents and the managers of a corporation are not liable for social wrong-doings. The only time that one will ever hear of a law suit involving the officers and directors of a corporation for alleged wrong-doing is when the wrong-doing has affected the owners, the capital stockholders.

The modern corporation's only objective and goal is to serve the interests of and maximize the benefits for the so-called owners. While corporate communications pay lip service to the concept that it seeks the benefit and welfare of customers, workers and suppliers—that is in fact a lie. The modern corporation exists solely for the benefit of its owners.

The purpose and objective of Wal-Mart is to maximize the wealth of the Walton family, the primary owners of Wal-Mart. The purpose and objective of the Ford Motor Company is to maximize the wealth of the Ford family, the primary owners of Ford. In a similar manner Samsung, LG Group, Carrefour Group, Fiat, Peugeot, Cargill, BMW, Hyundai, Koch

Industries, Bosch, ALDI, Motorola, Viacom, Novartis, Tyson Foods, Weyerhaeuser, Loew's, News Corp FOX, Michelin, Publix, Bombardier, Mars, Oréal, Lagardère, Gap, Philips, Louis Vuitton, General Dynamics, Anheuser-Busch, Hilton, Comcast, Sodexho, Winn-Dixie, and Ikea have as their sole purpose and objective the maximization of the wealth of their family owners. And there are tens of thousands of other family owned corporations.

Over 60 percent of US corporations are privately owned—60 percent. Privately owned corporations have a very small number of owners. These corporations range from small organizations with annual revenues in the hundreds of thousands to multi-national organizations with annual revenues in the billions with hundreds of thousands of employees. Cargill, Pricewaterhouse Coopers, Bechtel, Publix Super Markets, Love's Travel Stops & Country Stores, Ernst & Young, Pilot Flying J, Meijer, Cox Enterprises, Enterprise Rent-A-Car, Toys 'R' Us, Aramark, Fidelity Investments, First Data, Amway, SC Johnson, Caesars Entertainment, CDW, Giant Eagle, Gordon Food Service, Menard, Bloomberg, McKinsey & Company, Sinclair Oil, Wawa, Levi Strauss & Co, Hy-Vee, Wegmans Food Markets, Sheetz, Kohler, Graybar Electric, Perdue, Roundy's Supermarkets, Schwan Food, Burlington Coats, Del Monte Foods, Michaels Stores, Medline Industries, Neiman Marcus Group, McJunkin Red Man, Bass Pro Shops, Hallmark Cards, and Hearst are all privately held corporations whose sole objective is to maximize the wealth of the owners. And there are hundreds of thousands of small franchise based private corporations whose sole purpose is also to maximize the wealth of the owners.

The sole purpose of a modern corporation is to maximize the wealth of its owners. Workers spend their entire lives increasing the wealth of the owners of the modern corporations. This is similar to kingdoms whose sole purpose was the maximization of wealth of the king, queen, royal family and nobility. Is this just? Is this Christian? Certainly not!

One of the underlying principles (even though it is a false principle) of the modern corporation and its owners is that "it is neither right nor wrong, it is just business." This allows a corporation and its owners to hide behind the corporation in order to engage in virtually any kind of activity, moral or immoral, because it is just business. The owners, the officers of company, and the executives take the position that nothing that a corporation does should be construed as right or wrong in its pursuit of maximum profits. Corporations lie, though they do not consider falsehoods as lies, if it is advantageous to them. Corporations will cheat their employees, though they don't consider depriving their employees of their justly earned wages as cheating. Corporations will steal ideas, but they don't consider what they are doing as stealing, just doing business.

Legally, a corporation is an artificial person distinct from its owners. Those who are currently considered the owners of corporations use corporations to exploit the working class. Because the capitalist class has had extremely great influence on the US political system, they virtually control almost every facet of government: the executive, the legislative and the judicial branches—Federal, state, county and local. Through political machinations they have gotten laws passed that give superior rights and privileges to corporations and both protect and hide the owners from the wrong-doings of the corporation.

From a natural or philosophical point of view, what is a corporation? The word corporation is derived from the Latin word corpus which means body. A corporation is a body composed of people and has a life because it is made up of people. The corporation cannot be distinguished from the people who animate it because the corporation derives its essence from the people who constitute it. Buildings, equipment, or products do not give life to the corporation, only people. It is not really possible to have a corporation without people. A distinction needs to be made between the true and natural definition of a corporation and the artificial definition that has developed and which currently has legal status. The artificial definition of a corporation was developed with the objective of supporting and facilitating the goals of capitalists and denying the rights, objectives, and benefits of workers.

While the capitalist concept of a corporation has legal status today, that does not mean that it is the correct and true concept of a corporation. It is unfortunate that people blindly accept what is legal as being true and good. Historically, there have been many, many laws and things legal which were naturally immoral and false. Slavery, for example, was legal for thousands of years. It was even legal within the United States. Because it was legal, courts upheld the so-called rights of the slave owner over the slave. Of course, there is no right to slavery. No one has a right to own as property another human being. Yet, slavery was legal within the United States. It was certainly a contradiction for those individuals who signed the Declaration of Independence and the United States Constitution, both of which proclaimed the natural human right of freedom, to have actually been practicing slave-holders. The government of the

United States, all three branches of government, supported and facilitated slavery for almost a hundred years. It is necessary to point out that the vast majority of the members of the US government during this time were in their private lives capitalists. It also necessary to point out that it was the capitalists, the wealthy, who were the slave owners. Common, ordinary people who had to work for a living themselves did not own slaves. Common people did not own slaves primarily because they could not afford to own slaves and secondly because they did not really accept the notion of one class in society being superior to another class in society since they themselves felt the inequality of class hierarchy. Slavery thrived in the United States because of the close relationship between the capitalist class and the government.

The current legal notion of a corporation is based on a number of separate court decisions and not on a specific determination or law enacted by Congress. Unfortunately, this is a prime example of the courts legislating, a power not given to the courts by the constitution. This legal notion provides a corporation with personhood and corresponding rights, something which of course makes no sense at all. So, the courts have given corporations personhood, yet corporations have no social responsibility whatsoever. Corporations have the rights and benefits of a person but do not have the responsibilities of a person. In addition, this current legal notion of a corporation defines a very unique relationship between the so-called owners of the corporation and the corporation itself in that the owners are not legally responsible for wrongdoings done by the corporation. The owners have all the benefits and virtually no liabilities. This is wrong. This is unjust. This is totally contrary to all Christian principles. And yet, the majority of owners of corporations call themselves Christians.

While a corporation is actually a body of people working together for some common end, it is not legally defined that way. The current legal definition of a corporation is very different from what the corporation actually is and this definition actually frustrates the true purpose of the corporation. This legal notion provides a corporation with personhood and corresponding rights separate from the persons who comprise the corporation. Of course, this makes no sense at all. Only human beings are persons. A building is not a person. A car is not a person. Money is not a person. People are persons not corporations. In addition, while a corporation is incorrectly defined as a person, it does not have any social responsibility whatsoever. It has the rights and benefits of a person but does not have the responsibilities of a person.

The right of a person to own property is a natural right. A person can own land, furniture, equipment, money, cars, trucks, etc. A person's property is somewhat an extension of the person himself or herself. While this is a benefit, it is also a responsibility. If a person is injured or suffers some kind of damage from or through the property owned by another, that person can bring a legal suit in the courts against the property owner. In other words, the property owner is liable for damages and injuries associated with his or her property. The current legal notion of a corporation holds that the corporation is a person, yet it is the property of the stock holders. If a corporation is a person, isn't it slavery for one person to own another person? Furthermore, the current legal definition holds that while the corporation is the property of the owner, the owner is not liable for damages or injuries caused by the corporation. The stock holders of the corporation have the benefits of ownership but not the responsibilities and liabilities associated with property ownership. This is wrong and contrary to the natural order. Property is a natural right but it also involves responsibilities and liabilities in the event that some other person is harmed in any way by the property. Capitalists have worked to provide legality to this erroneous and deleterious notion of a corporation. Under the cloak of this false and unjust notion of a corporation, capitalists use corporations to pursue unjust and unfair practices meant to benefit the capitalist.

A corporation, according to the current legal though false notion, is an artificial person owned by real persons (stockholders) who are entitled to the financial benefits (profits) of the corporation but are not liable for the financial losses of the corporation or the social damages incurred by the corporation. Furthermore, according to the current legal though false notion of a corporation, workers are merely contractors to the corporation related through an implicit contract where their labor (creative, management, analytical, and/or physical) is exchanged with the artificial person of a corporation for money. Within this implicit contract, the worker has no rights whatsoever. This current notion of a corporation is false, unjust and unnatural, though unfortunately legal.

It is this false but legal notion of a corporation that is to blame for most of the problems affecting the current economy one of which is the unnecessary unemployment of millions of people. The only way to fix the problem of unfair layoffs is to change the current legal notion of a corporation. Since a corporation is truly a body of people working together for some common end, its structure and organization should be based on a democracy. A corporation needs to be defined as a body of people joined together for a common purpose, who are liable for their common and individual actions. The corporation is not an artificial person; it is the aggregation and integration of the people who comprise it. The corporation is not owned by some person or persons who contribute nothing but claim everything; it is owned by the people who comprise it. The workers in a corporation are not contractors to the corporation; they are co-owners of the corporation.

The only true and natural organizational structure for any social group is a democracy. In a democracy every member is able to vote to elect the management group, run for public office, submit initiatives, initiate recalls of those who have been elected, and participate in the process to create and or amend the constitution. The United States is theoretically democratic in most levels of its social structure. There are democratic processes at the Federal level, at the state level, at the county level, and at the municipal level. There are even democratic processes in place for school districts and library districts. While these democratic processes are not completely democratic, they are better than the king-noble structure that had existed for thousands of years.

A corporation is a social group that should and must be organized as a democracy. Every member of the corporation should have the ability to vote for the management team (the board of directors), run for a corporate office, submit initiatives, initiate recall petitions, and participate in the process to create or amend the corporate constitution. In a corporation, stockholders (capital shareholders) and workers (labor shareholders) should be considered equals, partners and co-owners. Both stockholders and workers should vote to elect the board of directors, the chief executive officer, and the members of the management team. The board of directors should be composed of an equal number of capital shareholders and labor shareholders. Both stockholders and workers should jointly decide the direction of the corporation, the organizational structure of the corporation, and the constitution of the corporation. Stockholders and workers should jointly make decisions regarding hiring policies, budgets, strategic plans, social responsibility policies, and layoffs. For large corporations, there should be multi-level democratic structures and processes similar to that of the Federal, state, county, and local levels of American society.

The monarchical, totalitarian notion and structure of a corporation that exists today and has legal status is a continuation of the structure of empires and kingdoms and is unjust and against the Natural Law. It has caused and continues to cause great harm to the majority of the people and to the economy. Of course, those who control the major corporations, especially the multi-national corporations will do all in their power to prevent the democratization of the corporation. They are not interested in what is right, what is just, and what is good for all; they are only interested in their own selfish pursuits. This current situation needs to be changed where workers have virtually no rights and capitalists have almost absolute authority over workers. Workers are equals with capitalists and must be treated as equals.

What drives the modern corporation? What especially drives the large, multi-national corporations that exist today ? There are two and only two goals or objectives for the modern corporation: the maximization of profits and unlimited growth. A corporation is not driven to merely be profitable; it is driven to achieve greater and greater profits. A corporation sets a goal to achieve a profit for one year of 10 percent. When that goal is reached at the end of the year, the next year's goal is a 12 percent profit. The pursuit of profit is continuous, relentless, and all-consuming. Secondly, the modern corporation is driven to grow and grow without limit. The small donut shop wants to open another site, and then another and another and another. The 2-billion-dollar corporation wants to become a 3-billion-dollar corporation, and then a 4 billion corporation and then a 5 billion corporation. Modern corporations want more and more profits and want to grow and grow. Modern corporations want to eliminate their competition either through mergers, acquisitions or by running the competition out of business. The modern corporation has as its growth strategy the 'king of the hill' strategy.

The chief executive officer and the management team of a corporation have incentive packages based on ever-increasing profits and ever-increasing growth. They do not make decisions based on what is good for their customers, their employees, the economy or society. Nor do they do not make decisions based on what is good for the company in the long term. They are only interested in achieving the profit objective and growth objective that will bring them their bonuses. The board of directors, the CEO, and the management team will do whatever is necessary to get their bonuses: mislead customers, lay off workers, close plants, out source jobs, avoid paying taxes, and sell unsafe products.

Again, what drives the modern corporation, from the smallest to the largest, multi-national corporations? The answer is greed. Corporations want more and more and more and more—without end. Modern corporations pursue aggressive policies to eliminate their competition because they don't merely want more—they want it all. Modern corporations do not pursue economic superiority, they pursue economic domination. Their pursuit of economic domination extends to suppliers, to customers, to countries, and to nations. Corporations are consumed by greed. Greed has blinded the intellects of corporate owners and management. Like an addiction to drugs or alcohol, greed drives corporations to lie, to cheat, and to steal in order to try to satisfy their desire. Yet, the desire for more and more cannot be satisfied. The more corporations feed their greed, the stronger their greed becomes. Driven by greed, corporations do not want more, they want all. Big, multi-national corporations will stop at nothing to pursue their lust for profit. Prices so high that they cripple the economy; kicking people out of their homes without any concern for where they will go, laying off workers (some of whom have dedicated their entire work careers to the corporation) without any concern for how they will pay their bills; financially enslaving people and countries with lifelong contracts, and starting and supporting wars are just some of the tactics that big corporations use in their drive for greater profits, greater market share, and greater market domination.

How can a Christian defend the modern corporation? How can a Christian lead or direct a corporation based on these unjust, un-Christian goals and objectives? The goals and objectives of the modern corporation are inconsistent with Christian economics. Would Jesus condone the pursuit of maximization of growth and profits at the expense of customers, workers, the economy and society? Certainly not, so how can Christians do so? The true purpose of a corporation is to provide a good or service while at the same time providing a living for the members of the corporation. Providing a living can be achieved without maximization of growth and profits. In fact, the maximization of growth and profits is incompatible with providing a living for the majority of society.

Terrorist attacks pose a potential harm which has been minimized due to the safeguards put in place domestically by the government. The harm caused by big corporations is not just potential; it is actual and has affected the majority of Americans. In the United States tens of millions of people have lost their jobs due directly to corporate greed and indirectly due to the lack of protection by the Federal government, the state governments and local governments. In the United States millions of people have been displaced from their homes due directly to corporate greed and indirectly due to the lack of protection by the Federal government, the state governments and local governments. In the United States hundreds of millions of people are suffering financially from out of control prices due directly to corporate greed and indirectly due to the lack of protection by the Federal government, the state governments and local governments. The greed of big corporations is out of control. Big corporations are out of control. The economy is out of control. The only thing in control is the Federal government, which is being controlled by Big Business and they control virtually all three branches of government within the United States. And unfortunately, modern corporations also control Christians.

History describes the cult associated with kingdoms. This cult manifested itself in not just respect for the king, the queen, the royal family and the nobility but reverence for these positions. The cult of kingdoms remains today and is seen in the fascination surrounding the royal weddings. In past times, people would bow for the king and queen and blindly followed the commands of the royal family and nobility without question. No one dared to criticize the royal family; whatever the royal family did was beyond reproach. This cultish behavior and attitude is also found within the modern corporation primarily among the salaried workers. Most salaried workers revere the so-called owner or owners of the company as well the CEO and management team. This reverence extends beyond the corporation to the general public through the mass media. Warren Buffet, Bill Gates, Sam Walton, Jack Welch and Steve Jobs are just a few of the CEO's who are looked upon as deities by modern society. No one dares to criticize them and most people are awed by their presence. These individuals are neither virtuous or good from a moral point of view. So why do Christians pay homage to them? The cult of modern corporations!

There are more kingdoms and empires now than throughout history: the kingdom of Walgreens, the kingdom of McDonalds, the kingdom of Raytheon, the kingdom of Northrop Grumman, the Wal-Mart empire, the Exxon-Mobil empire, the Bank of America empire, the Boeing empire, and the Lockheed Martin empire are just some examples. These corporations have kings, queens, royal families and nobility, they have cults and have unlimited growth and profits as their sole objectives.

Why have Christians allowed evil to flourish for the past 2000 years? For 2000 years empires, kingdoms and now corporations have promoted and started wars, engaged in physical and financial slavery, stolen people's land, property and ideas, and trampled on virtually every human right; and Christians have done not only nothing but have helped them. Why is it that Christians think that all they have to do is believe, pray and go to Church to be good and that their public, economic and political lives don't matter in the sight of God? Christian principles apply to economics, politics, geopolitics, social relations and international relations. There is such a thing as Christian economics. Why isn't there peace? Why are there still wars, genocide, and human trafficking? Why is there still extreme poverty? Why are there so many poor people? Why do 85 people have as much wealth as the lowest 3 billion people in the world? Why are approximately 14,000 people dying a day due to starvation and malnutrition? Why are there so many homeless? Because Christians do not apply Christian principles to their economic, political and social lives!

A true corporation according to Christian Economics consists of two or more individuals—there cannot be a corporation of only one person. Every person comprising the corporation has the same rights as every other person within the corporation and a true corporation is democratic by its very nature. Every corporate member has the right to vote; hold office within the corporation; help define the corporate charter, goals and objectives; and help decide policies and tactics.

Imagine the difference if corporations were true corporations based on Christian Economics. There would be no mass layoffs. There would be no outsourcing. Workers could have jobs for life. Workers would not fear layoffs. Workers would be fairly compensated and would share in the profits of the corporation. CEO's and the other members of the management team would not be paid hundreds of times as much as the average worker. Ruthless corporate competition would cease. Corporations would cease to control governments and countries and there would be fewer wars.

What needs to be done to correct the unjust structure and power of the modern corporation? The legal definition of a corporation needs to be changed to recognize the shared ownership of the corporation by both capital shareholders and labor shareholders and to promote the democratization of the corporation. Capitalism only works when ownership of the production system is as widespread as possible throughout the population.

The rule of law needs to be applied to corporations, the board of directors, the executives, the management and the owners of the corporation. No one and no corporation is above or outside the law. Stockholders, the directors of the company and the top managers of corporations must be held liable for the wrongdoings of the corporation. The government must regulate industries and supply chains in order to support competition and discourage practices that eliminate competition through ruthless pricing schemes and special and secret agreements with suppliers. Unfortunately, the Federal government has allowed corporations to eliminate their competitors to the detriment of consumers and the economy. Christians should act to promote the initiation of anti-trust suits against the major retail corporations, the major energy companies, the major food companies, the major banking and finance companies, the major insurance providers, the major communications companies, the major pharmaceutical companies, and the major news companies with the specific intention of breaking monopolies and oligopolies, promoting competition, encouraging new businesses and allowing small businesses to operate profitably.

All corporations by virtue of their nature and organization are public not private since they are composed of a society of people. As public entities, corporations must be open and transparent in their operations. Not all laws are just or designed to benefit the majority of the people. Many laws exist for the benefit of corporations and the capitalist class, and in fact are designed to allow and to facilitate the dominance and control of the capitalist class over the working class. These laws need to be repealed and Christians must act to repeal these laws and promote an economy based on Christian economics.

US Foreign Policy and the US Economy

THE PURPOSE AND OBJECTIVE of the US economy is to satisfy in the most efficient and effective way the natural needs and desires of all Americans for food, clothing, housing, a livelihood, education, healthcare, disability care, old age care, recreation, entertainment, social interaction, acceptance and respect. This statement which expresses the purpose and objective of the economy is a major tenet of Christian economics. The US economy needs to be organized and managed in order to achieve this objective. It needs to be organized and managed based on the principles of 'good is to be done and promoted, and evil is to be avoided', 'love your neighbor as yourself', the absolute dignity and equality of every person and natural human rights.

In a similar manner the purpose and objective of the UK economy, the French economy, the German economy, the Russian economy, the Chinese economy, the Indian economy and every other economy is to satisfy in the most efficient and effective way the natural needs and desires of their citizens and members for food, clothing, housing, a livelihood, education, healthcare, disability care, old age care, recreation, entertainment, social interaction, acceptance and respect. This is the true and only objective for every national, state, county and local economy now but it was also the only objective for every economy throughout history. And the primary focus of every government is to pursue this objective.

But if the purpose of every government is to pursue the economic good of every member of their country, then why have so many governments both today and throughout history pursed the goal of a global empire?

Throughout history much of the world has been ruled by empires. An empire is a large expanse of land and people that is politically and economically controlled by a monarch, an emperor, an oligarchy, or a foreign government. Empires are always controlled by a small group of extremely wealthy and powerful individuals.

Among the most well-known historical empires are the British Empire, the Mongolian Empire, the Russian Empire, the Spanish Empire, the Umayyad Empire, the French Empire, the Japanese Empire, the Roman Empire, the Macedonian Empire, the Ottoman Empire, the Rashidun Caliphate, the Yuan Dynasty, the Qing Dynasty, and the Egyptian Empire.

Empires have as their objective global domination. Driven by uncontrolled greed and a lust for absolute power, the people controlling empires have no regards for the rights of others, no morals and no conscience. Empires do not fit into God's design for humankind and run counter to Christian principles and economics. And yet, so-called Christians have led, promoted and supported empires throughout history and even today.

Every person recognizes the immorality of attacking one's next door neighbor and stealing their land, their resources and their possessions. Yet, why can't people see the immorality of a country attacking a neighboring country for the purpose of stealing their land, their resources and their possessions? Why have people been so blinded by false patriotism so as to be involved in helping the wealthy elite of their country to attack another country and steal their land, their resources and their possessions? How could the people of Britain help the wealthy elite of their country to attack, control and steal the resources of over 25 percent of the world's population? Britain, a little island country in northern Europe came to dominate the world, enslaving populations, and stealing resources and was at the peak of its power in 1921. And yet, the Christian leaders said 'nothing'.

And the same thing happened for every other empire in history and it is happening today. Empires are wrong: they are immoral, unjust and contrary to Christian principles and God's design for humankind. If the people of a country refused to fight for the wealthy elite, then there would have been no empires. If the people of a country protested against the imperial foreign policies of their country which sought to attack another country, then there would be no empires. If Christian leaders would have condemned as immoral the actions of the wealthy elite seeking to form empires and directed the people of such a country to refuse to cooperate in such actions, then there would have been no empires.

In spite of the fact that every empire in history has collapsed, the United States is promoting a global empire of financial and economic control. Through wars, military interventions, spying, the activities of the CIA, the activities of NATO, and the activities of the World Bank and International Monetary Fund; the wealthy elite of the United States are establishing a global empire controlling the resources and economies of other countries throughout the world. This is wrong. This is un-Christian, immoral and unjust.

The purpose of the United States government is to support and facilitate the people of the country in their pursuit of life, liberty and happiness and to support and promote the satisfaction of the natural needs and desires of all Americans for food, clothing, housing, a livelihood, education, healthcare, disability care, old age care, recreation, entertainment, social interaction, acceptance and respect. In terms of relationships, the government is subordinate to the people and is meant to serve or follow the will of the people. The word 'people' means collectively all the people living within the United States. It is not limited to a minority of the people but rather implies the majority of the people. Since the government is subordinate to the people, it needs to continuously dialog with the people directly and through surveys in order to know what is the will of the people regarding current events, issues and policies as well as long term strategies.

Foreign policy and domestic policy is a division of the strategies, tactics and activities of the US Federal government. Both foreign policy and domestic policy need to be directed toward the goal of life, liberty and happiness for the American people and should be in line with the people's express intentions and desires. The people, then, should define both foreign and domestic policy and it is the role of government, primarily the president and the administration, to execute the will of the people in this regard. This is God's design for society and government.

Unfortunately, the government has failed to communicate with the people regarding the foreign policy of the United States. For the past seventy years, the government has developed and pursued a foreign policy that is not focused on the goal of life, liberty and happiness for the vast majority of the people of the United States. The reason is that most government officials, while making reference to democratic principles, are not committed to serving the majority of the people. Instead, they seek to serve themselves and the wealthy class to whom they are somehow indebted. Because of this, US foreign policy has been focused on pursuing the best interests of corporations and the top echelons of the capitalist class, the top one tenth of one percent of the US population.

Unfortunately, this foreign policy has had a severely negative impact on the US economy and is a major factor in the current economic crisis. Foreign policy needs to be brought back into control, that is, made to serve the best interests of the majority of people in the United States, the 315 million.

Does the United States really need over 700 military bases in 130 countries? Imagine the cost to maintain these 700 bases? The money used to support these bases goes into the economies of the countries where the bases are located. These expenditures, which are obviously in the billions of dollars, benefit those foreign economies and provide absolutely no economic benefit to the US economy and to the majority of Americans.

The United States is buffered by two immense oceans and has a lengthy northern border and a southern border. How many military bases are situated on these borders and are used to patrol the borders? None! The United States has the greatest nuclear arsenal in the world with the ability to annihilate virtually every country on the face of the earth. Does the United States really need over 700 military bases in 130 countries to defend the United States? Certainly not!

Is Germany a threat to the safety of the United States? If it is not, then why does the US have military bases there? Is Italy a threat to the safety of the United States? If it is not, then why does the US have military bases there? Is the existence of military bases in almost every country in the world meant to safeguard the United States or pursue a global empire ? Is it moral for the United States to have military bases on other countries? What moral basis is there for the United States to have military bases in other sovereign nations?

How does the military engagements of the United States in Afghanistan, Iraq, Syria, Pakistan, Egypt, Colombia, Libya, Mexico, Venezuela, Yemen, Somalia, and the Ukraine reconcile with Christian morality and Christian economics? Are these military engagements moral?

The US foreign policy also includes renditioning, water-boarding, indefinite detentions, extrajudicial killings through the use of drones, mass surveillance of virtually the entire world, and the financing and training of individuals who plan to over-throw democratically elected governments. Do these activities reconcile with Christian morality and are these activities moral?

The United States has been spending over $1 trillion a year on so-called defense for the last 13 years. While the US government claims that this money is being spent on defense, is it? Where does this money go, or to whom does this money go? The US defense money goes to corporations for planes, drones, vehicles, bombs, missiles, guns, equipment, food, transportation, fuel, supplies, the construction of facilities, mercenaries, translators, and consultants; obviously these corporations favor the current US foreign policy and lobby the US government to continue spending money on so-called defense. Is this money spent by the US government really for national defense or to promote the empire of the wealthy? A great deal of the money that the United States spends on defense actually goes to foreign corporations and into the economies of other countries. How is this good for the US economy? This flow of money out of the country undermines the US economy.

The US government is responsible for sending far too much money out of the country. The excessive spending by the US government on so-called foreign policy actually runs counter to the principle of self-sufficiency. What benefit is there to the people of the United States from the billions of dollars spent on foreign policy by the United States government? Except for some humanitarian aid, virtually all money spent by the United States in terms of foreign policy is directed towards enabling US Big Business to gain and maintain an economic dominance over every other country in the world. The people of the world, that is, the majority of people in almost every country detest the United States government. These people feel that the US does not support or assist them but rather attempts to dictate and control them. Unfortunately, the primary focus of the United States government's foreign policy is to promote radical capitalism in virtually every country of the world with ultimate control residing here in the United States by Big Business and Big Wealth. This policy seeks to exploit both the natural resources and human resources of other countries.

Every other empire in history has failed; the Greek empire, the Roman empire, the Russian empire, the Japanese empire, the British empire, the Spanish empire, the Portuguese empire, the Dutch empire, the Mongolian empire, and all the others. They have all failed, most of them collapsing from within. Do Big Business, Big Finance and Big Wealth of the United States think that they will succeed in dominating the world? Imperialism and democracy are opposites. The current foreign policy of the United States government, as a puppet of Big Business, Big Finance and Big Wealth is imperialistic, un-democratic, un-American (it does not favor the majority of the people but rather a very small minority), and immoral. The US government puts more focus and emphasis on the global economy than its own economy. In fact, the US government's preoccupation with the global economy has directly led to the neglect of the US economy and the consequences are seen in the current crisis.

Domestic policy should dominate foreign policy and foreign policy should support and protect domestic policy as well as the pursuit of life, liberty and happiness for the people (all the people) of the United States. How does so-called 'free trade ' and globalization help the people of the United States? They don't. In fact, free trade and globalization are counter to the good of the people of the United States. The so-called free-trade agreements are only good for Big Business, Big Finance and Big Wealth. It is misleading to refer to these agreements as 'free'. Rather, they should be referred to as unregulated, unequal, unprotected, undemocratic and unjust. Foreign policy is out of control. It is not sub-ordinate to domestic policy and does not serve the good of the majority of the people. The current US foreign policy is primarily designed for and directed to the good of Big Business, Big Finance and Big Wealth. Foreign policy must be brought into control and made to serve all the people of the United States and not just the wealthy minority.

When will Christians do the right thing and begin to practice Christianity in their political, economic and social lives; doing good, avoiding evil and loving every person as themselves—every person no matter what nationality, gender, race, religion, or income level?

Spending by the US Government and the National Debt

Two essential principles of Christianity are service and stewardship: service to others and stewardship of the material things that God has given to humankind; natural resources and human-made resources. Everyone is obligated to serve others: parents are obligated to serve their children when they are young, children are obligated to serve their parents when they are old, people are obligated to serve the sick, the dying, those with special needs, the hungry, the homeless, etc. The mandate to serve others especially applies to those who are referred to as public servants: the President, the members of Congress, the Supreme Court justices, the federal judges, the military, federal agents, FBI agents, CIA agents, governors, state legislators, state and local judges, mayors, town council members, police officers, etc. Christianity requires that public servants serve the public, but do they?

Does the President really serve the public, all the people of the United States? Do the members of Congress really serve the public, all the people of the United States? The President and the vast majority of the members of Congress do not serve the people of the United States. Rather, they serve the selfish interests of Big Business and the wealthy individuals who own these businesses. In spite of the fact that the President and the majority of the members of Congress claim to be Christian, they ignore the mandate to serve the people. This is wrong, unjust and immoral. These people are not really Christians; they only pretend to be Christians in order to get elected.

Christians are called to be stewards. This is especially true for public servants. The President, his administration, Congress, governors, state legislators, mayors, town council members, and every other public servant has a serious moral responsibility to carefully manage the resources entrusted to them by the public. These resources involve natural resources such as water, land, energy, minerals, and elements; revenue money such as taxes and fees; and the public infrastructure such as roads, bridges, buildings, etc. Public servants must carefully manage these resources in a manner which benefits all the people as well as future generations of people. Unfortunately, most public officials do not manage the natural and public resources for the good of all people but rather seek to benefit the wealthy top one percent.

Spending by the Federal government, most state governments and many county and city governments is out of control. Through gross mismanagement, these governments have spent far in excess of the revenues that they have received and have resorted to borrowing to pay for these deficits. This has been happening for many years and has resulted in these governments having severe debt issues. The Federal government has squandered tax payers' money and has encumbered this generation and generations to come with severe debt. The current national debt is $21 trillion and has grown $17 trillion in the last 17 years. This is outrageous.

The People are responsible for all government spending even though they do not agree with all the things that the government does or how the government spends money. It should be clear that the money that the government spends should directly or indirectly benefit the People and not be spent on benefitting those in government or their friends. However, that is not the case. The President, his administration and Congress spend an inordinately excessive amount of money on themselves in terms of perks, travel privileges, etc. They spend the people's money on maintaining their power base. They spend the people's money on helping their friends through government contracts. And they spend the people's money on foreign policies that benefit the rich and not the working class of the United States.

In spite of the US government being in severe debt, it continues to spend far more money than it receives in revenues. Spending on foreign policy most of which as explained above does not benefit the majority of Americans is irresponsible and immoral because the government must be just stewards and servants of the people. The US government continues to send billions of dollars to other countries (most of which goes to the military of other countries) even though it does not have the money and has to borrow money to do so.

Unnecessary government debt is against Christian principles. The President, Congress, governors, state legislators, mayors, etc. have a serious responsibility before God and the people to manage their expenses.

It is immoral for those in government, most of whom call themselves Christians, to spend tax payers' money on things that do not benefit the tax payers.

The United States government should be fiscally responsible, that is, it must not spend more than it receives in revenues. Yet, the government especially over the last thirty-five years has been spending far more than it receives in revenues. As a result, the government has had to borrow not just millions of dollars, not just billions of dollars, but trillions of dollars. The current national debt is approximately $21 trillion dollars and has been growing at the rate of almost $4 billion a day since 2007. Almost 10 percent of the budget goes towards paying just the interest on the debt. How can any person, any organization, any corporation or any nation spend more money than it receives especially year after year?

The government borrows money in the name of the people. That means that the people are ultimately responsible for the debt incurred by the government. Currently, each man, woman and child in the United States owes approximately $67,000 because of the fiscal irresponsibility of the Federal government. It should be clear that the people do not agree with the uncontrolled and irresponsible spending by the government. How can the government which has the responsibility for managing the US economy not even manage its own budget ? The purpose of a budget is to manage expenses and revenues so that one does not spend more than what they receive. Obviously, the government is either not capable of doing so or is unwilling to do so. The people need to force the government to become fiscally responsible and stop borrowing money in their name. Budget approval and approval to borrow money belong to the people and the people need to take back that role from the government.

Fiscal responsibility extends to all branches and levels of government including state, county and local governments. Unfortunately, it most often happens that those who hold political office do not have the financial background or skills to make financial decisions on behalf of the people. The office of president of the United States is primarily a management function. Yet, most individuals enter that office with little to no management skills and experience. In other words, they are actually incapable of functioning as president. Senators and representatives are also managers. Representatives have the specific function of creating and managing the budget. Yet, most representatives do not have the required skills. The same can be said of most governors, state senators, state representatives, mayors, etc. The United States does not need politicians in its government; it needs managers—people who can manage an extremely complex economy and society. The primary focus and objective of a politician is to gain power, maintain it and increase it. The people of the United States do not need politicians in government, they need servants.

A serious problem in the midst of this current economic crisis is the fact that state, county and local governments are raising taxes instead of managing expenses. State income taxes are being increased, property taxes are being increased, sales taxes are being increased, and excise taxes are being increased because of the fiscal irresponsibility of government officials. The problem with increased taxes on the working class during this time is that they don't have the financial means to pay these increased taxes. The basic cause of the current economic crisis is the inability of the working-class majority to buy the goods and services that they want and need in the quantities that they want and need because of financial constraints. In other words, the working-class majority does not have enough money to pay for the things that they need and want. Increased federal, state, county and local taxes only make the problem worse.

The President, his administration, and Congress have a serious obligation to carefully manage the money entrusted to them by the people of the United States. Frivolous spending and spending far in excess of revenues undermines the balance and stability of the economy and is one of the causes of the current economic crisis. Government spending is out of control.

If the excess spending done by the government was directed towards the people in a manner designed to help bring the majority working class out of their financial slavery to Big Business, Big Finance and Big Wealth ; then excess spending for a short amount of time would be acceptable. But unfortunately, the excess spending by the government is not directed towards the people, the 200 million people who are financially suffering from this economic crisis. No, the excess spending by the government actually benefits the very wealthy minority who actually are not suffering from the current crisis and really don't need the money. The President, his administration and Congress are borrowing money against future generations in order to make the already wealthy even wealthier.

War, Business, the Economy and Christianity

THE UNITED STATES DEPARTMENT of War started in 1789 and was renamed the Department of Defense in 1949 obviously to make this department of government appear to be more acceptable to public opinion. The defense industry and the arms industry are businesses engaged in consulting, R&D, the production of weapons and military equipment, the distribution and service of materials and equipment, the construction and maintenance of facilities and the provision of personnel - all for the purpose of military engagements. These industries provide military aircraft, military sea craft, guns, ammunition, missiles, supplies and even personnel. Also, there are many businesses organized specifically as private armies or mercenaries, the largest of which is Academi (formerly Blackwater) which was started in 1997 and has been used by the US government in Iraq, Afghanistan, Ukraine, New Orleans for hurricane Katrina and many covert engagements throughout the world.

Businesses within the defense and arms industries are very profitable especially during wars. Since businesses have as their objectives the maximization of profit and growth, these businesses actively pursue more and more business both within the US and globally. They actively lobby the US federal, state and local governments as well as foreign governments to buy their goods and services. These industries are considered some of the most corrupt businesses in the world with respect to bribes. And their profits are based on the goal of killing people.

Fifteen percent of US manufacturing is dependent on the military industry. Twenty-one percent of the Federal budget is for military spending, the largest component of Federal expenditures. Obviously, this indicates the Federal government's main priority is not people, not education, not healthcare, not jobs but military spending and a foreign policy focused on military operations. Military spending is at the heart of

US foreign policy and now even domestic policy as seen with the Department of Homeland security and the militarization of local police. And this military spending must be considered within the context that the US does not face any real threats from any other country though it does fabricate perceived threats from other countries and so-called terrorist groups in order to justify the extreme spending.

Businesses within the defense and arms industries want to continue to sell their products and services and sell more and more. If the US Federal government has filled its warehouses with munitions, weapons and equipment, how can a defense business sell the US government more munitions, weapons and equipment? The US government will only buy more if it uses its munitions, weapons and equipment and they will only use these things if there is a war or military operation. This means of course that businesses within the defense and arms industries as businesses which operate under the philosophy that 'it is neither right nor wrong, it is just business' actively promote and pursue wars, military operations, potential threats, perceived threats and even artificial threats. They promote wars by lobbying and arming governments on both sides of a conflict or potential conflict. They influence the military hierarchies of both sides of a conflict, and they help promote propaganda campaigns for the purpose of coercing the people into supporting the war or military operation. They also help create false threats of a military engagement or attack in order for governments to buy arms to prepare themselves from these artificial threats.

In spite of all the rhetoric about Iran's nuclear ambitions or North Korea's nuclear program, the United States which has the largest nuclear arsenal in the world continues to build more and more sophisticated nuclear weapons. Does the United States really need more nuclear weapons? It already has enough nuclear weapons to destroy the civilized world. Why is the United States building more nuclear weapons? Is it because it is in the best interests of the defense and arms corporations?

While talking about peace and democracy, the United States government provides billions of dollars in military aid to other countries most of which are not democracies. In addition, the US government helps the US defense and arms industries by promoting sales to foreign governments. Because of this the United States is the largest exporter of arms in the world.

It is estimated that annually over $1.6 trillion are spent on military expenditures globally. Government contracts with defense and arms corporations are significant both from a political point of view as well as from a profit and revenue point of view for these corporations. President Eisenhower warned of the military-industrial-governmental complex which linked defense and arms corporations, the US Military hierarchy (generals, colonels, etc.) and members of Congress.

Arms sales are a significant part of the US foreign policy strategy. Since the early 1950's the US has been arming rebels, insurgents, dictators, and governments with serious human rights records, partly because of the intention of influencing global politics but also because the US Defense and Arms industries drive to sell their products and services. It does not take much thought to consider all the conflicts throughout the world today as having their driving force as weapon sales. If there was not such a proliferation of weapons throughout the world today, would there be so many conflicts affecting millions of people? While the US claims to seek and promote peace and democracy throughout the world, it in fact is the greatest single reason for war and conflicts associated with military operations. And that is because of the significant influence or almost control of the US government by the Military Complex of Corporations.

Presidents, senators and congressman claim to represent the People, when in fact most represent a different for-profit set of corporations. The political influence of the US Military Industry is extremely significant. The premise of the movie JFK is that the Military Complex conspired with high ranking US military personnel and some congressional personnel to assassinate President Kennedy because he was not going to escalate military operations in Southeast Asia. The movie attempts to show both the feasibility and probability that this was true. President Johnson's rush to escalate military operations to a full-scale war especially using the Gulf of Tokin lie seems to support Oliver Stone's premise. The war in Southeast Asia cost $600 billion and was obviously very good for the Defense and Arms industries. But with every war, what is good for the Defense and Arms industries is very bad for people: over 1.5 million Vietnamese, Cambodians and Laotians were killed and over 58,000 US soldiers were killed.

It is frightening to consider that the primary driver of US foreign policy is the financial benefit of corporations within the Defense and Arms industries. And it is even more frightening to consider the possibility that the Defense and Arms industries are so powerful that they conspired to assassinate the president of the United States. If this was in fact true, then it would certainly explain the control that they have over

WAR, BUSINESS, THE ECONOMY AND CHRISTIANITY   167

the Presidency today. Is it possible that presidents since Kennedy fear for their lives if they do not go along with the wishes of the Military industry?

As with every other business, so also is it true for corporations within the Defense and Arms industries, they hold to the philosophy that 'it is neither right nor wrong, it is just business'. While this nefarious philosophy results in human rights violations for most other corporations, within the Defense and Arms industries it results in death. How can any Christian support or work within any corporation which promotes increased sales and profits through military engagements and wars?

The influence of the Defense and Arms industries on US foreign policy over the last 25 years has had a major negative impact on the US economy. The national debt increased from $5.7 trillion in 2001 to $21 trillion in 2018 and the military operations in Iraq, Afghanistan, Pakistan, Syria, Libya, Somalia, Uganda, Turkey, Jordan, Chad, Mali and Ukraine represent a significant part of this rise in the national debt. Have these military conflicts since 2000 been necessary? Considering that the United States did not have the money to engage in these conflicts, have the benefits of these conflicts outweighed the expenses in dollars and lives? Absolutely not! If there have been no real benefits to these military engagements, then why does the US continue to spend billions of dollars building a global military empire and arming so many other countries throughout the world? The only logical explanation is that this is good for the corporations that comprise the US Defense and Arms industries.

Perhaps the most deceitful tactic used by the Defense and Arms industries is that military spending and military engagements are patriotic. Because of this people are afraid to criticize anything to do with the military lest they be considered un-patriotic. However, it should be clear that the corporations within the Defense and Arms industries are not patriotic. These corporations do not care about soldiers or civilians; they only care about profits, revenues and growth.

Seventy-five percent of Americans identify themselves as Christians. Obviously, the Defense and Arms industries have a significant number of stockholders and employees who are Christian. How can a Christian reconcile Christian principles with the business objectives and tactics of the Defense and Arms industries? How can the commandment to love your neighbor as yourself be reconciled with the objective of these corporations to sell more and more weapons including weapons of mass destruction? These corporations are out of control, but who can control them: the Federal government; Congress; the Supreme Court? Certainly not! Only Christians practicing Christian principles will be able to control the war monger corporations of the Defense and Arms industries starting with Christian stockholders and employees.

The Role of the Government within the Economy

THE ONLY BASIS FOR government is the will of the people that are governed. The government, every branch of government, and every level of government receives its authority, power and legitimacy from the people. The majority of people are members of some organized religion and virtually every organized religion holds that all power and authority comes from God or Allah or Yahweh or the Supreme Being. Yet this power and authority comes from God to the individual person. God does not interact directly with society and select a government. God does not give power and authority only to a select group of people. Monarchies, aristocracies, oligarchies, plutocracies, policeocracies, stratocracies (government by the military) and theocracies are all illegitimate forms of government even though they have existed in history and do exist today. God or Allah or Yahweh or the Supreme Being does not give authority to these kinds of governments in some clandestine way even though that is exactly what these governments tell the people that they govern.

The only legitimate form of government is a democracy where the power and authority to govern, to administer, to judge, to legislate, and to engage in war comes from the people. And this authority can be removed by the people. Unfortunately, most people do not understand this because they have been taught differently. People have been taught to be subservient and that authority comes from above them, from those who they are told are superior to them. This is false. People need to understand that they provide the President, Congress, the Supreme Court, the military and all other forms of government and branches of government with the power and authority to govern. People need to understand that the President, Congress, the Supreme Court, the military and all other forms of government and branches of government are subordinate to and should be subservient to the people. Once people understand this, they can start exercising their authority to bring control over the government.

The US economy is out of control because it is not controlled, managed and guided for the good of all the people in the United States. The US economy is in fact controlled by large banks and corporations, which in turn are controlled by a few very wealthy individuals. So, the United States economy is actually controlled by an oligarchy.

The United States does not exist for the sake of a few hundred thousand individuals. No, the United States exists for the sake of over 315 million people and those few hundred thousand individuals are included in the 315 million. The United States economy is not meant to serve and support a few hundred thousand individuals. It is meant to serve and support over 315 million people and those few hundred thousand individuals are included in the 315 million.

Currently, the United States government does not represent the majority of the people. Through lobbying efforts, through campaign contributions, and through the direct promotion of partisans for political office; Big Business has a significant influence on the majority of both elected and appointed officials of the Federal government. The influence of big corporations on the Federal government is so great that it approaches the point of total control. And this influence of Big Business on the government extends to all three branches of the government: the executive, the legislative and the judicial and the various levels of government: Federal, state, county and local.

The executive branch of the US government does not represent the majority of the people. No, the president and his administration represent and promote the interests of a very small minority. The legislative branch of the US government does not represent the majority of the people. There are over 315 million people in the United States. Over half the people are female. Are half the members of Congress female? Twelve percent of the population is black. Are twelve percent of the members of Congress black? Seventeen percent of the population is Hispanic. Are seventeen percent of the members of Congress Hispanic? Seventy-five percent of the population earns less than $50,000 a year. Did seventy-five percent of the members of Congress make less than $50,000 a year before they were elected to Congress? Eight percent of the adult population earn minimum wage. Did eight percent of the members of Congress earn minimum wage before they were elected to Congress?

Sixteen percent of the adult population is between eighteen and thirty years of age. Are sixteen percent of the members of Congress between eighteen and thirty years of age? Ten percent of the population are farmers. Were ten percent of the members of Congress farmers before they were elected? Ten percent of the adult population are restaurant workers. Were ten percent of the members of Congress restaurant workers before they were elected? Four percent of the adult population are teachers. Were four percent of the members of Congress teachers before they were elected? Fifteen percent of the population are students. Are fifteen percent of the members of Congress students? Two percent of the population are plumbers. Were two percent of the members of Congress plumbers before they were elected? Three percent of the population are nurses. Were three percent of the members of Congress nurses before they were elected? Two percent of the population are truck drivers. Were two percent of the members of Congress truck drivers before they were elected? Ten percent of the population is unemployed. Were ten percent of the members of Congress unemployed before they were elected?

Close to sixty-six percent of the members of the Senate are millionaires, and fifty percent of the members of the House of Representatives are millionaires. Older white males dominate Congress and law and business are the dominant professions practiced by the vast majority of the members of Congress. A person is known by the company that they keep. The wealthy associate with the wealthy! Lawyers associate with lawyers. Business people associate with business people. The wealthy do not have poor friends, lawyers do not golf with plumbers, and business people do not throw parties for their unemployed friends (for they don't have any).

It is claimed that when Marie Antoinette was informed that the people had no bread to eat (meaning that they were starving because of a disordered economy) she responded, 'let them eat cake'. She could not comprehend the situation where a person did not have anything to eat. She never experienced a lack of food, a lack of clothing, or a lack of anything whatsoever. All the people that she associated with were also wealthy and also had never experienced a shortage or absence of the basic necessities in life. Unfortunately, the attitude of Marie is very common among the wealthy. Most wealthy people cannot identify or sympathize with the plight of the financially less fortunate. In fact, many of those who are financially wealthy look down on the poor and the unemployed and they actually blame them for the situation that they are in.

How can a wealthy senator or wealthy congressman really understand the difficulties and challenges of a homeless person, an unemployed person, a person earning only minimum wage, a person whose home is being foreclosed, or the 150 million people in the United States who live from paycheck to paycheck? The vast majority of them can't. The majority of senators and congressmen have no idea regarding the difficulties and hardships the majority of Americans are facing within the current economy. Because of this they are incapable of representing the people who elected them. They are incapable of making decisions which will help the vast majority of working class Americans who suffer from this recession. The working class should place no confidence in the majority of their elected officials to do what is necessary to rectify the disorders, the imbalances, and injustices affecting the US economy.

A predominantly old, white, wealthy, male Congress composed primarily of lawyers and business people cannot represent the majority of the members of the US population with all its diversity. Only the working class can represent the working class. Only women can represent women. Only blacks can represent blacks. Only Hispanic can represent Hispanic. Only young people can represent young people. Only people who have earned minimum wage can represent people making minimum wage. Only people who have been unemployed can represent the unemployed. Only people who have been homeless can represent the homeless.

Currently, the United States government is not a representative government. The demographics of those who constitute the government do not reflect the demographics of the majority of Americans. The demographics of those who constitute the government reflect the demographics of a small and select minority of Americans: the wealthy and privileged. This is the major reason why the economy is grossly out of balance and out of order. Those individuals who have the responsibility of over-seeing, regulating, and managing the economy are biased in favor of the minority capitalist class. When the majority of senators and representatives are told that the people have no bread (they are suffering economically), like Marie Antoinette they respond, 'let the people eat cake'. When the majority of senators and representatives are told that the people have lost their homes due to foreclosure, they respond 'let the people live in their summer homes'. The majority of senators and congressmen have never suffered a lack of food, a loss of employment, a foreclosure, living from paycheck to paycheck, or earning minimum wage. They are blind to the realities of common life.

Neither is the current United States government democratic. It does not listen to the will of the people. The President does just about whatever he wants no matter what Congress or the majority of people thinks or want. Congress also does whatever it wants, ignoring what the majority of people think or want. The majority of people do not want another war, yet the President totally ignores the will of the People and does what he wants to do. The vast majority of people want food labels indicating whether it contains GMO's (genetically modified organisms), yet Congress totally ignores the will of the People.

Once elected, government officials have virtually no contact and communication with the people until it is time to seek their vote to be re-elected. There is no means for voter initiatives or voter referendums. If a person or group of people wants to initiate a change in law or policy, the only avenue of communication with the government is through a person's own senator and or representative. Unless a person is a constituent of a senator or representative, senators and congressmen are not willing to talk to that person. Yet, these same senators and congressmen spend countless hours with lobbyists who are not their constituents and often are not even citizens of the United States. There are over thirteen thousand registered lobbyists in Washington, DC. The vast majority of the time of senators and congressmen is spent meeting with lobbyists. Federal policies and laws are based primarily on the will of lobbyists or the companies and organizations that they represent and not on the will of the people. Who then does the government represent, the People or these special interest groups that represent Big Business and foreign entities? The phrase "government of the people, by the people and for the people" does not apply to the current government. Instead, the applicable phrase is 'government of the people, by the rich and for the rich and special interests'.

One of greatest problems for the United States, its economy and its way of life, is the fact that Big Businesses are multi-national corporations not affiliated with any specific country. They have no allegiance or loyalty to any country, no allegiance or loyalty to any government, and no allegiance or loyalty to the people of any country. The only allegiance and loyalty that multi-national corporations have is to themselves and their stockholders or rather those stockholders who have a controlling percentage of the shares of the corporation. These dominant stockholders control the corporation and the corporation is subservient to them.

Small and powerful groups of stockholders control multi-national corporations and manage them to be ruthless vehicles continuously working to feed their ever-increasing greed. In turn, these corporations have an almost stranglehold on the government of the United States and use the US government to help them increase in size, eliminate competition, increase their assets, and maximize their value. It is this small group of stockholders with and through the executive teams of the corporations that they control that is using the US government to bleed the US economy. For they do not care about the 315 million people who constitute the majority of the United States. They do not care about individuals or families. They do not subscribe to the principles of life, liberty and the pursuit of happiness for all. They do not care about anyone or anything except for themselves and their wealth. And they have been able to make use of deficiencies in the US constitution to place their partisans in Congress, the White House and on Federal benches. One of the primary purposes and functions of the government is the protection of its citizens. The government is supposed to protect its citizens from attacks, assaults, threats, and injuries by people, groups of people, corporations and countries. While the government makes an attempt to protect people against personal physical assault, it does virtually nothing to protect people against personal financial assault. In fact, the government does the opposite and protects those that financially assault others.

The only hope for the economy is for the people to restore true representation and democracy to the government of the United States. The people need to demand that Congress, the Courts and the President represent them, execute their will and serve their best interests. The government is out of control and only the people can bring it under control. This is the will of God and it is a Christian mandate.

Capitalism

ARE THE 3 MILLION people, who are billionaires, multi-millionaires and millionaires, more important than the other 312 million people living in the United States?

The main problem with capitalism is that it can be easily, directly and absolutely influenced by greed. Greed is the uncontrolled or unconstrained desire for and pursuit of material wealth. According to Saint Thomas Aquinas it is a sin directly against one's neighbor, since one man cannot over-abound in external riches without another man lacking them. It is a sin against God, just as all sin, inasmuch as man despises things eternal for the sake of temporal things. It is a disorder within the natural order of things.

Because human nature tends towards the infinite and can only be satisfied by the Infinite, greed also tends towards the infinite. It seeks more and more without limit. It is all-consuming. Rather than the person controlling greed, greed controls the person. Unfortunately, the person does not understand that they can never be satisfied by riches. They blindly pursue more thinking that when they have acquired more that they will be satisfied. But, when they have acquired more they are not satisfied, and greed drives them to seek more and more. This sad pattern ends with death, but the desire for wealth will continue into eternity. Greed can neither be satisfied in time nor eternity. Like all other mortal sins, it involves a cruel and debilitating slavery.

Human beings are distinguished from animals in that they have souls. Souls are real, yet immaterial and provide the capacity to think and will. Material things are limited by space and time, and only because the soul is united to a material body is it also bounded by space and time. And when death separates the soul and the body, the soul will enter into eternity and no longer be limited by space and time.

Human beings naturally seek happiness, and, because of their spiritual nature, happiness is a state of total, complete and enduring satisfaction and fulfillment. Since this propensity to seek happiness is rooted in the human soul, it is infinite. It is not infinite in the sense of an infinite capacity, but rather in the sense of a continuous, eternal movement towards infinity. Through reflection, humans form a perception of some good as the source of their happiness. They then will or choose that good and move or perform actions designed to acquire that good. While they may appear to choose multiple goods as the source of their happiness, there is always one good that dominates all others as the ultimate goal towards which they act.

What are the goods that humans choose as the goal of their activities? Some choose comfort, some pleasure, some material things including money; others choose power, still others control. Some humans seek truth or goodness or justice as their ultimate goal.

This pursuit of happiness can be so strong and over-powering that people can become slaves to what they desire clouding their reason and addicting them to what they seek. They will sacrifice all that they have and endure great difficulties in order to obtain the object of their desire. If they desire pleasure, they will desire more and more pleasure. If they desire fame, they desire more and more fame. If they desire money and material possessions, they desire more and more money and material possessions. Because there is no limit to these desires and because these things cannot completely satisfy or fulfill them; those who pursue these things as the object of their ultimate happiness will never be satisfied. Yet, they are almost constantly and continuously driven to seek more and more of these things. And these drives are so strong, that they will not allow anything or anyone to be obstacles to their ultimate pursuit.

While there is not an infinite amount of money and material things, the human that desires these things as the object of his or her ultimate happiness will continually seek more and more money and wealth. So consuming and enslaving is this drive, that this person will do anything and everything to achieve this perceived objective: the acquisition of absolutely all wealth. Unfortunately, money and wealth will never bring happiness to a person. Human happiness consists in the attainment of union with Infinite Goodness, Infinite Truth, Infinite Order, Infinite Wisdom, and Infinite Beauty; that is to say God, Who alone can satisfy a human's desire for happiness and Who alone will complete that person.

Greed, the disorder in which humans seek money and wealth as the object of their natural desire for happiness instead of God, has been driving human behavior since the beginning of civilization. As a disorder that blinds and enslaves, it drives those it controls to do whatever is necessary to seek its goal. People enslaved by greed will lie, cheat, steal, and even murder. In fact, virtually every war since the beginning of civilization has involved greed by one or both parties engaged in the war. While it is true that only one party may have started the war out of greed, if the side that was initially attacked wins then out of greed they will force the other side to pay reparations or give up control of something. Greed is involved before, during and after wars.

Currently, greed is the driving force behind the capitalism that is practiced today by Big Business, Big Finance, Big Wealth and the very wealthy individuals who control these organizations. Greed has blinded corporations, banks, financial institutions and the wealthy forcing them to act unpatriotically and unjustly, exploiting people and countries. Big Business, Big Finance and Big Wealth lie, cheat, scheme and manipulate in pursuit of their inordinate goal of more and more and more. Blinded by greed, nothing satisfies them. They care about nothing and no one, only about more and more wealth.

It is certainly very difficult to write critically about capitalism. For most people have been led to believe that capitalism is part of what it means to be American and also part and parcel with being democratic. Because of this, people look patriotically upon capitalism. Unfortunately, these people are naïve and confused, and through years of positive reinforcement of a very distorted and exaggerated notion of capitalism, they are not very open to discussions on the true concept of capitalism and the fact that the current practice of capitalism is out of line with the natural order of things. In addition, most people immediately assume that a person who criticizes capitalism must be a socialist or communist. Unfortunately, these mindsets and attitudes prevent a person from being open-minded about the subject of capitalism.

There are also many people who might be called 'disciples of capitalistic economics'. These individuals have accepted the teachings of modern capitalism and capitalist economics with a blind faith and enthusiastically promote its teachings. They have the same regard and devotion for capitalism that others have for religion. For these people, any criticism of capitalism is looked upon as heresy, an attack against the holy religion of modern man. Because they have an almost fanatical devotion to capitalism, they are dedicated to the spread of it throughout the world and attack anyone who even attempts to objectively criticize it.

In order to objectively analyze and evaluate the nature of capitalism, it is necessary to put aside any conceptions whatsoever on this topic. That is, one must ignore what the current laws are, what has been taught by one's education in history and economics, and whatever attitudes one has formed due to the circumstances of social class, profession or employment. Only by doing so will it be possible to evaluate capitalism, see it for what it is, and determine what needs to be done to correct its abuses.

Let it be clear that this discussion is not an effort to destroy capitalism, but rather an attempt to bring it under proper control for the good of all society. For true capitalism is a natural arrangement in the order of things. It therefore has its proper and appropriate place. It is unfortunate that capitalists have taken it far beyond it proper limits and severely encroached on the rights of labor. As a result, the proper relationship between capital and labor has been destroyed and the right balance between the two ordained by Natural Law for the benefit of both the common good and the individual good is grossly lacking.

Capital and labor are the two primary inputs into a productive system; a system which produces goods and services. Capital provides the funds which are used to buy materials and equipment and to pay for operating expenses. A capitalist is a person who provides capital to a productive system at its startup or inception until the productive system has reached the point where it is able to generate capital on its own through its profits. Labor is that set of activities that transforms raw materials into finished goods or finished services which are sold to generate a profit. Labor involves design, management, planning, fabrication, assembly, transportation, handling and every other physical and or intellectual activity involved with the transformation, transportation and delivery of the good or service to the final customer. It is clear that labor's role in the productive system is far more intimate than capital's role. Also, capital's role can occur only one time while labor's role is continuous.

It cannot be over-emphasized that the provision of funds by the capitalist occurs typically once at the beginning of the productive endeavor and that once the production system is working, the production system itself generates the capital needed by the system to continue to operate.

It is also clear that labor is critical to the production system while capital is not. For if a capitalist is no longer present, the organization can and will continue to function. However, if labor is no longer present, the organization ceases to operate and in fact ceases to exist. Given the true nature of an enterprise and the relationships between the enterprise with capitalists and laborers, it follows that the success of an organization lies almost entirely with the laborers.

An enterprise has two sets of objectives; one internal the other external. The internal objective is to provide an income to the capitalists and laborers. The external objective is to serve society by serving customers. Since the internal objective of a productive enterprise is to provide an income to both capitalists and laborers and since both capitalists and laborers contribute to the success of the organization (the laborers actually contribute far more than the capitalists); it follows that the profits of the organization should be shared between the capitalists and the workers. It further follows that the management of the organization should be democratic based on both capitalists and workers. It also follows that the ownership of the organization should comprise both capitalists and workers and it is most appropriate to refer to the capitalist as a capital shareholder and the laborer as the labor shareholder.

While all this is true from a natural point of view, it does not work that way within the present context of things. Within the present context, there are no labor shareholders only the capital shareholders. Within the present context, the management of organizations is not democratic, it is autocratic—the capitalists have absolute power. Within the present context, profits are not shared between capitalists and workers; they belong solely to the capitalists. Within the present context, there is only one objective for the organization - the maximization of profits for the capitalists and not the objectives of providing an income to the capitalists and laborers and serving society by serving customers.

The past forty years have seen a significant number of corporate acquisitions and the last twenty years have seen the dominance of private equity firms in this area. Many of these acquisitions have occurred through corporate raids and hostile takeovers. These acquisitions have resulted in extremely large corporations many of which are privately held. Private equity firms borrow money which is used to purchase companies. Once they have acquired the companies, they very often strip the assets of the company and layoff significant numbers of workers. Because the assets of a company (inventory, facilities, equipment, intellectual property) are often worth more than the price these private equity firms pay for the company, these private equity firms actually buy the company to break it up by selling its assets. The result is that the company is destroyed.

All employees lose their jobs. Customers lose their source of supply and vendors lose a customer. Employees lose, customers lose, vendors lose and the economy loses—but the private equity firm gains and they gain tens of millions, hundreds of millions and even billions of dollars. This is unjust and immoral.

Private equity firms do not always destroy companies by selling off their assets. Oftentimes, they hold on to a company waiting for an opportunity to sell it at a price higher than what they paid for it. While private equity firms hold on to companies, the employees typically suffer. Because the private equity firm borrowed the money needed to buy the company, they burden the company with the debt and the payments. As a result, there are no new hires, no raises, no bonuses, and reduced benefits. The company has become a slave to the debt used by the private equity firm to buy them.

Private equity firms do not care about people, they only care about themselves. Private equity firms do not care about the economy, they only care about themselves. Private equity firms do not care about the United States, they only care about themselves. They use virtually none of their own money for they borrow almost all of what they need to buy companies. They provide absolutely no good or service. They provide no value and make no contribution to the economy. They basically take money and wealth away from others because there is virtually no one and nothing to stop them. Private equity firms represent the ultimate in radical or inordinate capitalism. And they are increasing both in number and in the scope of companies under their control. Capitalism is out of control.

The State of the US Economy

CORPORATIONS HAVE BOTH GENERAL and specific goals, with strategies and tactics designed and managed to achieve those goals. Metrics are used to measure performance against goals and are reviewed annually, quarterly, monthly and even daily. These metrics are used to determine if the corporation is on track to meet its short-term and long-term goals. If company performance is not on track, strategies and tactics are changed with the objective of bringing the corporation back on track to meet its goals. The United States of America is a very large corporation. It is more than a thousand times larger than the largest corporation in the world. The US economy consists of over 315 million people, millions of production systems, millions of consumption systems, and billions of transactions occurring daily between these various entities. As an economy, it is one system. In order to be efficient and effective, it needs to function as one integrated system. Every part of the US economy (people, organizations and corporations) must work together to achieve the objectives of the US economy.

What are the general and specific financial goals of the United States as a nation, or as an organization or as a corporation? It is clear that the general financial goal of the US economy is to maximize the standard of living and the wealth of the people in the United States. It is also clear that this general goal involves the maximization of wealth of all the people and not a select minority of people. In a kingdom the goal of the economy is to maximize the wealth of the king. In an oligopoly the goal of the economy is to maximize the wealth of the privileged few. However, Christian Economics holds that the ultimate goal o f the economy is to maximize the wealth of the people, all the people.

In order to achieve a goal there has to be a managed effort toward that goal. To achieve an organizational goal, there has to be a managed, coordinated, collaborated effort in pursuing that goal. Every corporation must diligently manage its efforts in pursuing its goals. The United States of America is an immense corporation with an economic goal of maximizing the standard of living and wealth of all the people in the United States. Whose responsibility is it to manage and coordinate the efforts of the 315 million people, the millions of organizations, the millions of businesses and the hundreds of thousands of corporations in order to achieve the goal of maximization of wealth and the highest standard of living for all the people of the United States? It should be obvious that it the responsibility of the Federal government, the state governments, the county governments and the local governments—all working together.

What corporation can achieve its goals and objectives without management, direction, and supervision? How is it possible for 315 million people and millions of organizations, businesses and corporations to work together to achieve the common economic goal of maximization of wealth and the highest standard of living for all the people of the United States without management, direction and supervision? Truly absurd is the notion that the economy needs no management, direction or supervision. It is impossible for hundreds of millions of entities (people, organizations, businesses, and corporations) to function in an integrated, systematic manner and to achieve a common goal without management, direction and supervision.

What is the management function of the US economy ? Is it the Federal Reserve, a private organization? Is it the Bank of America? Is it Citibank? The management function of the US economy cannot be any private entity; it has to be a public entity. For a private entity has as its purpose the private good of only the owners of that organization. The management function of the US economy has to represent the interests of all 315 million people in the United States and not just a minority of the people. It should be clear that only the Federal government has the mission, responsibility and the authority to manage, direct and supervise the US economy. In a similar manner, only the state government has the mission, responsibility and the authority to manage, direct and supervise the state economy. The economy has to be managed to achieve its purpose and objectives.

Does the US government have an annual operating plan for the economy with goals, objectives, strategies, tactics and metrics? Does the US government have a strategic plan and long-term plan for the economy with goals, objectives, strategies, tactics and metrics? What are the strategies and tactics used by the government to keep the economy on track?

What metrics does the US government use to measure whether the US economy is on track to reach its goals? Does the US government have a balanced scorecard with which to see where the economy is out of balance?

If the US government had a balanced scorecard, the US would not now be in the economic crisis that it faces today. It is amazing to note that only in December of 2008 did the government realize that the US economy had been in recession since December of 2007. The Federal government does not understand its responsibilities to manage, direct and supervise the economy. Nor does it understand how to manage the economy.

In spite of the fact that the management of the economy is one of the primary responsibilities of the government, the Federal government does not have either an annual plan or a long-term plan for the US economy with objectives, strategies, tactics and metrics. Obviously, there are no such plans for if there were most people would be aware of them. While the government should and must manage the economy, yet it doesn't. And the main reason that the government does not manage the economy for the good of the people is the government is controlled by Big Business, Big Finance and Big Wealth. Big Business, Big Finance and Big Wealth want to manage the economy for their good and not the good of all the people. Therefore, they want the government (the President, his administration and Congress) to maintain a 'hands off' approach on the economy. And to the detriment of 315 million people in the United States, the government takes a virtual 'hands off' policy on the economy; they do little to nothing to manage, direct and supervise the US economy.

Within an economy everyone needs things. People need food, they need shelter or housing, they need clothes, they need furniture, they need appliances, they need electricity, they need to heat and cool their homes, they need healthcare, they need education, and they need entertainment as well as a multitude of other goods and services. While not impossible, it is neither practical nor efficient for everyone to try to provide on their own for the goods and services that they need. Instead everyone engages in the production of some good or service with the intention of trading the excess of the goods or services that they produce with the excess of the goods and services produced by someone else. And in order to facilitate the extensive trading that goes on money is used which is a medium of exchange. The 315 million people in the United States are both producers and consumers. Using money, consumers buy the goods and services that they need and want from producers (or from an intermediary distributor or retailer). The money that the producers receive from the sale of their goods and services is used by them as consumers to buy the goods and services that they need and want. This then forms the cycle of production, purchase/sale and consumption. Money flows from consumer to producer back to consumer.

The economy is the aggregation of all producers, consumers, distributors, retailers and the interactions and transactions between them. The goal of the economy is to maximize the wealth of the people. Wealth is made up of goods and money which can be used to buy services and more goods. In order to maximize the wealth of the people, the economy must maximize production. For only the production of goods and services generates wealth and value. The United States as a nation, as an organization, and as a corporation must pursue a goal of maximizing production. The US must maximize its production of food, housing, clothing, equipment, appliances, furniture, technical and electronic devices—everything that it is able to produce. Production is limited by consumption and consumption is limited by the amount of money the consumer has which is the result of the work that they do in producing goods and services. Maximizing the wealth of the people of the United States involves maximizing the production of goods and services by the people of the United States. Maximizing US production is dependent on maximizing consumption of and demand for US goods and services. The last fifty years has seen a continuing decline in US production of goods and services caused by corporations seeking to maximize profits. This has been extremely detrimental to the US economy, is one of the major reasons for the current economic crisis and must be reversed in order to rectify the problems with the economy.

Is the US pursuing a policy of maximum production? Is the President and his administration promoting and pursuing a policy of maximum production? Maximizing production implies maximizing worker utilization. How does the government pursue a policy of maximization of production output? It should be clear that every president since Nixon has helped to reduce the production of goods and services within the United States: good for corporations, very bad for the people.

Who manages the amount of money in the economy which is needed to facilitate the interactions between producers and consumers ? Is it the United States Federal government ? No, it is the Federal Reserve, a private banking system.

Who manages the US economy? Managing the US economy is one of the main responsibilities of the Federal government, yet it does little to nothing to do so. If the Federal government is not managing the US economy, who is? Is anyone managing the US economy or is it running aimlessly without direction? The US economy is actually run by a myriad of different and competing organizations, all of which can be labeled under the headings of Big Business, Big Finance and Big Wealth. These are not public organizations which seek to serve the general public but rather private organizations which seek to serve private individuals. Because of this, the US economy is in chaos. It is pulled in multiple directions. It lacks balance. It is not directed towards the good of all the people. It is not managed, it is mismanaged. It is out of control.

It is amazing to consider that seventy-five percent of Americans call themselves Christian, yet the United States government and businesses operate on principles and practices that are diametrically opposed to Christian principles.

Economic Disaster by Design

SOCIO-ECONOMIC CLASSES ARE A natural result of the differences in individual effort, personal creativity, and personal productivity. However, socio-economic classes are not based solely on these natural differences. For thousands of years, there have been people who have manipulated economies for their own selfish and greedy purposes and through this manipulation have succeeded in rising to very high levels within the spectrum of socio-economic classes. The upper class is dominated both in numbers and in power by these individuals who have acquired their position and wealth through economic manipulation rather than by personal effort, personal creativity and personal productivity. It should be clear that not everyone who is part of the upper class is there because of economic manipulation, but, unfortunately, the vast majority of the upper class is.

Those who have manipulated the economy have become super-rich. They are like kings and queens and they seek to become emperors. Some in fact wish to rule the world. While there have been national kingdoms, and regional empires; there has never been a global kingdom or empire in which the entire world, all peoples of the world are controlled politically and financially by an individual or small group of individuals. Yet, the global political and economic environment is witnessing the accumulation of such political and economic power that it is only a matter of time before there will be a global empire. This global empire will contain the most extreme difference between the haves and have-nots.

Currently, there are individuals whose wealth exceeds that of many national economies. Some of these individuals are known to the public and some are unknown to the public. And the wealth of these billionaires is increasing and this increase has accelerated during the current economic crisis where hundreds of millions of people in the United States have seen their wealth decrease. In fact, the cumulative decrease in wealth for the working class in the United States is equal to the increase in wealth for rich elite. This point needs to be emphasized: the economic crisis of the past fifteen years has resulted in a shift in wealth from the working class to the upper class. This obviously leads to the question, has this shift in wealth from the working class to the upper class happened by chance or by design?

Today there are individuals whose wealth is in the tens of billions of dollars and one person whose wealth exceeds $130 billion. There are families whose wealth is in the hundreds of billions of dollars and one family whose combined wealth is perhaps over a trillion dollars. Soon there will be more individuals whose wealth will be in the hundreds of billions of dollars and more families whose wealth will exceed a trillion dollars. And this accumulation of wealth will come at the expense of the majority of people who will see their wealth decrease correspondingly.

These individuals use techniques and mechanisms to extract wealth from the working class. They do not create, design, organize, manage, construct, repair, transport, teach, or nurse. They do not contribute to the Aggregate Production system of the United States whatsoever. Yet, they receive a disproportionate share of the created wealth through contrived techniques and mechanisms. And the last forty years have seen the most aggressive manipulation of the US economy by these very wealthy elite.

Has the economic crisis which started in 2007 happened by chance or by design? First of all, it should be clear that the current economic situation has been and is a crisis for the vast majority of people but not for all. For a very small percentage of people, this economic situation has been and is a great opportunity and a great event. While the vast majority of people are suffering financially (and some suffering immensely) and have been suffering from the economic situation of the last ten years, for some people these last ten years have been the greatest of times? During the last ten years these individuals have significantly increased their wealth, their control of wealth, and their political power—and they continue to do so.

The economic situation of the last several years has been caused by and continues to be caused by actions, tactics, and policies that have been intentionally put in place by these same people who have greatly benefitted from this economic situation. These people have intentionally taken these actions and have done so with the specific intention of increasing their wealth, their control of wealth and their political power. It should be clear that the current economic situation, which continues to be a crisis for between 100 and 200 million people in the United States, is by design and not by chance. Since the current economic crisis is by design and not by chance, it should be clear that this crisis will not change until the underlying causes are removed.

Contrary to what the Administration, Congress and the news media say, the economic situation is not getting better and in fact will get worse because the underlying causes are not being removed and because those who manipulate the economy for their own selfish and greedy purposes are implementing other schemes to further increase the imbalance in the distribution of wealth. The current Administration claims that the US economy is growing and is getting better. But for whom is the economy getting better? Is the economy or the share of the economy getting better for the 47 million Americans who are living in poverty? Is the economy or the share of the economy getting better for the 15 to 20 million people who have had their homes repossessed or foreclosed? Is the economy or the share of the economy getting better for the 9 million people who are unemployed? Is the economy or the share of the economy getting better for the 30 million people who are underemployed? Is the economy or the share of the economy getting better for the hundreds of thousands of college graduates who cannot find a job after they have spent or borrowed tens of thousands of dollars to finance their college education ? Is the economy or the share of the economy getting better for the 60 million people who live on Social Security? The fact is that the United States economy is not getting better for the lowest 60 percent of Americans, but it is getting better for the top 2 percent of Americans. And this is all by design and not by chance

Realizing that this economic crisis which has impacted hundreds of millions of people within the United States has been and is caused by some very rich people who are intent on becoming even richer and more powerful, one must consider the personalities and philosophies of these super-rich individuals who intentionally have developed schemes to take money from the poor and the working class to add to their already excesses. They have neither sympathy nor empathy for their fellow human beings. They have no concern about the millions of people who are homeless. They have no concern about the millions of people who have lost their homes through repossessions. They have no concern about the tens of millions of people who are unemployed or underemployed. They have no concern about the tens of millions of people who live in poverty. These super-rich people are in fact the cause of the financial, emotional and physical sufferings of these people and they don't care. Rather, these super-rich have contempt for those suffering from this economic crisis and actually blame them rather than themselves for their economic misery.

What makes matters worse is that these super-rich individuals have even more radical plans and schemes to take even more wealth from the lower classes and make it their own. These super rich individuals are promoting an even more extreme form of radical capitalism, where all common and community property will be privatized. In other words, they want to take private and personal ownership of property that is jointly and commonly shared by all people. They want to privatize all schools, all libraries, all roads, all bridges, all parks, and all police and fire departments. They want to privatize Social Security, Medicare, and unemployment insurance which will actually result in destroying Social Security, Medicare, and unemployment insurance. They want to privatize all services provided by the government and all community property. They even want to privatize the military.

What would happen if there were only privately owned schools, libraries, parks, roads, bridges, police and fire protection? Virtually, all people except for the rich owners would be financial slaves to those who owned the schools, libraries, parks, roads, bridges, police and fire protection services. What would happen if there was no public military protecting the United States but instead all that was available were private armies? The people of the United States would have no protection from foreign invaders unless they paid for such protection. But what would happen if they could not afford to pay for such protection?

What would happen if there was no social security, no Medicare, and no unemployment insurance? What would happen if there were no public services to help the unfortunate? The number of the homeless and the number of those living in poverty could increase to between 30 and 40 percent of the population, over 100 million people. Imagine over 100 million people in the United States living in poverty. Image the effect on the economy of 30 to 40 percent of the population living in poverty.

The history of recorded civilization spans almost 10,000 years. During the majority of that time the dominant political and economic system has been autocratic or oligarchic and totalitarian where almost all human rights were denied. One individual; a king, a queen, an emperor, or a dictator; or a small group of individuals claimed almost total economic and political control over all society.

The best and most complete enumeration of human rights is found in the United Nations Universal Declaration of Human Rights drafted in 1948 and the basis for international law. Among the many human rights listed are life, liberty, thought, speech, assembly, movement, security, privacy, freedom from arbitrary arrest or detention, property ownership, participation in government, access to public services, social security, the right to work, the right to a living wage and the right to form trade unions. It clearly identifies that the will of the people is the basis for government and the goal and objective of the government is the good of the people. It states that everyone has the natural right to take part in the government. It further states that all people have natural rights that are equal to the rights of others; no one has rights that others do not have, nor are the rights of some greater than those of others. The United Nations Universal Declaration of Human Rights expresses in detail the Christian principle of the absolute respect for the dignity of each and every human person.

Yet, for the greater part of 10,000 years most of these natural human rights were denied and disregarded by almost all autocratic and oligarchic governments. It has only been during the last two or three hundred years and at great personal expense (wealth, property and life) that many societies have been able to force governments to recognize their natural and human rights. Unfortunately, this populist struggle to force governments to recognize all human rights continues even today in many countries throughout the world including the United States where not all the natural human rights listed in the United Nations Universal Declaration of Human Rights are recognized.

The super-rich people who have been manipulating the economy and have caused the current economic crisis affecting over 150 million people in the United States are intent on having most natural human rights denied and disregarded by the various levels of government. The right to form trade unions, the right to a living wage, the right to participation in government, social security and the right to public services are currently under attack. And at a state and local level, even the basic right to a democratic government is being attacked by this most powerful elite.

The economic crisis that has greatly impacted the United States over the last ten years has been caused by design and not by chance and will continue, in fact getting worse, until the people understand the true causes of the crisis and do what is necessary to eliminate those causes. This design on the US economy and the global economy is diametrically opposed to God's design and the only solution to the problems affecting the economies of the world is the application of Christian Economics.

When will Christians begin to act like Christians in their business lives, their economic lives and their political lives?

PART II

Christian Economics—The Solution to the Economic Crisis

The Principles of Christian Economics

IF THE ACTIONS OUTLINED above were taken, balance would be restored to the United States economy, the current economic crisis would cease, and the United States would see economic prosperity for the vast majority of its citizens never paralleled in its history or in the history of the world. These actions require both legislation and policy changes on the part of the government. In themselves, such legislation and policy changes are simple and easy to implement. However, because the federal government is currently controlled by Big Business, Big Finance and Big Wealth these fixes and corrections to the economy would be rejected and opposed by them. While, it would be possible for a new president to bring about these necessary changes, it is doubtful that a person could be elected given the stranglehold that Big Business, Big Finance and Big Wealth have on the election process. And one person alone as president would have a difficult time in bringing about the necessary changes without the help and support of the majority of Congress.

What then can be done? If the government will not restore balance to the United States economy and political system, then who can and who will? The basic underlying cause of all the issues affecting the economy is the fact that the principles of Christian economics are not being applied. Christian economics can solve virtually all the problems affecting the economy but only if they are applied. And it is the responsibility of Christians to take an active interest in politics and economics, and apply Christian principles to these spheres.

People have heard of the phrase 'evil exists because good people do nothing'. This phrase is incorrect. Evil exists because there are too few good people to offset it. Evil can only be removed by good. Evil is the absence of good, and in order to remove evil good must consume it.

Christians are called to fight evil. Christians are called to overcome the evils in the economy by applying the principles of Christian economics.

All authority is derived from "the will of the people." The power and authority to rule, to legislate, and to judge resides with the people. And it is only by the people granting this power and authority to leaders, legislators and judges do these same individuals become leaders, legislators and judges. The President answers to and must obey the will of the people. A president who disregards the will of the people can and should be removed from office, and it is the people who should initiate this. This also applies to senators, congressmen, judges, governors, mayors, etc. Where does the US Constitution gets its authority? It gets its authority from the people. The people define and enact the constitution. The Constitution begins with the words "We the People" and that phrase represents the essence of the constitution. The constitution of a country: what makes the country what it is and what defines the country, are the People. The People are the constitution of the country. The People make the country what it is. The People define the country. Many people consider the US Constitution as the source and authority of all power within the United States. It is not. The constitution is a document expressing the will of the current people, the people living today—not the people who lived 200 years ago. Because of this, it needs to adapt to the will of the people.

The first three words of the Declaration of Independence are "We the People." The basis for the constitution, the basis for the government, the basis for the nation, the basis for all authority, the basis for foreign policy, the basis for domestic policy, and the basis for the economy are the People of the United States. Pseudo-scholars; constitutional, legal and historical, try to understand the minds and intentions of those individuals who penned the US constitution over 200 years ago not realizing that the current people of the United States are the owners of the constitution and only they have to power to amend and interpret it. Scholars, lawmakers, judges and lawyers need to consult the people for the interpretation of the constitution and for direction and understanding on the bases for all laws and policies. The writers of the original constitution are dead, but the actual owners of the constitution are living. 'We the People' imply that the owners of the constitution are the current citizens of the United States. The justices of the Supreme Court need to confer with the People regarding the interpretation of the constitution. They need to frequently communicate with the People in order to hear and understand the mind and will of the majority of the people.

Referendums represent a formal way for the people to express their will. The working class needs to initiate national referendums that will clearly tell the government; the President, Congress, and the courts, what is their will. And if the President or senators, or representatives or judges refuse to obey the will of the people, they need to be recalled.

What makes things extremely difficult is that the capitalist class currently holds a dominant position within the economy and will vehemently resist any attempt to rebalance the economy by bringing it under control. It must be clearly understood that the capitalist class uses every means to promote its dominance including lying, bribery, character assassination, and even war. Unfortunately, most capitalists have no concern for the difficulties and misery of the working class, the misfortunes of the poor, and the personal tragedies associated with war. They have no compassion. Capitalists only care about themselves and they use the government, the economy and the working class for their selfish good. There has and is a class war going on in the United States and it is the capitalist class that is at war with the working class. The working class must defend itself against the capitalist class. It must struggle against the capitalist class not to eliminate it but to bring it under control, and to bring about the appropriate controls of a balanced economy.

The people of the United States need to gain control of the government and the economy in order to correct the severe problems afflicting the United States. The United States is tending towards what could be the worst economic crisis in its history. Only by restoring the economic and political balance between capital and labor can this be avoided. It is up to the Christian working class to restore this balance by forcing the government to represent the people, both capitalists and workers, equally.

The Good of All the People, the Objective of the Economy

WHERE DOES THE PRESIDENT get his authority to act as leader of the United States? Where do the senators and congressmen get their authority to act as legislators? Where does the Supreme Court get its authority to judge? Where do the federal, state and local courts get their authority to judge? Where do governors, mayors, and every other type of government official get their authority to lead? Where does the military get its authority to engage in military actions of any kind whatsoever? Where do the CIA, the FBI, the Justice department, the state police, and local police get their authority to act?

All authority is derived from "the will of the people." The power and authority to rule, to legislate, and to judge resides with the people. And, it is only by the people granting this power and authority to leaders, legislators and judges do these same individuals become leaders, legislators and judges.

The ultimate and natural power and authority to lead, legislate and judge always resides with and in the people and can never be taken away from the people since the people receive this by nature. When the people grant to leaders, legislators and judges power and authority, it is only temporary and subject to the continued will of the people. The people can withdraw their power and authority from the President, the legislators, the Supreme Court, any governor, any mayor, any judge, any government official at any time.

The President (as well as the vice-president and entire administration) answers to and must obey the will of the people. A president who disregards the will of the people can and should be removed from office, and it is the people who should initiate this. This also applies to senators, congressmen, judges (at every level even the Supreme Court), governors, mayors, etc.

The military must realize that they serve the people and must obey the will of the people. They should only obey the commands of the President and Congress insofar as their commands are in conformity with the will of the people. They should ignore and refuse any command from a superior which does not conform to the will of the people. Patriotism is the love, respect, support and defense of one's country. The word country implies the people of the country. Patriotism is not blind obedience to the president or to Congress. When a significant majority of the people do not support the president's use of the military, the military needs to ignore the president and obey the people. For in such a case, it is the president who is insubordinate to the will of the people. To serve the will of the people is the highest duty of a soldier.

The CIA, the FBI, the Justice department, the Supreme Court, the federal court system, state courts, and police officers must realize that the will of the people is the highest law of the land. Whenever the will of the people is significantly at odds with the orders, directives, and commands of their superiors, they need to seek and obey the will of the people.

The constitution contains the principles, strategies, tactics and operating policies for a nation. The principles of a nation, since they are derived from nature, can never be changed; however, the strategies, tactics and operating policies of a nation can and should be changed. The original framers of the United States constitution identified many though not all the natural principles which should form the basis of this nation. It is absolutely necessary that the constitution be enhanced to include all the rights contained in the Universal Declaration of Human Rights. Furthermore, the constitution should state that human rights are derived from nature and are not limited to the jurisdiction of a nation.

There are many strategies, tactics and operating policies in the current United States constitution that are no longer relevant and need to be changed, and there are obviously some new ones that need to be defined. Voting procedures need to be drastically changed. The Electoral College needs to be eliminated and the plurality criterion for selecting representatives (the president, vice-president, senators and congressman are all representatives of the people) needs to be replaced by a majority criterion. All government positions involving an elected official need to have term limits specifically defined (including the Supreme Court and Federal judges). Voting must allow a voter to choose neither candidate and still have their vote count.

The election process (perhaps it should be expressed as the selection process since it is the process whereby the people select their representatives) needs to be totally re-engineered. It is clear that the gender, ethnic, racial, age and income makeup of the US Congress in no way reflects the statistical gender, ethnic, racial, age and income makeup of the US citizen population over eighteen years old. Having access to money, either personally or through a network of friends and associates, is an entry requirement to participation in the campaign process for all but the wealthiest of citizens. As a result, the pool of candidates is limited to those with money and those with more money and the people have no real choice in selecting candidates who they feel will truly represent them. Money should not be an entry requirement for an individual wishing to pursue public service. Candidates and campaigns should be based on principles, qualifications, and ideas—not money.

Since the government is meant to represent the will of the people, the people should have a greater role in electing most if not all individuals to fill positions within the government to include supreme court justices, federal justices, and secretary members. The nefarious practice of assigning judges (sometimes referred to as administrators or commissioners—yet having the same authority as a judge) needs to be abolished. No one should judge without having been elected by the people. And term limits must apply to judges, all judges. It is absurd for a person to rule or judge for life. And the behavior and performance of judges must be subject to regular evaluation and review by the people.

The people should have to vote for the budget to be approved (obviously the budget with all its details would have to be easily available for review by all citizens before the vote) as well as anytime the government must borrow money. The people should also have to approve any type of government reorganization such as the Homeland Security reorganization. The people and only the people should approve treaties, approve new amendments, and approve new powers for the president.

The ability to engage a nation in war does not lie with one individual such as the president, nor with a group of individuals such as Congress. No, this power and right belongs only to the people. It is the people of a nation who fight a war. It is the people who sacrifice their very lives and limbs, and who also bear the burden of financing the war. War can only be declared by the will of the people; by a significant majority vote of the general population. Once war is declared it cannot take on a life of its own. It is necessary that the general population periodically vote to continue the war, and it is the will of the people who should decide if and when to end the war.

In re-writing the United States constitution, the people (through their votes—not through their representatives) need to decide the final content and form. It would also be necessary for the people to be involved in the various stages of the new constitution's development.

Despite all the rhetoric about the United States being a democracy and the model for all nations, in actuality the United States is very far from a democracy where the will of the people guides, directs, and governs the nation. The people of the United States need to realize their supreme power and authority and do what is necessary to restore their will as the basis for this nation.

Why are Americans so afraid to talk about politics and political ideologies? When will people realize the difference between the will of the people and the will of the current president? When will people realize the difference between the common good and the good of special interests? When will people realize the difference between the truth and the propaganda and doubletalk of the current government? When will people realize that it is their right, their duty, and their responsibility to define, guide, and regulate this nation?

When will individuals working for the CIA, the FBI, the military, the Justice Department, Homeland security, law enforcement or any other government agency realize that human rights are derived by nature, cannot be limited by the government and are not limited to citizens of the United States? When will these same individuals realize that an order does not justify the morality of the act that is ordered; that an order that violates one's right to life, liberty and security of person is not a valid order and cannot and should not be obeyed; that an order that involves torture or cruel, inhuman or degrading treatment or punishment is not a valid order and cannot and should not be obeyed; that an order to subject a person to arbitrary arrest or detention is not a valid order and cannot and should not be obeyed; that an order that will deprive a person of a fair and public hearing by an independent and impartial court is not a valid order and cannot and should not be obeyed; that an order that subjects any person to arbitrary interference with his privacy, his family, his home, his correspondence, his honor or his reputation is not a valid order and cannot and should not be obeyed. "I was under orders," I was only doing my duty," I was only doing my job"; these are not excuses for doing something wrong. Virtually every atrocity within history was carried out by those following orders, and these atrocities could have been avoided if the orders were not obeyed.

In order for the working class to become active, they need to reduce the amount of time watching television, limit talk about sports, movies, celebrities, etc. They need to read more political and economic articles and less sports magazines, tabloids, and glamour magazines. The working-class majority should not be afraid to take a stand or express an opinion. High school students and college students need to wake up and make decisions for themselves. What happened to the days when college students were activists and wanted to improve the society in which they were going to live?

Working class members should email family, friends, and associates on issues and articles that promote equality between capital and labor. They need to start discussion groups, circulate petitions, and promote referendums. Referendums represent the most important political tool of the working class. Referendums represent the will of the people, and they are the basis and authority of the United States constitution, the government and the economy.

The People need to control the Executive Branch of Government. The People need to control the Legislative Branch of Government. The People need to control the Judicial Branch of Government. The Good of the People which is the objective of the economy can only be obtained in a democratic society, through a real democratic government, and within a democratic economy.

Natural law is the moral order which God established in order for humans to reach their final end. It consists of personal rights, the structure of society, and the relationships of individuals with society including politics and economics. What political system is part of the natural order: a monarchy, a representative government, an oligarchy, a plutocracy, a limited democracy, a complete democracy, or some combination? Any government having total control (totalitarian) over the rights and lives of the individuals of society is contrary to the natural order. This applies to every form of government except a democracy. An almost complete democracy is best and most in accord with the natural order.

Desired State

IMAGINE A SOCIETY WHERE virtually everyone who wants to work is employed and the unemployment rate is basically zero. Imagine a society where virtually no one is under employed, that is, employed in a position which does not correspond to a person's full potential. Imagine a society where workers, or worker shareholders, are never faced with a layoff situation. Imagine a society where workers and their families never have to endure a long period of being out of work with no income, never have to endure living off savings until their savings have been totally spent, never have to live off credit until they are enslaved by the unscrupulous and ruthless credit empire, never have to sell their home in order to use its equity to pay for food and daily expenses.

Imagine a society where a labor shareholder can start work at one company and retire from that same company forty years later. Imagine a society where health care expenses are both reasonable and affordable and where insurance is only needed for catastrophic expenses. Imagine a society where people can buy a home and own it entirely within fifteen years because the mortgage interest rate is between two to three four percent; there is no private mortgage insurance; closing costs are extremely moderate and property tax escrow accounts are interest bearing.

Imagine a society where interest rates for all types of loans are less than five percent. Imagine a society where there are no credit rates of 32 percent, personal loans rates of 35 percent and payday loan rates of up to five hundred percent.

Imagine a society where prices for goods and services are fair and stable and where prices are based on 'making a living' not 'making a killing'. Imagine a society where the philosophies of 'maximum profit', 'something for nothing' and 'it is neither right nor wrong, it is just business ' are considered fallacious and erroneous. Imagine a society where the just price principle and the balanced economy pricing principle are adhered to.

Imagine a society where the government is not a puppet of Big Business and Big Wealth and truly acts as a servant of the public and seeks only the common good. Imagine a society where legislators are not multimillionaires who put personal gain before and in place of the common good but truly represent the people with all their gender, income, age, racial, ethnic, and professional diversities. Imagine a society where the government seeks what is most beneficial to the majority and not the privileged few. Imagine a society where honesty, fairness, and justice apply and civil law is a mirror of the Natural Law.

Imagine a world where war is virtually non-existent because personal greed, exploitation and imperialism do not dominate a country's political and economic systems. Imagine a society where poverty has been eliminated and people possess the highest standard of living possible. Imagine a society where the Natural Law is recognized and obeyed, and where virtue is practiced for the sake of a higher good.

Can there be such a world? Is such a thing possible? The answer to these questions is 'Yes," and the solution involves the application of Christian economics and the control of capitalism. Notice that it is stated that capitalism needs to be controlled not eliminated. For capitalism has its proper role in nature. It is the excess of capitalism, taking it far beyond its correct limit within the economy and society that has resulted in the greatest difficulties and injustices inflicting all known societies since the beginning of civilization.

What is Capitalism?

A PRODUCTIVE SYSTEM IS any system that produces goods or services. While such systems can be classified as profit and non-profit, only those productive systems organized for profit will be considered here. There are obviously a wide range of for-profit, productive systems. Among the most common types of for-profit, productive systems are manufacturing organizations, distribution and sales organizations, banking organizations, construction organizations, entertainment organizations, educational organizations, consulting organizations, software organizations, telecommunication organizations and medical organizations.

There are two basic components to a productive system: capital and labor. Capital can either be land (and the natural resources on the land), equipment, material, intellectual property, technology or cash/funds which can be used to buy the necessary assets and materials required by the productive system. Labor can be either intellectual or physical. By intellectual is meant creative activities such as designing, developing, planning, organizing, managing, etc. Physical work covers a wide range of activities from those involved in manufacturing and construction to playing sports to singing and acting to talking to teaching to writing.

What is most problematic about discussions on capitalism is that most people have the wrong understanding of what capitalism is. While most people think that a capitalist is one who contributes 'capital' to a productive system, that is not completely true. In the vast majority of cases, the one who is considered the capitalist did not contribute any capital to the organization. (While it may appear confusing to use the term 'capitalist' for those who have not in fact contributed capital, this is the term that most people use to refer to this class of individuals. The real confusion lies in the realization that these individuals do not contribute capital to the organization.) Other than the case of a startup or initial public offering, capitalists have not contributed any capital whatsoever to the actual system. It is more appropriate to consider the capitalist as the purported owner or controller of the organization. (It must be emphasized that the role of capitalist as owner is based upon history and civil law and is not based on natural law. From a natural law point of view, the capitalist is the co-owner of the organization along with the worker.)

The vast majority of organizations are controlled and from a legal point of view owned by individuals who have provided virtually no money of theirs to this enterprise. In many cases people have inherited the legal ownership and control of a business. It may be true that those from whom they inherited control of the business may have invested some of their money at some time. However, that initial investment compared to the present worth or value of the business is usually insignificant. In many other cases, individuals have either borrowed or have used others' money to gain control of an enterprise. In most cases today regarding large corporations, the supposed owners are so-called investment groups who control, direct and manage the entire corporation in order to either increase the price of a share so that they can sell their ownership and make a profit or to increase the value of the corporation so that they can sell the corporation and make a profit. They are really not investment groups because they have become the owners by buying shares from someone else. In other words, they invested no money whatsoever in the company. Of course, many people see nothing wrong with this. It is portrayed as the American dream to own a property or a business and have others pay rent or work for you. "Something for nothing," "get rich quick," "buy property with no money down"; these expressions are sometimes referred to as the American dream. Getting something for investing nothing is really stealing. Taking the benefits of the production of others without having made any contribution to the productive process is exploitation and theft. Is stealing and exploitation the American dream?

People who own property or a business and do not work but rely on the labor and productivity of others are like kings and queens. They claim ownership of property or a productive system as well as the production of those who are coerced to work for them. They do not look upon the worker or tenant as an equal, but rather as a subordinate. In fact, the capitalist looks upon the worker or tenant as chattel, property that they own.

Most people have both the wrong understanding and the wrong impression of capitalism. And this is the direct and intentional result of capitalists who have endeavored to make themselves and capitalism itself appear good, appropriate and necessary. In order to understand capitalism, it is necessary to define and understand a capitalist and also to define and understand capital.

A capitalist is a person who uses a claim (either real or artificial) on capital (either real or perceived property) to receive an income and/or an increase in wealth from the work of others. The pure capitalist does not work but rather depends entirely on the productive work of others for his or her income and increase in wealth. Furthermore, the pure capitalist takes the position that he or she as a capitalist has rights superior to the rights of the worker. The pure capitalist also holds that the real or artificial capital that they own or claim to own has its own rights and that these rights are also superior to those of the worker. In its extreme form and application, this attitude has led to the absolute denial of any rights for workers, that is, slavery.

The pure capitalist does not work and makes no contribution to a production system or to the economy. They do not design. They do not create. They do not mine. They do not farm. They do not make. They do not assemble. They do not market. They do not advertise. They do not sell. They do not ship. They do not take orders. They do not teach. They do not nurse. They do not doctor. They do not counsel. The pure capitalist does not produce any good or service whatsoever. And yet the pure capitalist claims to own the goods and services produced by the workers and wants to own and control virtually all revenue, profits and benefits associated with the production, delivery and sale of the good or service while at the same time disowning any responsibility and liability for any negative result. The pure capitalist does not work and makes no contribution to a production system or to the economy and yet wants to own and control the entire economy.

Who are pure capitalists? Everyone who 'plays' the stock markets are pure capitalists. They do not work for nor make any contribution to the companies in which they own stock. Most people who play in the commodities market are pure capitalists. They do not add any value to the commodities which they temporarily own. People who own companies and have others manage these companies for them are pure capitalists. Many people who own copyrights and patents are pure capitalists. Private equity firms are pure capitalists. Corporations that own other corporations are pure capitalists. The pure capitalist does not work and makes no contribution to a production system or to the economy and yet wants to own and control the entire economy.

The pure capitalist makes a real or contrived claim of ownership on the capital used in a production system. In earlier times and still today pure capitalists claim to own land and all the resources above, on and below the land. Workers are employed to manipulate these resources and transform these raw materials into materials that can be sold and either used or consumed by others. In most cases, the land or raw materials have no value in themselves. It is the transformation process performed by workers that creates the value. A tree by itself has virtually no value. But the processes of cutting the tree down, taking the bark off, cutting it into rough lumber, planing the rough lumber into finished lumber, cutting the finished lumber into pieces for a door, gluing the pieces together, staining the door, attaching hinges and a handle to the door—these activities produce the value which will be realized by the person who buys and uses the door. And yet the pure capitalist claims to own everything because the tree was on the land that supposedly belonged to him or her. In this example the land and the tree are considered capital by the capitalist.

The following story will illustrate the principles of the present day, exaggerated and defective form of capitalism. (Capitalism is a correct principle but not the form of capitalism that exists today.)

The Little Red Hen

A LITTLE RED HEN was walking around the barnyard and came across some grains of wheat. She considered herself lucky and formed a desire to make some bread. However, she was averse to work of all kinds, manual and intellectual, so she devised a plan to get others to make the bread for her. Furthermore, being one that wanted to control everything, she decided that it was best that she be incorporated so that she was assured that she and only she held absolute control in this venture. So, the little red hen formed a corporation and then proceeded to persuade others at the barnyard to help her. She solicited the help of many animals around the barnyard promising them that if they helped her make the bread, she would give them a slice of it. Once the barnyard animals were selected, the little red hen explained to them that she needed to visit some relatives on another farm. She would not be back for a week, so would they please go about the tasks of making the bread.

So, the little red hen left and the others gathered together in order to organize themselves and agree on the right course of action to take in order to make the loaf of bread. About an hour into their meeting, the owl asked to speak. "While it is certainly a good idea to use the wheat to bake a loaf of bread, it would be better if we would use the wheat to grow even more wheat so that we could make many loaves of bread and not just one." The duck replied, "But, it would take three months to grow the wheat and we don't have that many grains of wheat to begin with. In fact, we only have enough to bake a single loaf of bread." To which the owl answered, "You are right if you only consider conventional methods of agriculture. However, using genetic engineering, hydroponics and greenhouses; we can produce as much seed as we need and achieve six growing cycles per year." Astonished by this information, the horse interjected, "Why, we can make enough bread for the whole barnyard for the whole year!" To which the owl, responded: "We can make bread for ourselves and bread to sell. Why don't we start a business! We can call it The Little Red Hen Baking Company."

Everyone at the meeting agreed and they quickly began to work on this business venture. When word reached the little red hen as to what the animals at her barnyard were doing, she decided to extend her visit not wanting to get involved in all the work and activity. Yet, she did want to keep informed as to the progress of the business.

The barnyard animals, without the help of the little red hen, set about to establish The Little Red Hen Baking Company. They researched genetic engineering techniques, developed greenhouses, designed and constructed state of the art baking techniques, perfected highly nutritious and quite delectable recipes for a wide range of bread products, assembled a highly sophisticated supply chain, and actualized a first class marketing and sales organization. Within two years' time, they had transformed the barnyard into a highly complex manufacturing and distribution facility generating sales of over five hundred thousand dollars a day.

When news of the success of The Little Red Hen Baking Company reached the little red hen, she was overjoyed and decided to immediately return to the former barnyard now Baking Company. When she arrived, she wandered around the campus in complete amazement. As she went from the greenhouses to the bakeries to the distribution center to the corporate offices; she kept repeating, "All mine, this is all mine." When word reached the executive office that the little red hen had returned; the owl, the duck, the horse and the other original animals went out to greet the little red hen. As they approached her, they heard her say, "All mine, this is all mine." Rather confused, they asked her what she meant when she said, "All mine, this is all mine." And the little red hen replied, "Why, this is all mine. The Little Red Hen Baking Company is all mine." To which the owl responded, "Well, you really mean that this is our company. You provided the initial few seeds of wheat, but through our creativity, resourcefulness, and hard work we have transformed those few seeds into a three hundred-million-dollar organization." "No, you are quite mistaken. This company is my company. I am the owner. You are merely employees. I have the papers to prove it." "But," the owl retorted, "You only provided a few grains of wheat which you found. We have worked mentally and physically for the past two years to make this company what it is today. Surely, you can see that we have contributed far more to the success of this venture than you have. It is only right that you consider this our company; yours and ours." "I am sorry," said the little red hen. "You are mistaken. I am the owner of the company; the law says so. And, I will take you to court to prove my point and have you removed from my property."

And the little red hen and the barnyard animals did go to court and both sides presented their case before the judge. And the judge scolded the barnyard animals, "How dare you come into my court with such a frivolous case. You have no rights whatsoever. The little red hen is the owner of The Little Red Hen Baking Company and she is entitled to all profits and benefits." The barnyard animals replied. "Judge, the little red hen only provided a few grains of wheat years ago and did nothing afterwards. We have worked long and hard to build this company into what it is today. It was our labor that built this company into a multi-million-dollar organization. What is her meager investment of a few grains of wheat compared to our investment in labor, creativity, and organization? What is her meager investment of a few grains of wheat compared to the multi-million-dollar value of the company today? And the judge ignored them and ordered the barnyard animals to vacate the premises of The Little Red Hen Baking Company. And he sent the sheriff and dozens of deputies to enforce his order. And as the deputies accompanied the barnyard animals off the premises of the Company, the little red hen took a loaf of bread, broke it open and handed each barnyard animal a single slice of bread. "See," she told them, "I am a very fair individual. I told you that if you helped me make bread, I would give you a slice of it." And so, the barnyard animals who had used their creativity, their resourcefulness, their time and their energy for two long years in the development of this company now worth hundreds of millions of dollars; walked away with nothing to show but a slice of bread. The little red hen, on the other hand, who had done virtually nothing to develop the company, was now a multi-millionaire.

Anyone who is open-minded will admit that this was not fair. How could this happen? How could the little red hen who contributed virtually nothing be the owner of and receive the benefits of the company which was the complete result of the creativity and work of so many others who in the end received virtually nothing? In this story the little red hen is a capitalist according to the present-day form of capitalism. She provided the capital, a few grains of wheat, to start the business. Note that the amount of capital she provided was almost insignificant compared to the value of the company after two years. Also, note she was not involved in any way with the management, the intellectual work, or the physical work that were the key factors in the success of The Little Red

Hen Baking Company. Yet, the law considered her the owner of the company and, therefore, master of all assets, royalties, intellectual property and profits. Is this fair? Is this just? Absolutely not! Yet, this is the state of our current economic system. And not only is this the state of our current economic system, it has been the state of most economic systems throughout history.

People have been educated to accept this capitalistic view as correct. Starting with the first kings, queens and so-called nobles, there has been a concerted effort on the part of the capitalists to convince the workers that such a system is right and proper. First the kings claimed to own the land and all natural resources on the land: water, trees, animals, minerals, etc., and in many cases even the people who occupied the land claimed by the king. While such a claim was totally false and contrary to the Natural Law, people were forced to accept this claim because the king maintained an organization of enforcers who executed his orders and subjected all the inhabitants of the land to the will of the king. People who worked either on their own initiative or through the coercion of the king's enforcers were made to understand that the results of their labors; food, animals, buildings, furniture, etc., belonged to the king because he owned the land, and its resources. Besides the unnatural claim that the land and its resources belonged to the king, the claim that the products resulting from the human activity called work (manual and intellectual) being applied to natural resources also belonged to the king was also false and absolutely contrary to the Natural Law. The entire royal economic system, as well as the legal system that was developed to support the economic system, was based on gross injustices. Originally and at diverse times people realized these injustices and attempted to rebel against the king to correct these injustices. Of course, these rebellions were squashed by the king's enforcers and the people were intimidated and coerced into accepting the claims of the king. Kings and their administrators soon found it necessary to indoctrinate the people with the principles of this exaggerated capitalism. Through documents, literature, news and formal education ; these false principles were propagated. These original masters of propaganda gave their unjust principles a positive spin by inventing such standards as loyalty to the king, patriotism, the divine right of the king, and the notion that the king was God's representative on earth. This last notion was carried to such an excess that many kings and emperors claimed to be 'gods' themselves. This was such an abuse of the truth to marry the false principles of exaggerated capitalism to the principles of religion. Such actions were both marvelously brilliant and marvelously devious at the same time.

The economic and political model of kings and queens was replicated on smaller scales by noblemen and lords, then by landlords, then by business owners and this has continued for centuries. While the workers are now theoretically free, yet their subordination and subservience to the owner is not much different than that of serfs to lords and subjects to kings and queens. In other words, not much has changed regarding the rights of workers down through the years.

This perception of capitalism extends back thousands of years. A person would make a claim on land, usually a vast expanse of land which he controlled through military force. The actual ownership of the land was only based on a claim by the capitalist who defended his claim by force if necessary. Because the land by itself had no value, the capitalist had to use workers to create value from the capitalist's land. Since there were few people thousands of years ago in relation to so much land, it was only by force that the capitalist could use workers to work his land.

To clarify this point, the vast majority of people or families would make a claim to their own land and work their own land to hunt, farm, produce furniture, make tools, etc. If another person came and proposed a labor contract where the second person would work for the first person, the first person would have total ownership of all the productive efforts of the second person, and the first person would pay the second person whatever he wanted to; obviously the second person would refuse the proposal stating that he and his family would rather work their own land and have total ownership of what they produced. There was no logical reason for a person to work for another person while there was so much land. The only logical way in which the capitalist could succeed with such an arrangement was for him to force the second person to work for him. It should be clear that the original forms of capitalism were based on ownership of the worker by the capitalist—forced slavery. The capitalist had to physically control the workers on his land and prevent them from leaving. Since the capitalist did not want to work and had to depend on the work of others, he had to physically control the workers and their families through force. Slavery, which is an extreme form of capitalism, has existed for thousands of years. While slavery has continued to this day, it was gradually replaced with slightly less extreme forms of capitalism such as feudalism, share cropping, company towns, child labor, indentured servitude, consulting; temporary employment agencies; and services agencies such as house cleaning, babysitting, etc.

Origin and Historical Development of Inordinate Capitalism

THE ORIGINS OF CAPITALISM coincide with the beginnings of civilization. Initially, families and extended families worked together to satisfy the needs for human life: food, clothing, and shelter. Virtually everyone with the exception of very young children, the very old and the sick engaged in work in order for the entire extended family to eat, be clothed and be sheltered and safeguarded from the natural elements. Things functioned well within this mini-society and mini-economic system. There are a few interesting principles involved in this first socioeconomic system. First, there was the belief that everyone was required to work both for their own good but also for the common good. There was no thought of 'something for nothing', never having to work because others work for you, ownership of the fruits of someone else's labor, control of others, or taking more than one's fair share. Within the family, everyone who was capable of working was expected to work and did work. In fact, if a family member who was capable of working did not work, then they would not be entitled to eat and the other family members would resort to coercion in order to bring the inordinate individual back into order.

Another principle of these initial societies was the respect for the very young, the sick and the very old; those who were incapable of working. Though these individuals could not work, yet they still required the basic necessities of life. In fact, because of their physical condition, their necessities for life were greater than normal. They required care and assistance from others which they could not provide for themselves because of their condition. It was understood by all the members that the economy and organization of this mini-society should account for and take care of these individuals. Work, then, was organized into those who generated food, clothing, tools and shelter; and those who provided care. All workers understood that they would benefit directly from and in proportion to their labors, but also that a percentage of the fruits of their labors would go towards those in the community who were not able to work. This principle was based partially on the fact that everyone in this society was related, but also on the realization by those who worked that someday because of age or health they would be in a position where they would have to rely on someone else for food and care. It was an initial and natural form of social security.

One of the greatest strengths of this initial mini-society was its structure. It was a community of families, all of which were related to each other by blood. Each family constituted a mini-society in itself consisting of workers (providers and care-givers) and those who required care. Each member was ordered not only to their own good but also to the common good of the family as a whole. In turn, the larger community was composed of families. These families were ordered not only to their own good but also to the common good of the community. For each family realized that their survival and the attainment of their own personal happiness could only come about through cooperation with the other families in the community. This society of families was based on personal work ethics, as well as individual and distributive justice.

In early civilizations hunting predominated as the primary source of food though farming soon followed. Natural resources such as land, animals, plants, etc., were available to all. Ownership of personal property which was the direct result of one's labor was respected as a natural right. Ownership of land and natural resources was limited to the land and resources within the direct use and control of each family. In other words, families did not lay claim to more land than they needed. There was also common ownership of land and resources by the larger community of extended families. This common ownership was based on the common good principle and involved resources which needed to be shared by all. In the event that an individual attempted to control and claim ownership of a natural resource which was needed by the entire community, then the community at large would do what was necessary to rectify this situation. Everyone seemed to have a natural understanding of personal rights and community rights and the proper relation between the two. And these early communities of extended families were primarily democratic. Each family had a vote or voice in the decisions affecting the entire community.

How, then, did capitalism develop, for it would appear that capitalist principles did not exist in these initial communities? It is almost impossible to consider a positive way in which capitalism developed, for it is inconceivable to think that anyone who labored would voluntarily work for and hand over all rights to his production to someone else who did not labor manually or intellectually or who worked less than everyone else. It might be proposed that capitalism originated from those in a leadership role within this mini-society. For those more capable at organization, direction, and management could easily take over total control of the entire society. While this is plausible it is not probable especially given the democratic political system of these communities. Given that there were such individuals in positions of leadership and authority within the community (obviously elected by the families), as soon as the leader would have proposed an unjust or unfair distribution of the production from the cooperative efforts of the individual members of the community, the individual members would have immediately complained and if necessary removed such an individual from his position. What would be even more absurd would be a claim by the leader that all property and all production generated through the use of the property belonged to him. Such a claim would not only be refused and resisted, but the one making the claim would probably have been removed from the community itself, lest he try to make such a claim in the future.

Perhaps, some examples may help. A capitalist, one who desired to live off the work of someone else, would propose to a hunter that the hunter kill a deer and that both would share the deer. Obviously, the hunter would realize that the capitalist contributed nothing in this venture even though he was able to. There would be no logical reason for the hunter to go along with such a proposal. Another situation would involve the capitalist proposing to a laborer that the laborer should work on the land of the capitalist and that the capitalist would pay the laborer with a certain amount of the produce generated by the laborer. Since the land was free and there was more than enough land, there would be no benefit for the laborer to work for someone else and not receive all the fruits of his labors.

It is certainly plausible to think of a situation in which there was cooperation between two individuals; one individual producing weapons and tools and the other using the weapons and tools to generate the food. In this situation, both individuals are equals and would look upon the food generated as equally theirs. It would be inconceivable for the hunter/farmer to accept a claim by the tool maker that all of food belonged to the tool maker and that the tool maker would give what he thought was fair to the hunter/farmer. The hunter/farmer could only accept the fact that the food was the result of both the work of the tool maker and himself and therefore proportionally theirs.

Even though within the first pristine communities things functioned well, there arose cases where individuals did not accept the work ethic. Because of laziness, these individuals sought ways to avoid work. They contrived ways to get others to do their share of the work. Of course, such attempts to avoid work did not succeed. For those who worked and accepted the ethic of work quickly realized the injustice of those who were able to work failing to do their share.

How then could a situation arise in which one person or a group of people worked for another person who did not work or worked far less than they and accept the claim that all rights to what was produced belonged to the person who did little to no work? It only could have happened by coercion and force. The capitalist could only make the laborer accept his claim to all of the rights of the production of the laborer by using force and coercion. The way in which they could accomplish this was to organize a group of mercenaries who would force the laborers to work for both the capitalist and the mercenaries. This is the only reasonable explanation of the origin of capitalism.

As it would happen within the initial communities, there were some individuals who through laziness, a lack of acceptance of the work ethic or both; rebelled from the order of this pristine social and economic system. They chose not to work or to do less than their share of the work. Eventually, either through personal choice or the decision of the community, they removed themselves or were removed from this society. Once on their own, they were faced with the difficult task of having to work or starve. However, being disinclined to work, they reasoned that it would be easier to steal rather than work. So, these individuals began to steal from the communities to which they previously belonged as well as other communities. Stealing was successful for a time, until individuals began to protect themselves from theft. When faced with this obstacle to their livelihood, these social outcasts resorted to robbery, stealing using intimidation and violence.

These individuals continued to use robbery for some time to obtain food, clothing and other necessities of life. And it happened that these individuals began to form groups, since a gang of individuals was more powerful that the one or two individuals that were being robbed. This mode of operation for the social outcasts was successful, but it only provided them with food and objects that they could carry with them. It did not provide them with shelter. It did not take long for these individuals to come to develop the idea of taking control of the entire community. Why should they rob from a part of the community, when they could control the entire community? By controlling the entire community, they would have food, shelter, and whatever else the community provided. In addition, there was the element of revenge. For this community had expelled some of these individuals because they would not work.

So, the plan was made to attack the entire village with the goal of occupying it, controlling it and taking ownership of everything that belonged to it as well as everything that was produced by it. And hence these individuals became the very first capitalists. Only by depriving the laborer of his rights and freedom could extreme capitalism be foisted upon the laborer. This initial form of capitalism which has lasted for thousands of years was in fact slavery.

Were kings and queens capitalists? They certainly were. They claimed ownership of the land and all the natural resources on it which was the main source for the production of food, clothing, furniture, housing, etc. Those who worked the land and produced food, clothing, furniture, tools, buildings, etc., could make no claim on what they produced because the king, as capitalist, claimed to be the sole owner and master of all the fruits of production since he claimed to own the land. Of course, this was dictated by the king who made the laws and enforced them. The so-called nobles who formed the government of the king were also capitalists. The king would give these nobles parcels of land so that they could also generate revenue through the labor of those who worked their land. In return for making the nobles capitalists, the king expected both a share in their revenues as well as their loyalty in keeping the working class in subjection and in his pursuit of extending his capitalist kingdom when he waged war against neighboring capitalists.

Kings, queens, royal families, nobles, royal courts, etc. are usually depicted by historians, writers and journalists as good and virtuous people deserving of respect by all people. Yet kings, queens, royal families, nobles and royal courts were and are (there are still kingdoms) ruthless capitalists who have exploited people, living outrageously extravagant lives at the expense of countless people. Kingdoms were established by military means where peoples' lands were stolen from them by armies and police. The king claimed ownership for all the land and controlled it and the former owners through a network of lords (sometimes called nobles) and armies. Imagine the event where soldiers arrive at the farm of a peaceful family and announce that their land now belongs to the king, they must work for the king and they must blindly obey the king in all things. And this event occurred millions of times over thousands of years all over the world where ever there were kingdoms and empires.

Understand the reality of this. A person makes a claim to own all the land within a particular area and through force and violence enforces that claim over the real owners of the land. This person then calls himself 'king" and begins to rule his kingdom through the military and the police. The real owners of the land are made to work for the king and everything produced by the people belongs to the person who calls himself king. This is the essence of pure and absolute capitalism. A person makes a claim to own capital. In the case of the king, it is all the land within a particular area. And then he uses unjust means to enforce that claim over the claims of the real owners. He further exploits the real owners by claiming to own and control what they produce. In a similar manner, people will make a claim to own a business, which is a collection of workers, by dishonest but legal means and claim to own what the workers actually produce even though what the workers produce is actually owned by the workers themselves. These people call themselves the owners of the business and force and coerce the workers into working for them.

Kingdoms as a totalitarian political system and capitalistic economic system dominated societies for thousands of years. And there are still kingdoms that exist today, the most notable one being the Saudi kingdom. While there are few kingdoms that still control specific countries, most of the capitalistic economic systems that formed the basis for most kingdoms over the past 5000 years have transformed themselves into the dominate economic and political force within all democracies. For democracies are democratic in theory only. They are in fact still dominated by a small and elite group of extremely wealthy individuals who actually control both the politics and economy of the country.

Within kingdoms, it was quite clear who was in control: the king and the nobles. The king and nobles laid claim to total ownership of all resources. Within democracies it is more difficult to determine who makes similar claims though it is clear that corporations, especially large multi-national corporations, have the same goals and aspirations of kings—they claim ownership and control over everything (workers, suppliers, customers, and societies) that fall under their sphere of influence.

But who controls these corporations—individuals and very small groups of individuals?

Every production system is based on two essential elements: capital and labor. Capital is used to provide facilities, equipment, materials, funds, etc. in order to operate the system. Labor provides the ideas, designs, philosophy, direction, management, physical work, etc. that is required to generate the goods and services which will be sold by the organization. In the initial or start up stages of the production system, the capital is provided by individuals or capitalists. After the production system is operating in a profitable mode, the capital is no longer provided by capitalists but rather generated by the system or organization itself. If an evaluation is made of both capitalist and laborer at the time of startup, it would appear that both play an equal role and have an equal value. However, once the organization is functioning in a positive manner, it is obvious that the laborer is far more significant to the organization and plays an almost exclusive role in generating the profits. This is because the organization generates its own capital and is no longer dependent on capitalists. This is true for any organization that has endured beyond start up. It does happen in a few instances that the organization decides to obtain additional capital through capitalists as opposed to loans.

Most organizations which have been in existence for quite some time have virtually no capitalists. Those individuals who provided the capital to help start these organizations are no longer living. There are, of course, individuals who have acquired either through inheritance or purchase the partial ownership of the organization associated with the original capitalists. These individuals are shareholders and as will be explained later they should be defined as capital shareholders to distinguish them from labor shareholders. What role do these capital shareholders play within the production system? They do not provide capital; the capital is generated by the organization itself. They are not directly involved in the management of the organization, though they do play a role depending on the number of shares that they hold or control in the selection of the board of managers or directors. They do not provide ideas, develop strategies, acquire customers, develop products and services, sell products or services, make products, or deliver products and services.

While laborers receive compensation on a regular basis, it is only by convention that the capital shareholders do not receive compensation in a similar manner. In fact, providing the capital shareholders with compensation on a regular basis is not only most appropriate but the only way that capital shareholders should receive compensation. For the usual scheme of buying stock at a low price and then selling it at a higher price is harmful to both the corporation and the economy. For a person, group, or institution which engages in buying and selling shares of stock actually undermines the long-term good of the corporation by focusing on increasing the share price in the market rather than on what is best for the company. Such individuals, groups and institutions actually exploit the companies that they hold shares in. In order to increase share price so that they can sell their shares and make a profit, these individuals, groups and institutions force the corporation to engage in practices and activities that are actually detrimental to the corporation. There individuals, groups and institutions do not care about these corporations, they do not care about the workers, the suppliers or the customers. They only care about making a profit and they are using the corporation as a means to do this. Layoffs of valuable workers, outsourcing and the sale of assets are schemes which these individuals, groups and institutions use to drive the share price up at the expense of the corporation. Capital shareholders must be forced to be partners and not exploiters of the corporation and providing the capital shareholders with compensation on a regular basis is the appropriate way for capital shareholders to realize benefits. In fact, buying shares and then selling them after a short time should be discouraged by a federal sales tax system.

It is often thought, though incorrectly, that there is an implied contract between the capitalist and the laborer with respect to the laborer's role within the production system. This contract is usually considered to be an employment contract. Of course, the worker will deny that any such contract exits. This notion of an employment contract where the worker hands over all rights to his work to the capitalist is contrived, false, and contrary to the Natural Law. For the true and natural relationship between capitalist and laborer is that of partners, equal partners in a production system that is co-owned by both and should be co-managed by both. The notion of the labor contract has been contrived and while it is an improvement over the slave relationship between capitalist and laborer that existed for centuries; it none the less represents a superior-subordinate relationship between capitalist and laborer. While generally and naturally there should be a relationship of equality between capitalist and laborer, if there can ever be an inequity between the two then it should be the capitalist who should be subordinate to the laborer.

Now, before moving on there needs to be some consideration of the position that the legal systems of most countries have taken with respect to capital and labor. In the case of kingdoms where the king is the highest and almost absolute capitalist within the country, the entire legal system which is of course under the control of the king is designed and managed to maintain the king's claim to and control of his capitalist position. Kings hold that they own in varying degrees virtually all property, all means of production as well as the fruits of production. The laborer is looked on as the property of the king. The legal systems of current governments still blindly follow the false philosophy that capital is superior to labor and that labor is subordinate to capital. This is an obstacle to rectifying the economy which needs to be overcome before the natural relationship between capital and labor can be restored.

The Dignity and Excellence of Labor

HUMAN LABOR IS AN expression of the character of the laborer. Consider music. The musical composition is a product of the work of the musician. It is an expression of the musician and tells something of the character and personality of the musician. In a similar manner a work of art is an expression of the artist. It tells something about him or her. This relationship between the worker and the product of his or her work applies to all labor. It applies to the architect, the construction worker, the plumber, the mechanic, the teacher, the nurse, the farmer, the homemaker, the cook, etc. So true is the expression from the Bible, "by their fruits you shall know them." People most often answer the question, "Who are you?" with a reply involving what kind of work that they do. That is because a person's actions reflect who they are and what they are. A person can be evaluated by what they do or what they have accomplished. When a child is born, they are known or somewhat defined by their relationship to their parents, since they have not as yet accomplished anything on their own. Once they begin doing things on their own, their actions reflect their personality.

Labor is natural to human beings and part of God's design. God intends humans to express themselves through their work; their work being a reflection of their personality and character. Hence, labor represents one of the most important activities of a human being. (It may be necessary to recall that by labor is meant productive human activity: creativity, design, organization, direction, as well as physical labor.) Because labor is natural to human beings, it is a necessary activity to human fulfillment. Humans have a natural tendency to act, to accomplish things. Humans that have desires or goals that do not pursue their goals by actions or work are incomplete as humans and unfulfilled. It should be understood, then, that labor is necessary for human beings. Labor should not be looked upon as a burden, but as a means of expressing oneself. Because of this, there is a natural dignity to human labor, as long as it is voluntary. For work makes humans more human.

A person's work is intimately related to them as a person. It is their work, it belongs to them: it is their property whether it is physical or intellectual. In fact, all human work is both intellectual and physical.

Even though a person's work belongs to them by nature and by God's design, it happens that others steal the work of people through deceit, manipulation, coercion and even force. They deny and disregard the true nature of work and its intimate relationship to the worker. These people have no respect for the rights of workers and deny the most basic right that work belongs to the worker and the transformation of a material into a product is the property of the worker. Because of this, these people steal the work of others. They make every effort to avoid work and seek to have others work for them or serve them. And this is the essence of inordinate capitalism which is prevalent today.

The capitalist may provide wood, but the worker transforms the wood into a chair, a table, a cabinet, a dresser, etc. What is more important in this process, the wood or the work? Clearly the work! And yet, it is the capitalist who claims absolute ownership of the work and final product, and capitalists over time have manipulated legislators to pass laws supporting this unjust, immoral and anti-Christian claim.

Inordinate capitalism disregards the rights of workers. Within most organizations, those in management take credit for what others have accomplished. It is interesting how a manager lists on his or her resume not only the things that they personally have accomplished but also what was accomplished by their subordinates even though they had nothing to do with the actions of the subordinate. Inordinate capitalists use every means possible to undervalue the work of others. They want to determine the value to be paid for work. Capitalists disregard the equality between themselves and workers.

Capitalists and workers are equal and they are partners in the production process. Truly absurd is the notion that a person works for another or is employed by another—they are partners, they work together. 'Working for' or being 'employed by' implies subordination, the worker being subordinate to the capitalist. That is wrong, incorrect and unjust. Every person that is part of a corporation either in a part time or full-time role is a partner with everyone else who constitutes the corporation. The notion that a corporation can be owned by one or a few people even though the corporation consists of dozens, hundreds or thousands of people is contrary to the Natural Law; it is counter to Christian principles; it is immoral.

While most people think that they understand what capitalism is, they are unfortunately very confused. The confusion results from the immense difference between what capitalism should be and the false and exaggerated practice of those who clothe their actions under the cloak of capitalism.

False capitalism is all about control. A capitalist is one who seeks to control an individual, a group of individuals, or a society of individuals with the objective of claiming total ownership of the results and products of the labor of those individuals. These results and products of labor are intellectual, artistic, organizational, and physical. In complete opposition to true capitalism, this false capitalism desires to make no contribution whatsoever to the productive process and claims the right and title to all the results of the production system. On the other hand, a true capitalist actively contributes capital to the production process and claims only a share of the results realizing and acknowledging that capital and labor are equal members of the production process and naturally should share the results equally. In order for a capitalist to be a true capitalist, that is, a capitalist in accordance with the Natural Law and Christian economics they have to provide capital (cash, property, equipment, materials, etc.) to the production system. False capitalism is based on the principles of 'something for nothing', inequality, and exploitation. True capitalism is based on collaboration, equality, and distributive justice. Most of the so-called owners of corporations and businesses today have provided absolutely no cash, property, equipment, or materials to the corporation or business and yet they claim to be the owners.

An illustration of false capitalism is where an individual or company purchases controlling shares of Company X from some other individual or company. This individual or company does not contribute anything to the productive process of Company X. They provide no capital, they do not contribute to the organizational management, the design of new products or services; they do not labor. In effect, they contribute nothing and do nothing with respect to the productive process and system of company X. Yet, all profits supposedly belong to them. Any increase in the assets of Company X supposedly belongs to them. Any new designs, any new ideas, any new intellectual property supposedly belongs solely to them. By current law, the laborers of company X have no right whatsoever to the profits, assets and intellectual property of Company X even though the profits, the increase in assets and the development of new intellectual property was solely the result of their labor. Unfortunately, false capitalism is the norm today.

One of the main issues with capitalism is that it can be easily, directly and absolutely influenced by greed; the uncontrolled or unconstrained desire for and pursuit of material wealth.

Because human nature tends towards the infinite and can only be satisfied by the Infinite, greed also tends towards the infinite. It seeks more and more without limit. It is all-consuming. Rather than the person controlling greed, greed controls the person. Unfortunately, the person does not understand that they can never be satisfied by riches. They blindly pursue more thinking that when they have acquired more then they will be satisfied. But, when they have acquired more they are not satisfied, and greed drives them to seek more and more. This sad pattern ends with death, but the desire for wealth will continue into eternity. Greed can neither be satisfied in time nor eternity. Like all other sins, it involves a cruel and debilitating slavery. It is amazing how the expression 'greed is good' is not only popular in this day, but also accepted by many people. However, when capitalism is directly under the influence of greed, it is morally wrong.

Inordinate capitalism seeks more and more without end. Inordinate capitalists seek more than their fair share and seek to deprive others of what is due to them naturally by their work. Inordinate capitalists want something for nothing. That is, they want wealth without either work or investment. Inordinate capitalism is driven directly by greed and indirectly by pride because the inordinate capitalist assumes that he or she has superior rights and privileges. Capitalism, when it is subject to the Natural Law and Christian economics is not influenced by greed and is a good and necessary part of the economy.

The Current Economic Crisis

THE UNITED STATES IS currently experiencing a continuing economic crisis. A crisis not reflected in the wealthy class but in lower and middle classes. It should be clear that this crisis involves the lack of consumption. It should also be clear that there is no problem with the desire to consume and/or the need to consume. People want and need to buy food, clothing, transportation, furniture, housing, healthcare, education, entertainment, etc.

Production is driven by and is dependent on consumption ; consumption by the majority of the people. If people were to increase consumption as they need and want, production would increase to match or satisfy consumption. While the majority of the people want and need to consume, they are prevented, limited or constrained from consuming because of a lack of money. Millions of people want to buy homes but cannot because they don't have the money. Millions of people want to buy cars but cannot because they don't have the money. Tens of millions of people want to buy furniture but cannot because they don't have the money. Tens of millions of people want to buy clothes but cannot because they don't have the money. Tens of millions of people want to buy food but cannot because they don't have the money. Tens of millions of people need healthcare but cannot obtain it because they don't have the money. Tens of millions of people want an education but cannot receive one because they don't have the money. There is absolutely no problem with consumption within the US economy or at least the need and desire to consume. And there is absolutely no problem with production capacity within the United States. People want to work and are able to work. If there is no problem with consumption and if there is no problem with production capacity; then what is the problem with the poorly functioning and inefficient economy? Why isn't it working or rather why isn't it working for the benefit of the majority of Americans?

The current economic crisis is not going to be resolved by the so-called economic stimulus packages or reduction of taxes for corporations or the wealthy class. In fact, these expenditures, financed by the government borrowing the money, will actually make the economy worse. Stimulus implies that the only problem with the economy is that it needs a little help to move it in a positive direction. Stimulus implies the structure of the economy is fine and that there are no significant problems. The fact is the US economy has significant structural problems that cannot be fixed with ten trillion dollars of expenditures by the government with borrowed money. (If the engine in a car is broken, all the gasoline in the world will not get the car going again.) The problem with the economy is that it lacks balance, coordination and management. Critical elements of the US economy are out of control and causing the lack of coordination, collaboration and balance. Until these structural problems are fixed, until the out of control elements are brought under control, the government can spend hundreds of trillions of dollars and the economy will still not work efficiently and effectively for the financial good of all.

It should be clear that the economy is broken. It is not merely sluggish, or asleep, or groggy; IT IS BROKEN. The actions, policies, and inactions of the previous five administrations and Congresses have caused serious imbalances and defects in the economic machinery of the US economy. The economy will not move in the right direction until the defects are removed and the imbalances are fixed. The actions taken by the Obama administration to reverse the recession were not successful. He did not do what was necessary to eliminate the causes of this economic crisis.

While the people who elected Barak Obama or Donald Trump realized that they were not experts in economics, they assumed that they would choose the right economic advisors; individuals who understood/understand the real causes of the current economic crisis. Unfortunately, Obama and Trump surrounded themselves with multi-millionaires who could not and cannot identify with the vast majority of Americans. Their economic advisors did not and do not know what it means to live from paycheck to paycheck. Their economic advisors have never experienced foreclosure, or continuous harassment from bill collectors, or unemployment. Their economic advisors have never experienced the emotional horror of not knowing how they going to pay their bills, or where they are going to go when their home is re-possessed. Their economic advisors were and are unaffected by this economic crisis on a personal basis and their only exposure to the hardships of this crisis is through the media. Their economic advisors did not and do not grasp the severity of the current economic situation. Because they are not personally impacted by this crisis, they suffer from the Marie Antoinette syndrome "let them eat cake." The people whom Barack Obama and Donald Trump have chosen to give them guidance on how to lead the United States out of the continuing economic crisis (the crisis affecting tens of millions of Americans) are blind to the causes of this crisis. And, since they do not understand the causes of this crisis, they do not know the solution. What makes matters worse, many of these economic advisors have actually contributed to the current crisis through the policies that they either promoted or followed during previous administrations.

Reaganomics is one of the primary reasons why we are experiencing the current economic crisis. The economy is not driven by investment ; the economy is not driven by supply; the economy is driven by consumption. The basic dynamic of an economy is the continuous cycle of demand, production, sale, and consumption in which demand reflects what will be consumed. The economy is driven by consumption and jobs are created because of consumption. When consumption is down, jobs are lost. When consumption is up, jobs are created. Businesses only create jobs in response to demand for consumption.

Consumption drives the economy ; not the minimal consumption by the upper one percent of the population as is espoused in Reaganomics, but the consumption by the lower 99 percent of the population. Who will buy the ten million cars made each year in the United States? Who will buy the millions of homes built each year? Who will buy the tens of millions of appliances made each year? Who will buy the hundreds of millions of articles of clothing made each year? Will the three million people of the upper class buy ten million cars each year? Will the three million people of the upper class buy the millions of homes made each year? Will the three million people of the upper class buy the tens of millions of appliances made each year? Will the three million people of the upper class buy the hundreds of millions of articles of clothing made each year? Absolutely not! Not even the most exuberant greed would amass possessions of such quantities. But the 315 million people of the middle and lower classes will buy all these things and more if they have the money to buy—not the credit to buy, but the money to buy. The middle and lower classes want to work and they want to buy things: goods and services that they want and need to preserve life and liberty and to pursue happiness.

The basic problem with the economy is a lack of consumption. And this problem does not involve the top 20 percent of the population; it involves the bottom 80 percent—over 240 million people.

Christian Economics

CHRISTIAN ECONOMICS IS BASED on many principles. It is based on morality, doing good and avoiding evil, loving one's neighbor as oneself, the absolute respect for the dignity of each and every human person and the equality of all human persons. No human person has greater economic rights than any other or should be given special economic privileges that others do not have. The president is not above the people. Senators and congressmen are not above the people. Governors, judges, mayors, police officers, and generals are not above the people. CEO's, CFO's and vice-presidents of corporations are not above the other workers.

The source of all economic authority lies with the people. Every dimension of society must be democratically governed both politically and economically: the Federal government, the state government, local governments, communities, and corporations. Every group of individuals engaged in economic activity that interacts with others is by its nature public. Within Christian economics there is no such thing as a private corporation; every corporation is by its nature public. Human beings have the right to own private property, yet not all property is private. Public property is property that needs to be jointly owned by the members of society since this property is to be shared by the members. Public property cannot be made private property. Common property is property that is owned by a community of people or a corporation. Yes, the property of a corporation is common property owned collectively by both capital shareholders and labor shareholders.

Because natural resources are finite and because there are a finite number of human beings, the economy will always be finite. Because the economy is finite there are limits to the amount of property that an individual, a group of individuals, or a corporation can own. The amount of property owned by an individual, a group of individuals or a corporation cannot be so great as to prevent others from owning the minimum amount of property needed to sustain and support life, liberty and relative happiness. Christian economics requires that the economy be shared by all. This sharing applies to community or common property, to what is produced by the nation as a whole and to what is produced by corporations or groups of people. This principle of sharing dictates that the share that a person receives corresponds to the contribution made by that person in the productive endeavor. Sharing implies fairness not equality.

Christian economics has as its objective the good of all. Through mutual collaboration all people work towards both personal and common goals. All people and all corporations are subordinate to the goal of maximization of wealth for all.

The Nation: A Community: One for All and All for One

WHILE MOST PEOPLE HAVE heard of the expression "one for all and all for one," most people do not realize that this phrase expresses one of the most basic principles of a community, of a corporation, of a society, of a nation and of an economy. But first, what is a community, what is a corporation, what is a society, what is a nation, what is an economy? Community, corporation, society, nation, and economy are different perspectives or views of the same entity: a group of people (human beings) interacting for the mutual benefit of all members of the group. It is very important to emphasize that the essential elements of a community, a corporation, a society, a nation and an economy are people. The notion that a corporation is an artificial person with the same rights and privileges as a human person is totally false and is the source of many of the underlying problems with the current economic crisis.

One of the primary and essential reasons for establishing a society or a nation is economic. People as individuals cannot provide for all the goods and services needed to sustain life, preserve liberty and pursue happiness. Because a person cannot provide themselves with food, clothing, housing, healthcare, education, etc., they enter into an association with others where the people collaborate with each other to jointly provide the goods and services which they all need and desire. For the sake of both efficiency and effectiveness, labor is divided so that people specialize in a particular form of work. Each person labors both for themselves and for society as a whole. Each person contributes their work to support society and to support themselves. This is especially true for the United States as a nation. The United States is a society. It is a collection of individuals (human beings) who have entered into the association of the United States primarily for economic reasons. While defense from foreign enemies is also a purpose of this nation, the primary purpose and reason for the existence of the United States is economic. The People of the United States want to collaborate with each other for their mutual economic benefit. Since the primary purpose of the United States is the economic welfare of all its citizens, the economic welfare of all citizens is also the primary purpose and responsibility of the US government. It should be clear that the primary purpose of the nation of the United States is the economic benefit of all its citizens and not just a few of its citizens, 'one for all and all for one'.

True Patriotism and the Economy

PATRIOTISM IS ONE OF the bases for an effective and efficient economy. The United States is a nation with over 315 million members. It exists as a nation for the mutual support of and collaboration with its members towards the goals of life, liberty and the pursuit of happiness. Life, liberty and the pursuit of happiness are essentially physical, economic and social. True patriotism is based on Natural Law and has as its basis the love of family. True patriotism means love, respect, support, and protection of those around you. First, patriotism involves the immediate family and then the extended family (grandparents, aunts, uncles, cousins). This circle of patriotism grows from immediate family to extended family to community to society to nation. The entire nation, from a patriotic view, can be considered as one's family. True patriotism is synonymous with brotherhood. A common expression used to indicate the love and commitment to one's family, one's extended family, one's community, one's region, one's state and one's nation is 'family takes care of family'.

In times of difficulty family members should take care of one another. If one family member does not have enough to eat, the other family members should share what they have with that person. If a family member within the extended family loses their job, everyone within the extended family should assist that family member until they are employed again. If someone's house burns down in a community, people within the community should help that family. The Amish are a great example of a community which helps each other as in the case of barn-raising. In like manner when a natural disaster occurs, members of a region or even the nation should help those who have been affected by the disaster.

Are the foreclosure actions of banks which could use forbearance instead of foreclosure/repossession patriotic? Are layoffs which are done so that the CEO can obtain his or her bonus patriotic? Are price increases of 10 to 20 percent in one year patriotic? Is outsourcing patriotic? Are wars to expand corporate empires patriotic?

True patriotism naturally applies to economics. Each member of a family should be interested in the economic welfare of all family members out of patriotism. In turn, every person should be interested in the economic welfare of everyone in their extended family. In a similar manner, each person should be desirous of the economic welfare of all members of his or her society and nation. True patriotism then applies to the local, regional, and national economy. Should not every citizen be concerned about and support the economic welfare of every citizen within the nation? Should not every citizen be concerned with and support the economic welfare of the entire nation as a whole? Should not the entire nation be concerned with and support the economic welfare of each and every citizen? Yes! Yes! Yes! For one of the primary reasons for establishing a society and a nation is the collaboration between members and the mutual support of each other regarding the economic welfare of all, 'one for all and all for one'. The economic good of every individual is dependent on the economic good of the entire nation. In turn, the economic good of the entire nation is dependent on the economic good of all its members.

True patriotism is centered on the physical and economic welfare of the members of the family, the community, the corporation and the nation and is not blind obedience to those in management positions. In fact, blind obedience is a vice and not a virtue. It is very unfortunate that the notion of patriotism has been interpreted as blind obedience to the leader. Blind obedience is not patriotism and is counter to true patriotism. Yet, this false notion has been prevalent for thousands of years and has been the cause of countless crimes and atrocities. The atrocities committed by the Germans during World War II were performed out of patriotic duty. The German military and people blindly followed Adolph Hitler and did not question his orders. That was false patriotism.

True patriotism is at its foundation democratic. It is based on the principles of equality, human rights, and the brotherhood /sisterhood of humankind. Patriotism tends towards cooperation and assistance and not domination and control. The government is meant to serve the People and exists to coordinate and regulate the activities of the people in the pursuit of life, liberty and the pursuit of happiness. Since one of the primary purposes of the nation of the United States is individual and aggregate economic welfare, the government is responsible for managing economic activities with the goal of supporting the economic welfare of all. The members of government should be driven essentially and entirely by patriotic principles and not by the desire for personal gain or fame. And not just the members of government but all individuals within society that have positions of management and authority must be driven by patriotic principles: love of nation, society, community and family. Any person and every person in a management position is in that position to serve the group and not to be served by the group.

The government should serve the People and exists to coordinate and regulate the activities of the people in pursuit of life, liberty and the pursuit of happiness. The vast majority of citizens agree that it is the role of the government to develop and manage programs that help and support people in their pursuit of life, liberty and the pursuit of happiness. These programs are called social programs because their objective and focus is people. Such social programs as Social Security, Medicare, Medicaid, Unemployment Insurance, educational grants and guaranteed student loans, Food Stamp programs, and job training programs are just some of the social programs that the government administers because the majority of Americans want these programs. In addition, these social programs are consistent with Christian principles and Christian economics.

However, not all citizens favor social programs. The members of the wealthy, capitalist class have no need of such social programs. And most of them disapprove of social programs and want to end them in spite of the fact that the majority of Americans need these social programs during some time in their lives. Many of the upper one percent of the population would like to end virtually all social programs including Social Security, Medicare, Medicaid, Unemployment Insurance, educational grants and guaranteed student loans, and the Food Stamp program. The patriotism of such individuals should be questioned since they certainly seem to be lacking in love, respect, and support of the majority of Americans.

The Balanced Distribution of Income and Wealth

THE US GROSS DOMESTIC product GDP is over $18.6 trillion dollars. With a population of 315 million people, the GDP per capita is over $57,000. That means that if the GDP was divided equally among the 315 million people, each person would receive over $57,000. Imagine if the average family of 3.1 people had an income of $57,000 per person. That would be a family income of over $176,000. If the average family income right now was $176,000, what would happen to the economy? The current average family income is $72,000 and the current median family income is $60,000. That means that half of all families in the US earn less than $60,000 a year. Ninety-three percent of all families (293 million) make less than $176,000 a year. If every family making less than $176,000 a year had their income increased to $176,000, what would they do with the money? Obviously, they would buy things. They would buy homes. They would buy cars. They would buy furniture. They would buy clothes. They would buy healthcare. They would buy education. They would buy entertainment. And what would happen to production when people started to buy homes, cars, furniture, clothes, food, healthcare, education and entertainment? It would obviously increase to meet and satisfy demand. Would this stimulate the economy? It would drive the economy wild.

The previous administrations tried to stimulate the economy by providing between 2 to 3 trillion dollars to banks, insurance companies, corporations, state governments and local governments. If $2.5 trillion dollars was given to the 315 million people in the United States, each person would receive over $8000 and the average family of 3.1 people would receive over $25,000. Did the $2.5 trillion given to the banks, insurance companies, corporations, state governments and local governments stimulate the economy? Did the $2.5 trillion given to the banks, insurance companies, corporations, state governments and local governments provide employment to the 15 million people who were unemployed? Did the $2.5 trillion given to the banks, insurance companies, corporations, state governments and local governments trickle down to the 315 million people who drive the economy by their consumption and production? Absolutely not! If the government gave the $2.5 trillion dollars to the people instead of to the banks, insurance companies, corporations, state and local governments, would that have stimulated the economy? Yes! If the government gave the $2.5 trillion dollars to the people instead of to the banks, insurance companies, corporations, state and local governments, would that have provided employment to the 15 million people who were unemployed? Yes!

The current US economy can be compared to 100 people who collaborate together to make a pizza to eat. Each person's objective is to have some pizza to eat. Once the pizza is made, it is cut into 100 pieces. Now one person takes 25 pieces, the next 4 people take 15 pieces, the next 5 people take 10 pieces, and the next 10 people take 15 pieces. That leaves 35 pieces to be shared between 80 people. All 100 people were involved in the production of the pizza in different respects and it should be clear that the pizza must be shared by all 100 people. Since each person did not contribute equally in the production of the pizza, it would be unfair and unjust for all 100 people to receive an equal share of the pizza. Yet, it is also unfair and unjust for one person to receive 25% of the pizza, ten people to receive 50% of the pizza, and twenty people to receive 65% of the pizza. Since 80 people have to share 35 pieces of pizza in an unequal manner, it happens that a significant number of people end up with an unjustly small amount of pizza in spite of their contribution to the production of the pizza.

Since the distribution of the pieces of pizza is certainly unfair and unjust, it should be clear that the process of allocating or sharing the pieces of pizza is not democratic. For the 80 people who have to share 35 pieces of pizza in spite of their contribution to the production of the pizza certainly think that they deserve a greater share of the pizza than they receive. Since the distribution of the pieces of pizza is not democratic, it is done by a minority of people who have almost total control over the entire process of sharing the pizza. The few people who take most of the pizza obviously control the process of allocating or sharing the pieces of pizza. Such a situation is obviously good for a few people, but detrimental for the majority of people. Again, this example of the production and distribution of a pizza reflects the US economy.

In the US economy, a small minority of people control the distribution of income and wealth. They do so through market manipulation and through corporations and with the support of the government. This small minority has such influence on the administration and Congress, that it can be said that the President, his administration, and the majority of the senators and representatives are puppets of this powerful, elite and extremely wealthy group of people.

Because the amount or quantity of property, income and wealth is not infinite; property, wealth and income must be distributed throughout the entire population. That does mean that everyone should have an equal amount of property, wealth and income. What it means is that one person or a few people cannot own or control an amount of property, wealth and income which will prevent others from owning property, wealth and income. The goal is sufficiency and balance. Each human person must have a sufficient amount of property, wealth and income to support life and liberty and to pursue happiness. While every person must have a sufficient amount of property, wealth and income; it is also true that the amount of property, wealth and income will vary from person to person.

There is a lower limit to a person's wealth which the government must see to it that no one's wealth or income falls below what is necessary to preserve life and liberty and to pursue happiness. And because the total amount of national wealth is limited, there has to be an upper limit on the wealth of any person. For if the amount of property that one person (or a few people) own or control is so large that it deprives or prevents others from owning the basic necessities for supporting life and liberty (a house, furniture, a car, etc.), then the economy is out of balance—it is not functioning efficiently nor effectively and is failing to achieve its goal of maximizing the wealth of all of the people. It is the responsibility of the government to prevent such an imbalance and if such an imbalance exists, the government must correct the imbalance through graduated income, asset and sales taxes, minimum wages and other means.

All people are equal and have equal rights. That means that no one person is superior to another. No person should have special privileges or be treated as special. Every person is in fact special and their uniqueness must be respected and protected. Capitalism applies to all people by nature and not merely to a small, select group of individuals. That means that everyone should be allowed to own property: a home, a car, furniture, appliances, etc.

There is a natural and moral obligation on everyone to limit the amount of their wealth because excess wealth deprives others from what they need for life, liberty and the pursuit of happiness. This also applies to corporations and businesses. More is not better; it is morally worse. An excess of wealth does not indicate 'blessing', it indicates greed. There is only so much wealth available, it is not infinite. An extreme excess of wealth for one person involves a deficit of what is necessary for life, liberty and the pursuit of happiness for many others. How can a person consider themselves blessed when they see so many others living in poverty? How can a person consider themselves blessed when they see so many others who are homeless ? How can a person consider themselves blessed when they see so many others unemployed?

Communism is a political and economic system in which the government owns the wealth and income of the nation. Communism denies the basic right of a human being to own property and because of this is a naturally corrupt system. On the opposite end of the political and economic spectrum, limited or selective capitalism is a political and economic system in which a very select minority owns and/or controls the vast majority of the nation's wealth and income. (Free market capitalism is another name for limited or selective capitalism.) Limited selective capitalism deprives and prevents the majority of people from what is due to them economically and actually prevents them from exercising their natural right to own property. While limited selective capitalism does not deny the theoretical right of a human being to own property, it does so in practice. For radical, free market capitalists propose and seek to have no government regulation of the economy, allowing them instead of the government to control and manipulate the economy for their selfish purposes. By controlling the economy, the free market capitalists seek to maximize their wealth almost without limit. Since the economy is finite, the maximization of the wealth of a few results in the minimization or elimination of wealth of many. It is one of the main responsibilities of the government to manage the economy, prevent selective capitalism and promote and support universal capitalism; the capitalism that applies universally to everyone and not just a select few.

The main cause of the current economic crisis is the re-distribution of wealth that has been occurring over the last thirty years and has accelerated during the last sixteen years. This re-distribution of wealth which was once referred to as 'trickle down' economics has in fact been the exact opposite. Wealth has not trickled down from the upper minority (the top wealthiest three million people) to the lower 312 million people in the United States. No, instead wealth has flowed (emphasis on "flowed") from the working-class majority up to the already excessively wealthy top one percent of the population. This re-distribution of wealth has caused a significant imbalance in the economy. The majority of people are not able to buy the goods and services that they need and want because their wealth has been taken away and given to the extremely wealthy three million. Why is the US automobile industry struggling? The US automobile industry is struggling financially money because they cannot sell cars. Why can't the automobile companies sell cars? They cannot sell cars because the working class cannot buy cars. Why can't the working class buy cars? The working class cannot buy cars because they have lost a significant amount of their wealth to the already wealthy upper one percent of the population.

Giving money to banks, insurance companies, automobile companies or any other company and reducing the tax rates for corporations and the wealthy will do absolutely nothing to fix the economy. The only fix for the economy is the elimination of the current economic imbalance by a reversal of the re-distribution of wealth that has occurred over the last thirty years. This can be done without the Federal government creating or borrowing any money whatsoever. The tax burden needs to shift from the working majority to the wealthy minority. The tax rates similar to those during the golden years of the US economy need to be put in place permanently: 4 percent for the lowest income bracket and 95 percent for the highest income bracket. And there should be absolutely no distinction between income resulting from work or income resulting from so-called capital gains. Income is income. There should be a graduated asset tax on assets greater than $1 million for individuals. This tax would apply to all assets; cash, real estate, personal property, stocks, bonds, and businesses. And since corporations are defined as legal persons, they too must be subject to the exact same graduated income taxes and asset taxes as real persons. Lastly, there needs to be a graduated, Federal sales tax which applies to all personal sales and the sales of corporate assets.

Unfortunately, the economic policies of the Federal government are supporting the wealth imbalance by taking money away from the middle and lower classes and giving it to the upper class. This has to be reversed before the economy completely collapses. The policies of the last thirty years need to be reversed and done so immediately.

If this re-re-distribution of wealth was put into effect immediately through structured income, asset and sales tax systems, the US economy would see an immediate reversal of stagnation and significant and sustainable growth. The working class needs to see their tax obligations reduced significantly by shifting the tax burden to the wealthy, the very wealthy and the extremely wealthy. And tax-avoidance schemes need to be eliminated for both individuals and corporations.

This re-re-distribution of wealth from the wealthy, the very wealthy and the extremely wealthy is moral and just. For these individuals have dishonestly and deceptively taken money away from the working class through means that are unfortunately legal though contrary to Christian principles.

The Economy and the Living Body Analogy

AN ECONOMY AS A system is similar to the human body. As the human body is composed of living cells, the US economy is composed of living human beings. There is an inter-dependency between the body and the cells and there is an inter-dependency between the US economy and the 315 million individuals in the United States. Cells are organized into organs which provide specific functions for the body. Individuals are organized into families, organizations, corporations, businesses, communities, municipalities, counties, and states.

A healthy body is a body that is in complete balance without any excess. Its temperature is neither too hot nor too cold. Its blood pressure is neither too high nor too low. The body supports the life of every cell and every cell supports the life of the body. The body provides for every cell and those cells that do more work receive more sustenance. The body has an elaborate network of control sub-systems to keep everything within the body within balance. And all functions, all activities, all coordination, all control is managed by the brain. The brain manages, controls, coordinates and directs the body with all its organs and with all its cells for the good of the entire body and the good of each and every cell.

An efficient and effective economy is similar to a healthy human body. Every part of the economy must be in balance without any excess. In an efficient and effective economy, every person contributes to the economy and the economy supports every individual. An effective economy facilitates the attainment of its objective to satisfy the natural needs and desires of all Americans for safety, food, clothing, housing, a livelihood, education, healthcare, disability care, old age care, communication, recreation, entertainment, social interaction, acceptance and respect. This applies to every individual and those individuals who do more work receive a greater share of the wealth generated by the economy. Everything within the efficient and effective economy is balanced and under control. There are no extremes, there are no excesses. As the body cannot function without the brain to manage, control, coordinate and direct; so, the economy has to have a central function which manages, controls, coordinates and directs. Absurd is the notion that the economy does not need to be managed, controlled, coordinated and directed. It is not possible for a complex organization such as the United States economy which consists of hundreds of millions of individuals interacting daily through billions of transactions to achieve its goals of life, liberty and the pursuit of happiness for all without a management function. For the pursuit of a goal involves planning, management, control and coordination. And the government, which is the central management and control system for the economy, must manage, control, coordinate and direct the economy with all its sub-systems (consumption, production, and monetary), its businesses and its individuals for the good of the entire economy and the good of each and every individual.

The efficient and effective economy provides for every member of society because the good of the entire economy is dependent on the good of every member of society. Every member of society, every family, every organization, every community and every business must work for the good of the entire economy; for the good of the economy is necessary for the good of every individual, every family, every organization, every community and every business. True patriotism, which is love of country, involves the support and defense of country. Every individual, every family, every community, every organization, every business and every corporation must support and defend the economy of the nation to which it belongs. This is patriotism. Every individual, every family, every community, every organization, every business and every corporation must work together for the good of each other and the good of the nation. No individual, no family, no community, no group of people, no organization, no business, no corporation is above the good of the nation and the good of the economy. The good of the nation and the good of the national economy are the same good.

A person who acts against the good of the economy is unpatriotic. A family which acts against the good of the economy is unpatriotic. A group of people who act against the good of the economy is unpatriotic. A community which acts against the good of the economy is unpatriotic. A business which acts against the good of the economy is unpatriotic. A corporation which acts against the good of the economy is unpatriotic.

The good of every person, every family, every group, every community, every business and every corporation is intimately connected with the good of the economy.

One of the most basic and natural human rights is freedom. People are free. Yet, freedom is not unlimited. The freedom of one person is limited by the freedom of other individuals. A person is free to swing their arm, but that person is not free to swing their arm in the space occupied by another individual. A person is free to drive down the street and pass through an intersection. But that person's freedom to pass through an intersection is limited by the freedom of the other people who also wish to pass through the same intersection.

A person is free to engage in business selling goods and services. But a person is not free to sell goods and services that he or she does not own. A person is free to set a price and realize a profit on what he or she sells. But the person is not free to charge whatever price that they want. The freedom to set a price is limited by the ability of the consumer to afford the good or service within the context of all the goods and services which the person requires for life, liberty and the pursuit of happiness. Absurd is the notion of 'let the buyer beware' implying that the seller can set whatever price he or she wants and it is the responsibility of the buyer to decide whether or not to buy. A consumer has to buy the goods and services required to sustain life and preserve freedom: food, clothing, shelter, transportation, education, healthcare, etc. They have no choice whether or not to buy these things; they have to buy them. The moral, ethical, and patriotic responsibility to control prices lies with the seller. In a balanced, efficient and effective economy prices must be controlled; controlled by the seller (individual, business or corporation). When a person does not respect the rights and freedoms of others, the government must intervene to correct the abuse. So also in the case where a corporation abuses consumers and undermines the balance of the economy by charging inordinately high prices, the government must intervene to correct the abuse.

Is a corporation free to charge whatever price it wants for gasoline? Is a corporation free to charge whatever price it wants for food? Is a corporation free to charge whatever price it wants for electricity? Is a corporation free to charge whatever price it wants for natural gas, heating oil, or propane? Is a corporation free to charge whatever price it wants for water? Is a corporation free to charge whatever price it wants for medicine? Is a corporation free to charge whatever price it wants for a medical procedure such as an operation? No, no, no, no, no, no!

Over the past 50 years, there has been a movement within the Economics schools that holds that there should be no regulation of business practices by the government. Businesses should be allowed to conduct business, set prices, set wages, create contracts, hire and fire employees, and do virtually whatever they want without any government interference. Promoted under the deceptive phrases of 'free trade', 'let the market decide' and others; this false principle has permeated the thinking of most academics, business practitioners, and government officials. The idea that a business which is organized for selfish purposes should be allowed to operate without any limits is truly ridiculous. Rules and regulation bring order and harmony, and lead to the attainment of objectives. A lack of regulation and limits always lead to an imbalance. Laws, rules, and regulations are limits meant to maximize the aggregate freedom and welfare of everyone. Limits are a consequence of and necessity for living in a society, especially a democratic society.

Basics of Christian Economics

CHRISTIAN ECONOMICS IS THE application of Christian principles to business and economics both in theory and in practice. It is a subject that has been neglected and ignored for too long. Christian Economics promotes justice, fairness, balance, cooperation, and mutual respect within business, economics and politics and is based on three principles: good is to be done and promoted and evil is to be avoided; love your neighbor as yourself and the absolute dignity and equality of each and every human being.

Within an economic system all people are consumers and most people are producers. Children do not produce, yet they are consumers. The elderly do not produce, yet they are consumers. The sick do not produce, yet they are consumers. Most consumers are producers. In fact, the vast majority of consumers have to be producers since it is through production that people receive the goods or money necessary to support their consumption. Goods and services are demanded by consumers, produced by producers, and exchanged with or sold to consumers. Money is traded or exchanged between consumers and producers and is used to facilitate the billions of transactions of goods and services between consumers and producers. Money is considered to be an exchange medium and the amount of money within an economic system needs to be sufficient to support the exchange of goods and services between the millions of individuals, groups, organizations and businesses.

What is the Purpose of the Economy?

The US economy consists of over 315 million individuals, over 126 million families, over 132 million homes, 155 million workers, over 5.7 million businesses, approximately 10 thousand banks; there are over hundreds of billions of transactions annually and the US annually produces about $18 trillion of goods and services. It should be clear that the US economy is very complex.

What is the purpose of the US economy? Every theory on economics must first start by clearly stating what it holds as the purpose and objective of the economy. For the principles of an economic theory are the means towards achieving the objective. Unfortunately, most economic theories do not specify the objective and purpose of the economy. However, by analyzing the principles of an economic theory, a person can determine what objective the economic theory holds. Most people, in fact the majority of Americans, agree that the purpose and objective of the US economy is to satisfy in the most efficient and effective way the natural needs and desires of all US citizens for food, clothing, housing, education, healthcare, disability care, old age care, communication, recreation, entertainment, social interaction, acceptance and respect. Given this objective then it follows that the complex US economy must be managed in such a way as to achieve this objective. It is really almost absurd to think that the US economy can achieve its objective of satisfying the natural needs and desires of all US citizens without any management, coordination and direction. And yet, that is exactly what most capitalistic economic theories hold. Though it must be stated that most capitalist economic theories do not support the objective that the economy's purpose is to satisfy the natural needs and desires of all US citizens in the most efficient and effective manner. Instead they hold that the economy should support the survival of the fittest principle where the objective of the economy is the good of the elite who have superior rights over the rest of society. Radical capitalists hold that the government should not regulate or have any control over the economy. Popular capitalistic economic theories such as laissez-faire, classical liberal, free market capitalistic, right libertarian, anarcho-capitalistic, and neoliberalistic economic theories all hold that the government should not regulate (or minimally regulate) trade, all property (all property) should be private, there should be no taxes or tariffs (or minimal taxes and tariffs), productions systems should be largely or entirely private and operated to achieve a maximum profit, maximization of capital accumulation, and that the market (businesses) should manage the economy.

Should businesses or corporations manage and direct the economy? The objective of every business is to maximize its profits and its capital, or more specifically the profits and capital of those individuals who own the business. Businesses want to grow and grow without any limit. Businesses grow by eliminating most if not all their competitors. Once businesses have grown to a point where there are only a few giant corporations within an industry, they dominate the market: suppliers, workers, customers and governments, all levels and all branches and collectively these giant corporations dominate the economy. And since these corporations are owned by individuals, it is these individuals who dominate the market and the economy. While it is legitimate for a business or an individual to realize a profit, it is wrong for a business or an individual to seek to maximize profits and capital. This is because resources or capital and profits are finite. The capitalistic theories which support the principles of maximization of profits and capital which lead to the domination of the US economy are wrong and counter to the principle that purpose and objective of the economy is to satisfy in the most efficient and effective way the natural needs and desires of all US citizens—all US citizens.

People need to realize that these capitalistic economic theories are wrong and are actually responsible for both the economic and the political crises that the US is facing today and unless something is done will face for generations to come. People need to realize that the US economy is for all Americans, is co-owned by all Americans and that the purpose and objective of the US economy is to satisfy in the most efficient and effective way the natural needs and desires of all US citizens for food, clothing, housing, education, healthcare, communication, recreation, entertainment, social interaction, acceptance and respect—there is no other purpose and objective. People need to understand those tenets of the various capitalist theories that are false and why they are false. Why can't Christians see the discrepancies between the teachings and philosophy of Jesus and these various capitalist theories? Unfortunately, most Christians want their cake and they want to eat it too. They want to be called or considered Christians thinking that they will merit the benefits or rewards but they also want to receive the benefits of extreme capitalism.

Principle of Economic Self-Sufficiency

WITHIN AN ECONOMIC SYSTEM consumption and production are interdependent. Production depends on consumption and consumption depends on production. The vast majority of people need the income or money received from their role in the economy's production system in order to be able to consume. Because of the inter-dependence between consumption and production, it is a necessary condition for the consumption system to consume or utilize as much as the production system is capable of producing. In simpler terms, it is critical that US consumers primarily consume and utilize the goods and services of the US production system. Consumption of imported goods and services which are available or can be produced by a nation's production system represent a gross imbalance in the economic system. And if not corrected this imbalance will lead first to economic stagnation, then to economic decline and lastly to economic shutdown. This is because consumption of imported goods and services decreases the production of goods and services within the nation. Since the vast majority of people need the revenue from their jobs as producers to be able to buy and consume, a decrease in national production because of imported goods and services has a significant negative effect on the economy.

It is very difficult to measure how much in goods and services are imported by the United States ever year. While the amount of goods imported is approximately $750 billion, it is difficult to estimate the amount of services performed outside of the US that could be performed by workers within the US. There has been a significant increase in the amount of services performed outside the United States resulting both in the elimination of jobs in the US as well as the change in US jobs from ones that pay a living wage with benefits to ones that do not pay a living wage and have no benefits. Outsourcing has been very beneficial to multi-national corporations but very detrimental to workers and consumers within the United States. Outsourcing is both un-patriotic and contrary to the proper balance within the economy between production and consumption. While denied by those who blindly follow the religion of free market capitalism, outsourcing is in fact a contributing factor to the current economic crisis. And until outsourcing is brought under control, the economy will remain out of balance with the resulting negative consequences. Initially, outsourcing only involved manufacturing, but now it has extended to customer service, accounts payable, human resources, purchasing, planning, engineering, software development, radiology and others.

The purchase of imported goods and services has crippled the US production system which in turn has led to reduced consumption because consumers have less income to spend. In addition, the purchase of imported goods and services has sent money out of the US economy resulting in an imbalance in the monetary system. Spending money outside the monetary system of the economy also leads to an imbalance. The Federal government spends an inordinate amount of money outside the US economic system financing wars, supporting over seven hundred military bases and spending billions of dollars on aid to foreign governments. This money is actually spent on goods and services not provided by US workers. The amount of money within the US economy must support the transactions that occur between consumers and producers. It is the government's responsibility to carefully monitor the economy for imbalances and act to correct the imbalances before they cause significant harm. Anything undermining, constraining or limiting consumption by individuals needs to be eliminated. Anything undermining, constraining or limiting US aggregate production needs to be eliminated. Anything undermining the monetary system needs to be eliminated.

Money needs to be managed; the amount, the availability, the expansion and the contraction of the money supply. The management of money for the US economy is the responsibility of the Federal government. It is clearly not the responsibility of private or non-governmental businesses since government is chosen by and responsible to the people and private and non-governmental businesses are not. The government is meant to serve the people, while business is meant to serve a few people. Businesses are selfish and self-serving. The government, at least in principle, is meant to serve all the people.

The guiding principle for money management is balance. Money must be managed to maintain the balance and equity between consumers and producers, facilitate transactions between consumers and producers, and promote the maximization of wealth for the maximum number of people. Money management must not be, as it is today, a vehicle to maximize the wealth of a few at the expense of the majority. For these same reasons, the central banking function of the United States which is currently performed by the Federal Reserve System must be owned, controlled and managed by the Federal government. The Federal Reserve System is not a branch of the government and is in fact a private banking system. Again, the government is meant to serve the people, while private businesses (the Federal Reserve System) are meant to serve a few people. Private businesses (the Federal Reserve System) are selfish and self-serving, while the government is meant to serve all the people.

Investment—Yes! Speculation—No!

THE US ECONOMY LIKE any organization needs to be run efficiently and effectively. Efficiency in part is based on the elimination of waste. Anything that does not add value must be eliminated. Speculation adds no value. It increases prices but adds absolutely no value whatsoever. The vast majority of transactions within stock markets, commodity markets and exchange markets involve speculation and do not involve investment. Except for initial public offerings or when a company is trying to raise capital by selling stock, in every other stock purchase the money that is used to buy the stock does not go to the company in which the shares of stock are involved. No, it goes to an individual, group or institution who currently owns the stock. In these latter purchases which represent over 99.99 percent of the stock transactions, the intent of the stock buyer/holder is to buy stock with the hope that the stock price will rise. When the stock price rises sufficiently, the stock will be sold at the higher price to realize a profit. These activities provide absolutely no value to the company itself, to the workers, to the customers, to the suppliers and to the economy in general. In fact, these buying and selling activities are detrimental to the long-term growth of the company, since the majority stockholders exert pressure on the corporate management to focus on doing what is necessary to raise the stock price and not on what is necessary for the long term good of the company. Most majority stockholders are institutions and they have been responsible for forcing companies to do things that are in their best interests and not in the best interests of the company itself, the workers, the customers, the suppliers and the economy. And this has had a very harmful effect on the entire economy. Companies cannot be run based on the short-term greed -based objectives of these majority stockholders who are stockholders of the company today but not tomorrow. A true investor is a lifetime partner within the organization and not a temporary pseudo-owner.

Since it is the responsibility of the government to manage the economy efficiently and effectively, it must prevent, reduce and eliminate speculation within the stock market, commodity markets and exchange markets. Currently, there are no constraints whatsoever on buying and selling stocks, bonds, commodities, etc. A purchase of stock one day and the sale of the same stock a week later is not an investment in the company. A purchase of stock one day and the sale of the same stock a year later is also not an investment in the company. Even a purchase of stock one day and the sale of the same stock five years later or ten years later is not an investment in the company. True investment leads to ownership and partnership. Ownership and partnership relationships are lifetime relationships.

Preventing speculation within the stock market involves the elimination of short term buying and selling of stock. Preventing or eliminating short term buying and selling of stock can be accomplished easily through a sales tax system where the sales tax applies only if the sale occurs within a short term and the selling party has to pay the tax. Such a tax would be graduated based on the amount of time short of the required term to hold the stock. For example, if the term was set to ten years, an individual, group or institution would have to hold the stock for at least ten years before they could sell it. If they wanted to sell the stock sooner than the ten-year term, then they would have to pay a sales tax based on the amount of time between the date of sale and the ten-year term. For example, using the table below, a mutual fund institution that wants to sell some stock after holding it for only five years would be subject to a 46% tax on the sale, not the profit. Obviously, the tax would offset the profits that they may realize assuming that the price of the stock has risen and would be a disincentive to selling before the ten-year term.

Ownership Period	Sales Tax
One year or less	91%
More than 1 year but less than 2 years	82%
More than 2 years but less than 3 years	73%
More than 3 years but less than 4 years	64%
More than 4 years but less than 5 years	55%
More than 5 years but less than 6 years	46%
More than 6 years but less than 7 years	37%

More than 7 years but less than 8 years	28%
More than 8 years but less than 9 years	19%
More than 9 years but less than 10 years	10%
Ten years or more	0%

Another market which involves extensive speculation is the commodity market. The vast majority of transactions within commodity markets involve speculation and do not involve investment. Individuals, groups, and businesses buy commodities without any intention of ever taking possession of the commodity they are purchasing. They buy oil, natural gas, heating fuel, propane, industrial metals (copper, aluminum, lead, zinc, etc.), agricultural items (grains, corn, wheat, soy beans, flowers, vegetables, eggs, coffee, cocoa, sugar, cotton, etc.), livestock, meats, and precious metals. They never take physical possession of these commodities because they are not capable of receiving, storing, transforming or transporting them. Nor do they want to take possession of these commodities. Because they never take physical possession of the commodities that they buy, they add no value whatsoever to the commodity. They only buy the commodity in order to sell it at a price higher than they bought it for. Hence, their actions increase the price for the final end user and yet provide absolutely no value to the end user. These traders undermine the efficiency and effectiveness of the economy and their activities need to be prevented, yes prevented, through regulation, legislation, and litigation if necessary.

Within any system anything that does not add value is considered waste. Efficiency and effectiveness is based on the elimination of waste. Speculative transactions within the commodity markets do not add any value and are therefore waste in terms of the economy. Since it is the government's responsibility to manage the economy in order for it to achieve its objectives (maximization of wealth for all citizens), the government is responsible for eliminating such transactions that are actually detrimental to the economy.

Property

CAPITALISM IS A NATURAL right of individuals. Every person by virtue of their humanity has the right to own property: to own land, to own a home, to own furniture, to own appliances, to own a car, to own a phone, etc. The right to own property only applies to human individuals as humans and as individuals. Groups, organizations, corporations and governments do not have a natural right to own property. In fact, groups, organizations, corporations and governments do not have any rights whatsoever. Only people, living human beings have rights. Groups, organizations, corporations, and governments cannot own property. They can only manage property which is owned by the individuals comprising them. In other words, a group cannot own property; it can only manage the property which is owned by the individuals in the group. An organization cannot own property; it can only manage the property which is owned by the members of the organization. A corporation does not have the natural right to own property; it can only manage the property of those individuals who comprise the corporation. The government does not have the right to own property; it can only manage the property of its citizens.

Because property ownership is a natural right of human individuals and because property ownership is necessary to preserve life and to allow a person to pursue happiness; it is the goal of the economy that virtually everyone possesses property (land, a home, furniture, appliances, a means of transportation, a means of communication, etc.). While property ownership is an absolute right, it is not unlimited. A person's right to property ownership is limited by every other person's right to property ownership. One person, a small group of people or a minority of the people cannot own everything. Truly absurd and contrary to Natural Law was the idea that the king owned everything and truly absurd and contrary to Natural Law is the idea that the State should own everything.

What is considered property and hence what is subject to ownership by the natural right of a human being is also limited. One human being cannot own another human being. Nor can a group of people or a corporation or a government own a human being. Property ownership does not extend to human rights. A person, a group, a corporation or a government can never own a person's right to life, to privacy, or to vote. Nor can a person, a group, a corporation or a government ever own a person's liberty, thought, speech, creativity, or work. For a person's life, liberty, thoughts, creativity, privacy, and work are so personal and intimate to the individual person that they only belong to that person and can never belong to any other person.

There are two types of property: personal, private property and common, community property. Personal, private property belongs to a human person by natural right. Land, a home, a car, furniture, appliances, tools, jewelry, etc. are examples of personal, private property. Common or community property is property which is held jointly by a group of human beings. The group can be small or large. The property of all corporations is common, community property. Civil corporations such as cities, counties, states and nations jointly share streets, parks, buildings, etc. Non-civil corporations such as non-profit and profit corporations have property which is jointly owned by the various stakeholders.

Another categorization of property that is often used involves physical property and intellectual property. Physical things are tangible (subject to the senses) and subject to time and space constraints. Because physical things are subject to time and space constraints, they are quantifiable, that is, they can be measured. Intellectual things are intangible, not subject to time and space constraints and they are not quantifiable. The ownership of property involves individual physical possession and control of the property. In the case of physical things, the person who physically owns and possesses the things is clearly identified and because of that reason physical things are subject to being held as property, primarily personal and private. Intellectual things, an idea or set of ideas, can only be ascribed to an individual as long as it remains with that person. As soon as the idea is communicated, the possession and control of the idea is now owned by everyone to whom the idea was communicated. For this reason, intellectual things cannot be personal and private property but are rather common and community property. This fact is not clearly understood by the wealthy elite and the court systems. They have incorrectly allowed intellectual things to be considered as private and personal property.

If a person builds a house and lives in it, it is clear that this person is the owner of the house and the house is his or her property. If a person conceives an idea and communicates the idea to 100 people, the idea is now shared by the 100 people. It does not belong to the originator of the idea because it is no longer possessed by the originator. The originator should get credit and perhaps compensation for the idea if there is value to the idea, but the idea now belongs to the 100 people to whom it was communicated. Doctor Jonas Salk, the inventor of the first polio vaccine, took the right position on his invention. He did not seek a patent on his discovery admitting that the vaccine belonged to the public domain. Unfortunately, patent laws and copyright laws are biased in favor of the false opinion that intellectual objects fall into the domain of private property. Within the context of this biased and erroneous view of intellectual objects as private property, the rights to these intellectual objects can be transferred from one individual to another individual who then has absolute ownership of the idea which was conceived by another. This is most detrimental to the economy and the common good. For ideas are meant to be shared for the good of all and not controlled and restricted for the benefit of a few. Intellectual property which should be common property and used for the good of all cannot be under the absolute control of a private individual, group or institution. Private individuals, groups and institutions do not have the good of society as their main objective but rather their own personal good as their objective. How often are life-saving drugs, the basis of which should be common property, made so expensive that many people who need these drugs cannot afford them? This is because of the extremely strong influence of the very wealthy and corporations which seek to maximize profits and operate under the philosophy 'it is neither right nor wrong, it is just business'.

Price Management Principles

THE PRODUCTION SYSTEM OF the economy produces goods and services which are needed and desired by consumers. The producers are consumers, and the consumers are producers. Consumers can only buy the goods and services provided by the producers in so far as they have the money to pay for the goods and services. Consumers receive money in their capacity as producers when they produce and sell goods and services. In an effective and efficient economy there is a delicate balance in the interactions between consumers and producers. The prices that producers charge for their goods and services must have limits. The price cannot be too high lest consumers not be able to afford what they need for life, liberty and the pursuit of happiness. Nor can prices be too low lest producers, as consumers, not have enough money to buy the goods and services they need for life, liberty and the pursuit of happiness.

Because people, businesses, and corporations function economically as part of the US national economy, transactions between these entities must be viewed within the context of the national economy. It is assumed that the US economy as a whole should be balanced, integrated, and always growing because the population is growing. The US economy is composed of consumers, producers, a monetary system, and a management system. Economic activity consists of production by producers, consumption by consumers, and the trading or buying/selling of goods and services between producers and consumers. It is this economic activity (production, consumption and exchange) which must be kept in balance and functioning most efficiently and effectively. Production and consumption must be kept in balance within the US economy. And transactions involving the exchange of goods and services between producers and consumers must not undermine the delicate balance between production and consumption.

A sale is a transaction between a seller of a good or service and a buyer or consumer of the good or service. The vast majority of sales transactions involve a business or corporation as the seller and an individual as the buyer/consumer. The natural basis of a sales transaction involves an equal or fair exchange sometimes referred to as quid pro quo. Unfortunately, most sales transactions today are neither fair nor equal. Because of the political power of corporations, the business determines the price which the buyer or consumer must pay. The current pricing strategy is based on the maximization of profit for the business and is sometimes referred to as "whatever the market will bear." This means that the business will attempt to charge as high a price as possible without regard to fairness, justice or the possibility of causing an imbalance in the economy. This is in complete opposition to the just price principle, which holds that the price must be fair to both seller and buyer, as well as the balanced economy pricing principle. Proponents of the maximum profit pricing principle have long labored to undermine the just price principle and the balanced economy pricing principle by holding that the market should be totally free, un-regulated, and un-managed; without any rules or management whatsoever.

Every sales transaction must be viewed within the context of the economy ; it is not a separate, isolated activity. This is especially true regarding transactions where one party is a business or corporation. The vast majority of prices involving consumers are not negotiated; they are set by the seller. The buyer has no choice regarding the price. Nor can a buyer assume that the price of a good or service is fair because of the notion of a competitive market. Many markets are dominated by a few gigantic corporations which indirectly collude in setting and maintaining unfairly high prices. In many situations there is an absence of a truly competitive market in which the consumer has choices. And in some cases, the buyer or consumer has no choice whatsoever regarding whether or not to buy. A consumer has to have food. A consumer has to use transportation. A consumer has to have medical care. They have no choice.

Sales transactions are part of the economy and either support the balance within the economy or undermine it. Sales transactions will support or undermine the necessary balance within the economy based on the fairness of the price charged for the good or service. The income of two-thirds of American consumers is less than the average income, while these same two-thirds produce three-quarters of the goods and services within the economy. These two-thirds of the consumers have limited purchasing potential because their expenses equal or exceed their income. This is a fact that few within the upper one-third and almost no one within the upper one percent of the income spectrum are able to comprehend. (Unfortunately, most of Congress, the President, and the Federal courts fall into the upper one percent bracket.) These two-thirds of the consumers receive a paycheck and then pay their mortgage or rent, pay for food, pay for utilities, pay for healthcare, pay for transportation, pay for education and pay for the other necessities in life—and they have nothing left over. Nothing!

What happens to consumers and what happens to the economy when the price of food rises five percent a year because food prices are not managed by the government and food prices are driven by the principles of "maximization of corporate profit" and "whatever the market will bear"? What happens to consumers and what happens to the economy when the prices of healthcare and prescription drugs rise eight percent a year because healthcare and prescription drug prices are not managed by the government and healthcare and prescription drug prices are driven by the principles of "maximization of corporate profit" and "whatever the market will bear"? What happens to consumers and what happens to the economy when the prices of electricity, natural gas, and heating fuel rise ten percent a year because the price of electricity, natural gas and heating fuel are not managed by the government and these prices are driven by the principles of "maximization of corporate profit" and "whatever the market will bear"? What happens to consumers and what happens to the economy when the price of gasoline rises twenty percent in a year because gasoline prices are not managed by the government and gasoline prices are driven by the principles of "maximization of corporate profit" and "whatever the market will bear"? What happens to consumers and what happens to the economy when interest rates increase ten percent in a year because interest rates are not managed by the government and interest rates are driven by the principles of "maximization of corporate profit" and "whatever the market will bear"?

When the price of one basic necessity (food, utilities, transportation, etc.) rises so high that it prevents the consumer from buying other basic necessities; the economy is thrown off balance. When consumers are prevented from buying the goods and services which they need because they are now spending an inordinately high amount of money on some other good or service, then the economy actually contracts. This is what has happened in the US economy from 2006 to 2010 and continues to be one of the main causes of the current economic crisis.

Un-managed price increases undermine the stability and balance of the economy, and if the price increases are high enough they will slow, stop or reverse economic growth. In such a case the excessive price increases need to be controlled and in some cases reversed. In other words, businesses would need to reduce their prices back to acceptable limits. Can such a thing be done? Absolutely! Corporations want to maximize profits. They do not want a reasonable profit, they want as much profit as they can get no matter what impact that has on individuals or the economy.

Just Price Principles

WITHIN A SOCIETY WHICH is organized around the principles of mutual support of and collaboration with its members towards the goals of life, liberty and the pursuit of happiness; the prices of goods and services are subordinate to the aggregate economic welfare of society. Because of the large number of members of the US society (over 315 million) and the magnitude and complexity of transactions between these members, balance must be maintained in order to achieve efficiency and effectiveness. Justice involves the proper ordering of things. Everyone would agree that there has to be order in society, there has to be order in the economy, and there has to be order and balance between the various interactions and transactions between the members of society including those transactions involving the exchange of goods and services. Every human person has rights equal to every other person. Every person has the right to life, liberty and the pursuit of happiness and these rights are both physical and economic.

The just price principle involves the price for a good or service provided by a seller to a buyer. Simply stated, a just price is a price which is fair to both the buyer and the seller. It is most especially applicable to the basic necessities in life: food, shelter, energy, transportation, clothing, appliances, furniture, healthcare and education. The prices for these things must be fair, which means affordable within the context of the totality of all things. The consumer must buy a range of different products and services for life. The price of one thing cannot be so great that it prevents the person from buying other things which they need for life and liberty. This must be viewed within the context of goods and services which the person needs to purchase on a regular basis such as food, energy (electricity, natural gas, or heating oil), transportation, healthcare and communication. Price increases, especially on the basic necessities of life, must be fair and must be just. And the only way to achieve just prices is management and regulation.

The seller, business or corporation, has a twofold responsibility and purpose: to make money and to serve society. Serving society means providing the society to which it belongs with goods and services which the people need for life, liberty, and the pursuit of happiness (the principle of national and economic community). Serving society is part of one's patriotic duty and is incumbent on all members of society. All businesses are bound to follow the just price principle. They cannot raise prices to a point where the buyers, fellow members of society, cannot afford to pay all their expenses to maintain life and liberty. Obviously, the just price principle is incompatible with the current pricing principle expressed by the phrases of "whatever the market will bear" and "maximization of profits."

The just price principle serves the individual and the community, the business and the community, and the individual, the business and nation. The just price principle is based on fairness, equality of rights, the principle of community and the principle of patriotism. The maximization of profit pricing principle ignores fairness, denies the principle of community and is anti-patriotic. The maximization of profit pricing principle is based on individual greed, contempt for the rights of others, contempt for community and contempt for country.

The just price principle places a limit on prices, or more specifically on price increases and applies primarily but not exclusively to those goods and services necessary for life: food, clothing, housing, education, healthcare, transportation, disability care, old age care, communication, and recreation, entertainment. The key to the limit on price increases is affordability, where affordability is based on a living income. Prices cannot rise faster and higher than median personal income increases.

While the first aspect of the just price principle involves those goods and services which involve the basic necessities for life (food, housing, clothing, healthcare, transportation, and education), the second aspect extends to all goods and services. The second aspect of the just price principle is that every transaction must involve a fair or equitable exchange of goods and services. The equity in the goods and or services exchanged has to do with the actual value of the goods and services and not the perceived value which can be artificially manipulated. This means that the just price principle applies to all goods and services and not just to those goods and services which are considered necessary for life.

Were the gasoline prices in the US during the latter half of 2007 and the first half of 2008 where the average price for a gallon of unleaded gasoline was over $4 just? Is the price of an airline ticket purchased three days before departure which is significantly higher than the price of a ticket purchased three weeks earlier just? Is a $35 fee for an over-draft for having a five dollar deficit in a person's checking account just? Is a continuous $35 fee charged on a daily basis for having a five dollar deficit in a person's checking account just? Is the price (interest) of a payday loan where the interest rate can be as high as 400 percent just? Is the price of credit where the interest rate is over 20 percent just? Is the price of a beer or a hotdog at a sports arena just? Is the price of an appendectomy just? Are the prices of most prescription drugs just? Is the price of electricity just? Is the price of the usage of a cell phone where a person has exceeded their monthly limits just? Is the price of a college education just?

Prices are just when they are affordable. Every transaction must be seen within the context of the entire economy because every person, every business, and every corporation is part of the economy. Every transaction must have a positive effect on the economy. Transactions based on the just price principle will always have a positive effect on the economy because they are fair to both buyer and seller. Transactions based on the maximization of profit pricing principle will always have a negative effect on the economy because they benefit the seller and hurt the buyer and thereby cause an imbalance in the economy.

What are acceptable limits for price increases? First of all, price increases should only be allowed during a growing economy and not during a recession. For price increases during a recession are counter to reversing the negative growth of the economy. Next, price increases must be limited to the growth factor of the economy. If the economy is growing at the rate of 3 percent, then a 3 percent price increase is acceptable. But a more interesting question is "Why are there price increases?"

If a business is generating a reasonable, steady profit year after year, then why would they have to raise prices? Unfortunately, businesses have used price increases to increase their profits operating under the pseudo-principles of "maximization of profits" and" whatever the buyer will bear." And equally unfortunate is the fact that consumers have become numb to price increases because they feel that they cannot do anything about them. So, prices spin out of control and wreak havoc on the economy, leading to stifled consumption, reduced production, layoffs, bankruptcies, foreclosures, repossessions, and other economic disorders.

Labor

IN THE PAST TWENTY years millions of workers have lost their jobs. Why? Did these people do something wrong? Were they bad workers? No. The only thing that they were doing wrong from the company's point of view was they were earning a paycheck. Corporations are driven by greed to maximize profits. Employees are considered an expense. In a few cases companies had lost money (their expenses had exceeded their revenues) and they laid off employees in order to reduce expenses assuming that their revenues would remain the same. However, in most cases companies just wanted to increase their profit margins or the CEO wanted to achieve his or her objectives in order to receive his or her big bonus. Laying off workers may be good for a CEO or for a company in the short term but it is not really good for them for the long term. However, laying off workers is extremely bad for the workers and very bad for the economy. And what is bad for the economy is also bad for business. From an economic point of view, millions of laid off people are no longer productive members for the economy. Their means of earning money with which to buy the goods and services that they need for themselves and their families has been eliminated. Aggregate economic demand is lessened which leads to less production which in turn leads to more layoffs.

What about the poor worker who has been laid off? Seventy percent of Americans live from paycheck to paycheck and have virtually no savings. So, if and when they are laid off from work, they have no funds to help them survive financially. While unemployment insurance keeps people from starving, it does little to prevent the drastic effects of unemployment. Unemployment is one of the leading causes of home foreclosures. People who have lost their jobs reduce if not totally deplete the equity in their homes. They are forced to move into an apartment, sell their furniture, sell their cars, sell their jewelry, stop going to college. The vast majority of the unemployed have no health insurance. Depression, divorce, alcohol abuse and drug abuse are extremely high among the unemployed. Many people who are unemployed resort to crime which can be seen by the high correlation between crime rates and unemployment rates. And why are these people unemployed? Why do they suffer financially, socially, and emotionally? The unemployed and their families suffer financially, socially and emotionally because corporations want to increase their profits and because CEO's want to receive their bonuses.

Most workers are apprehensive and fearful of being laid off. If profits are down, people begin to fear that a layoff may be coming. Companies lay people off in many different ways, some are respectful of the employee and some are cruel and demeaning to the employee. Some companies lay people off by calling them into an office individually and notifying them of the layoff. Some companies will bring employees together as a group and make a general announcement that everyone in the group is being laid off. In some rare cases, people have been notified by email that they have been laid off or they have been notified that they were laid off by security when they have been prevented from entering the building. When a person finds out that they have been laid off, they immediately experience shock, confusion, anxiety, and depression. Dozens of questions cycle through their heads without answers. How will I tell my family? What about our family plans for a vacation? Will my son or daughter have to drop out of college? How long will it take me to find another job? What will we do about health insurance? Will we have to sell our home? Where would we go? Who will hire me? Will I be able to get the same pay? These questions cycle through a person's head within the first few moments of being notified that they have been laid off and they continue cycling through the person's head day and night.

Are layoffs really necessary? Are layoffs fair? Are layoffs moral? How is it fair to those people who have provided ideas for new products, who have brought in new customers, who have built facilities, or who have built high quality products? How is it fair to those people who have dedicated their entire careers to the company and are responsible for making the company what is it? The vast majority of layoffs are neither necessary nor fair nor moral? They are the result of poor decisions, mismanagement, and a false, unjust, and undemocratic though legal management structure as well as the greedy, immoral and unpatriotic principle of maximization of profits.

Layoffs are actually immoral. Workers are co-owners of the business. They are not employees, they are not the help; they are co-owners.

They have the same rights to the profits and equity of the corporation as do the so-called capitalists, and in most cases the workers have superior rights. Every person working for a company whether full time or part time is a co-owner. As co-owners, they have property rights which must be respected. To lay a person off and deprive them of their share of the ownership of the corporation is immoral. In addition, workers have the right to a livelihood which cannot be taken away. To deprive a person of their livelihood in order to increase profits is immoral. What about the tens of millions of workers who have lost their jobs due to outsourcing? These people were deprived of their livelihoods for the sole purpose of increasing profits. When will people who call themselves Christian begin to act like Christians in their business lives?

The personal negative effects of one layoff can impact a family for between five to ten years. That means that it can take between five to ten years before the family can completely recover from a layoff. Unfortunately, a significant percentage of the US workforce has experienced multiple layoffs in their working careers. If one layoff causes economic hardship for five to ten years for a family, multiple layoffs for the same individual over his or her lifetime can translate into a lifetime of economic hardship.

Layoffs are bad for the economy even when the economy is growing because they reduce economic growth. Layoffs during a recession are extremely bad for the economy and undermine economic recovery. Unfortunately, there is no government management of the US labor force and control of corporations in the elimination of workers. Could and should the Federal, state and local governments manage and control the elimination of workers by corporations? Yes! Governments have the responsibility of managing the economy. Anything that undermines the balance and stability of the economy needs to be eliminated and or controlled. Layoffs undermine the balance and stability of the economy and therefore need to be controlled by the government. In addition, layoffs represent an injustice to those who are laid-off. The job of government is to protect people's rights and prevent injustices.

How can the government control layoffs? The government can tax corporations based on layoffs. Imagine if there was a $50,000 tax for each person that a corporation was laying off? The corporation would think twice about laying off workers if they were faced with such a tax. Taxing corporations for laying off workers would force corporations to improve their management and planning functions. There are so many irresponsible corporations that instead of planning better resort to regular cycles of hiring and firing. That is poor management. And there are many layoffs which are the result of poor management.

What is more critical is the continuing outsourcing of jobs to other countries where there are much, much lower wages and poor employee protections. Every job that is outsourced results in one or more lost jobs within the United States. The US economy needs more jobs to grow the economy not less jobs. People need more job opportunities in the US not less opportunities.

How can the government control outsourcing? The government can tax corporations based on outsourced jobs and jobs lost due to outsourcing. Imagine if there was a $50,000 tax for each person that whose job was outsourced? The corporation would think twice about outsourcing if they were faced with such a tax.

Home Ownership

FOR THE VAST MAJORITY of individuals and families, their home is their greatest asset, their greatest expense and their greatest source of personal security. Home ownership is a natural right and one of the objectives of the economy. An economy is most stable when every family or individual possesses their own home. For the stability of the economy is based on the constant, continuous consumption of the majority of the population. The majority of the population can only consume according to their needs and desires when they are not over-burdened by housing expenses for their entire lives. It is therefore one of the duties of the Federal government to facilitate home ownership with the goal of full home-ownership, that is, everyone who desires to have a home has a home and is able to pay-off their mortgage in a reasonable amount of time—and 30 years is too long of a time.

Unfortunately, the banking industry has had a stranglehold on the home loan industry almost forever. They dictate the terms of the home loan and the interest rates. Since the banking industry, which is still controlled by inordinate capitalists, has been and is driven by the principle of 'maximization of profits', it operates counter to the national economic goal of full home-ownership. The home loan industry sets too high interest rates making it difficult or impossible for many people and families to buy their own home and for those who are able to purchase a home these excessively high interest rates reduce the family's ability to consume. For example, on a $250 thousand home loan there is $500 difference per month between a loan with a 5.5% interest rate and a loan with a 2% interest rate. Five hundred dollars a month is a large amount of money for most families. If the family did not have to pay the $500 dollars to the home loan company, they would obviously use that money to buy other things. Five hundred dollars a month paid to a home loan company does not help the economy ; it merely goes into the pockets of the already wealthy people who own the home loan company. Five hundred dollars a month spent buying food, clothes, furniture, education, healthcare, and other goods and services does help the economy. And $500 a month for 30 years equals $180,000.

But is it feasible to assume that the objective of promoting full home-ownership with interest rates that do not severely constrain a family's monthly budget can be pursued with very low interest rates such as 2 to 3 percent? The central bank of the United States is supposed to maintain economic stability. Since the central bank, currently the Federal Reserve which is a private for-profit corporation, creates money and issues it to banks at very low interest rates, currently less than 1.5 percent, it is both feasible and in the best interests of the overall economy that the Federal Reserve or central bank (assuming that the US Federal government took control of the money supply from the private corporation the Federal Reserve) issue home loans at 2 percent. Other corporate banks would then be forced to match the FED's 2 percent home loan interest rate. Since the Federal Reserve System or central bank creates money, whatever interest rate it charges represents the same percent as gross profit.

Interest rates on home loans need to be very low. A family should not be encumbered by an extremely high monthly payment for thirty or more years. Thirty years represents the greater part of a person's working lifetime. Nature intends a person or a family to enjoy life during the majority of their lifetime. Extremely high monthly payments on a home loan due to excessively high interest rates consume too much of a person's income and represent too large a percentage of a person's net income. Home loan interest rates need to be controlled by the Federal government so that a family can pay their loan off in fifteen to twenty years instead of thirty to forty years and not financially suffocate the family on a monthly basis. It is in the best interests of the economy that home loan interest rates be very moderate. Moderate home loan interest rates would actually improve the stability and growth of the economy and help families pursue their goal of life, liberty and happiness.

Contracts

ALL CONTRACTS NEED TO involve equal parties. There cannot be a superior-inferior relation or a dominant-submissive relation between the parties. It is the role of the government to act as an impartial third party to oversee contracts and assure equity and fairness between the parties. Consider the situation where an individual wishes to enter into a contract with a finance company or bank to purchase a car. The finance company or bank is comprised of hundreds or thousands of individuals and perhaps dozens or even hundreds of lawyers. A written contract has been prepared by the finance company's or bank's legal department or legal firm. This written contract contains thousands of words in a syntax referred to as 'legalize', a language intentionally cryptic in order not to be understood by a layman. Virtually, all contracts are biased in favor of the bank or finance company or payday loan company. Who is there to referee such a situation and make sure that the contract is fair? It has to be the government, there isn't anyone else. It would be as simple as having all contracts pre-approved by the government and written in plain language to the average person. The individual should also have the ability to seek government council free of charge and in the event of a complaint, potential breach of contract, or what appears to be something done unfairly by the bank, finance company or payday loan company the individual should have the ability to pursue litigation on their own without having to pay an attorney.

The contract between the worker and the capitalist within a corporation also has to be over-seen by both a collective unit of the same corporation and by the government. Again, how can one individual go against the combined resources of a large corporation? The rights of workers to form unions, to bargain collectively, to negotiate contracts, and to vote for board members must be supported by laws and be part of every contract between the worker and the capitalist. Also, the rights of a worker to privacy, to a living wage, to be recognized for work done, and to mandatory severance in the event of a layoff sufficient to enable the person to live without having to be set back financially until they get another job—all these rights must be supported by laws and be part of every contract between the worker and the capitalist.

The contract between a borrower and lender has to be regulated by law and over-seen by the government. A contract should not be transferable from one party to another. For a contract defines an intimate relationship between two parties and only those two parties since the agreement, which is the basis of the contract, was between only those two parties. Even if there is language in the contract saying that this is possible, it is wrong. Contract terms that express something unjust or inequitable are false, invalid and non-binding. It is therefore wrong for one party to sell or transfer the contract to a third party which had nothing to do with the original agreement between the two parties. Obviously, this implies that the whole practice of mortgage securitization is wrong.

Corporations

Rights only apply to human beings by their nature and cannot be attributed to persons artificially created by the government such as corporations. Corporations have no rights. Corporations do not have the right to vote, the right to privacy, the right to own property or any other right natural to human beings. Nor should corporations have to right to contribute to political campaigns. Because of this corporations should not be allowed within the political sphere of the United States.

A corporation cannot be separated from the people who animate it. A corporation regardless of the false definition that it currently has does not have an existence separate from the people who animate it. A corporation does not think—people think. A corporation cannot speak—people speak. A corporation does not live—people live. What is a corporation? Is it a building or a collection of buildings? Is it machinery? Is it material? No, a corporation is a group of people working together for their own good and the good of society. The corporation is the aggregation of all people animating it, capital shareholders and labor shareholders (both full-time and part-time).

A corporation is a body of people; living human beings who are joined together for a purpose. An organ of the body is composed of cells. It performs a function which is subordinate to the good of the entire body. The organ serves itself and it serves the body. The organ exists for itself and it exists for the body. In a similar manner, the corporation consists of people who work together and perform a function for the good of the people comprising the corporation, the people that the corporation serves and the good of the entire economy. A corporation is meant to serve itself and to serve the economy. An organ such as the heart or the kidneys serves the entire body. The health of the body depends on the proper functioning of the heart and the health of the heart depends on the proper functioning of the body. The corporation is not an end in itself. It exists to serve the entire economy. Automobile corporations must understand that they have a duty to serve the US economy and the people of the United States. Banks must understand that they have a duty to serve the US economy and the people of the United States.

A corporation is a group of people and does not have an existence distinct from the people who animate the corporation. The notion that a corporation is an artificial person with the same rights and privileges as a human person is entirely wrong. Corporations are jointly owned by investor shareholders and worker shareholders both of which are equal owners. Natural Law dictates that corporations should be democratically governed and managed by both investor shareholders and worker shareholders. Corporations are liable for their actions and subordinate to the rule of law. Those that manage and direct corporations can and should be held responsible for wrongdoings done by the corporation since they and the rest of the investor and worker shareholders are the corporation.

The Balanced Economy Principle

THE UNITED STATES ECONOMY is a complex system involving hundreds of millions of entities. These entities consist of individual people and people organized into families, groups, organizations and businesses. There are two main functions of this economic system; production of goods and services and consumption /utilization of goods and services. There are billions of transactions occurring daily involving the exchange of goods and services between producers and consumers and money is used to facilitate these exchange transactions and is considered a medium of exchange.

One of the main conditions for the US economy to function efficiently and effectively as a system is that it has to be in equilibrium, that is, in balance. The various elements, activities, and interactions of the economy must be in balance. Balance involving millions of entities and billions of interactions and transactions cannot occur without management—it will not occur naturally. Management involves organization, direction, regulation and control. And yet there is virtually no management of the US economy. There is no direction to the US economy. There is no regulation of the US economy. There is no control of the US economy. And the results are obvious. There is no control, there is only chaos affecting not just tens of millions of people in the United States but hundreds of millions of people. The only people not affected by the unmanaged, undirected, unregulated, and uncontrolled economy are the wealthiest top one percent of the population.

The current US economy is not in equilibrium, it is out of control. The main reason why the economy is out of control is the Federal government does not exercise its responsibility to organize, direct, regulate and control the economy. Unfortunately, the vast majority of those occupying positions within the Federal government represent a very small and select group of wealthy individuals whose purpose is to use the Federal government to pursue its goal of economic domination. These individuals oppose a balanced economy.

The common phrase "the rich get richer and the poor get poorer" is lacking in precision. The poor or the working class in general gets poorer because the rich or capitalist class gets richer. This is based on net worth, the difference between a person's assets and his/her debt as well as the aggregate of all assets and debt. The wealth of the wealthiest one percent in the United States has grown considerably within the last twenty years while the wealth of the lower middle class and lower class has decreased. This is because the total wealth is finite. The more that the wealthy one percent take, the less that is available there is for everyone else.

Balance implies the lack of extremes with respect to wealth, income, work, and power. An economy has to be balanced in order for it to be efficient and effective. The US economy is neither efficient nor effective because it lacks the appropriate balance with respect to wealth, income, work and power.

Balance must be sought by the government, all levels of government and all branches of government.

The Most Appropriate Economic System

WHILE SOCIALISM AND CAPITALISM are basically complete opposites, both extreme socialism (communism) and extreme capitalism lead to totalitarianism. Totalitarianism is a political and economic system where absolute authority and control resides in the ruling elite and where every aspect of public and private life is regulated by the ruling elite. The ruling elite maintain this control through propaganda, threats and either police or military violence against the people. Furthermore, virtually all human rights are denied and ignored by the ruling elite. It should be clear that both uncontrolled socialism and uncontrolled capitalism lead to totalitarianism.

While both uncontrolled socialism and uncontrolled capitalism lead to totalitarianism, socialism and capitalism can be balanced and blended into an economic system which combines the benefits and advantages of each system while at the same time eliminating the harm and disadvantages of each system.

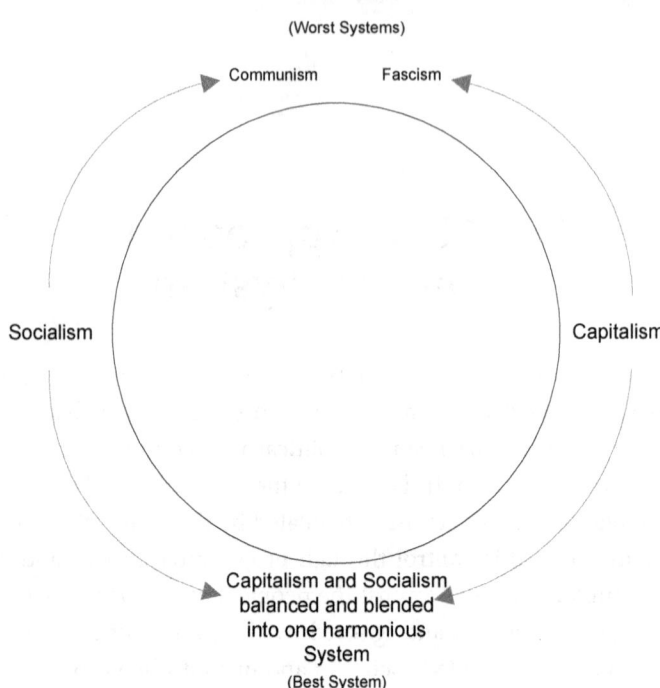

The diagram above shows the relationship between Capitalism, Socialism and Totalitarianism. Capitalism and Socialism can act as a 'check and balance' against each other preventing each from approaching and reaching Totalitarianism.

Capitalism of its nature is individualistic and its main objective is the acquisition and control of private property. Because of this, capitalism of its nature is selfish. The synonyms for selfish are: thinking only of oneself, egocentric, egotistic, greedy, mean, mercenary, miserly, narcissistic, narrow-minded, out for number one, self-centered, self-indulgent, self-interested, self-seeking, stingy, and wrapped up in oneself. A certain amount of selfishness is natural and good. However, when selfishness impacts others, denying others their natural rights and depriving others of what is due to them; then selfishness is wrong. This applies to capitalism as well. Limited capitalism is natural and good but it must be kept within limits and prevented from denying others their natural rights and depriving others of what is due to them.

Socialism of its nature is altruistic. The synonyms for altruism are: generous, liberal, charitable, caring, kind, unselfish, self-giving, and public-spirited. Ethics regards the good of others as the end of moral actions. Socialism involves cooperation and collaboration and is based on community. Socialism is at the foundation of most religions especially Christianity. Unfortunately, capitalists because of their animosity for socialism have waged a smear campaign on socialism and have succeeded in making most people think that socialism is something bad. They attempt to equate socialism with Marxism and Communism. Most people do not understand that public roads, public museums, public libraries, public schools, Social Security, Medicare, Unemployment Insurance, public parks, public beaches, police forces, fire departments, the US Postal Service and a myriad of other Federal, state and local agencies are all socialist programs. These things benefit all the people and not just a few. And if these things were eliminated or privatized (that is, people would have to pay for them), then the only ones to benefit will be the already rich and everyone else will suffer a significant lowering in the quality of life.

Where is the United States today on the above chart? Is it closer to Totalitarianism or closer to the ideal state where the best of capitalism and the best of socialism are blended together for the good of everyone and not just the good of a few? Unfortunately, the United States is moving rapidly in the direction of Totalitarianism on the arc of capitalism and away from the ideal state. Extreme capitalists are intent on eliminating every aspect of socialism in the United States. These radicals want to eliminate Social Security, Medicare, unemployment insurance, the postal system, and subsidies and social safety nets for the poor and children. They want to privatize virtually everything: education (yes, they would like to destroy the public-school system), water, energy, safety protection (police and fire departments), roads, bridges, and parks. And they want absolutely no government regulation of their capitalistic pursuits no matter what their methods and no matter who they exploit and/or harm in the process. This radical capitalism has its sights not only on the United States but also on the entire world.

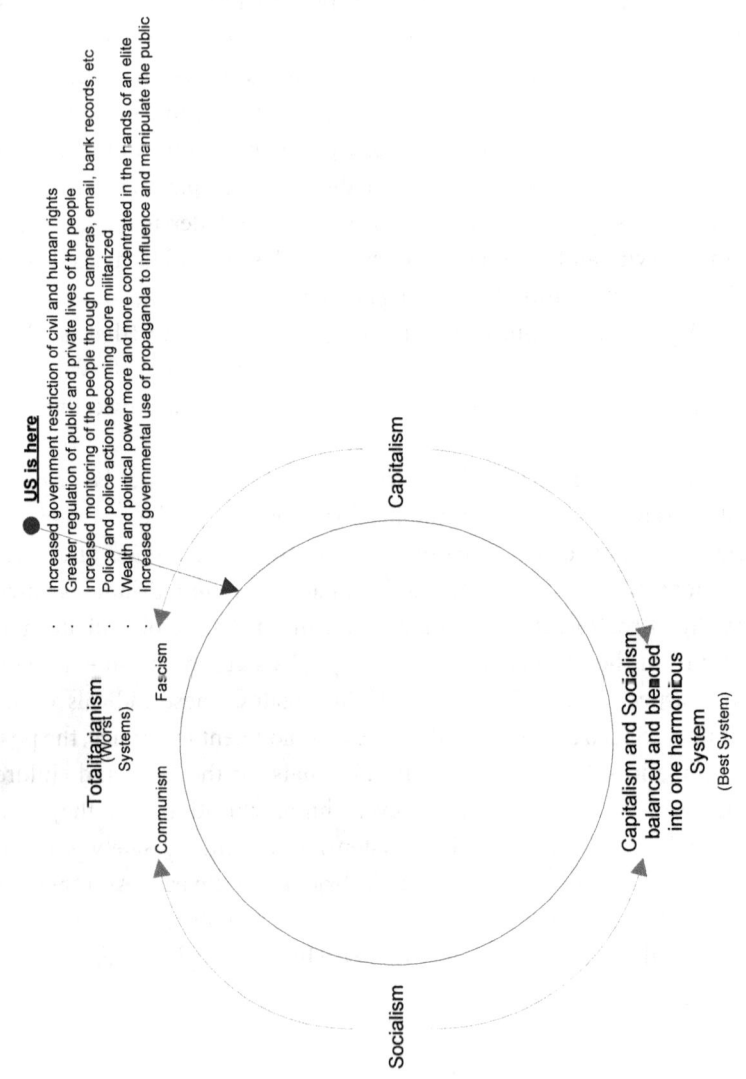

Socialistic Capitalism or Capitalistic Socialism

CAPITALISM WHICH IS NOT controlled leads to Totalitarianistic Capitalism. Socialism which is not controlled leads to Totalitarianistic Communism. However, Capitalism and Socialism can be blended together into one system retaining the positive aspects of each and eliminating the negative aspects of each. When Socialism and Capitalism are blended together forming Socialistic Capitalism or Capitalistic Socialism, each balances or offsets the negative aspects of the other.

Capitalism has dominated the history of the world with kings, emperors and the privileged class claiming private ownership of virtually everything: the land, natural resources, corporations, and the people themselves. Socialism has not had an impact on history until recently, the last hundred years, and unfortunately a radical form of socialism (communism) and the social evils resulting from this erroneous form of socialism has allowed the capitalists to malign every form of socialism.

Communism, like Extreme Capitalism, denies the rights of others. Communism holds the state as the highest good in society, while extreme capitalism hold the individual (more correctly some individuals) as the highest good. While Communism subordinates everything and everyone to the State, Extreme Capitalism subordinates everything and everyone to the elite class. It should be noted that theoretical Communism subordinates everything and everyone to the State, while the communism of the Soviet Union, China, and Cuba actually subordinated everything and everyone to the elite class and in this sense, was/is similar to Extreme Capitalism.

The greatest difference between communism and capitalism involves property. Communism holds that all property belongs to the state, while Capitalism holds that all property is or should be private. Communism controls all property especially the property associated with manufacturing, distribution, infra-structure and services. Capitalism also seeks to control all property and allows individuals to seek control of property by virtually any means and without regard to the needs of others. Capitalism allows the individual to pursue the acquisition and control of property without limit and without any constraints and regulation by society or government. Both of these ideas are wrong.

Private property is a natural right that comes from nature and not from the state and this right belongs to all people. Both Communism and Extreme Capitalism deny this right. Communism denies the right of private property absolutely and Extreme Capitalism denies the universality of this right. Extreme Capitalism does not think that everyone should possess private property, only a privileged few, the exceptional people. Communism, as does the other forms of Socialism, accepts the principle of community or social property, while Extreme Capitalism denies the principle of community or social property. Communism holds that all property is community property, while Extreme Capitalism holds that all property is or should be private. Both are wrong.

Property is limited, it is not infinite. There is a limited amount of land, water, minerals, petroleum, natural gas, coal, iron, copper, tin, zinc, silver, gold, uranium, trees, etc. Because property is limited, one or a few individuals cannot be allowed to control virtually all or most of any finite resource which is needed by everyone. One individual's right to private property is limited by the rights of others to private property. Within the US society of 315 million people, one person's right to private property is limited by the rights of 315 million other people. Within the global society of 7.6 billion people, one person's right to private property is limited by the rights of 7.6 billion other people. Because of this, there is a limit to the amount of private property that one person or a small group of individuals can own or control. These limits must be defined by law and regulated by the government. Because of the natural right to private property, everyone should be able to acquire and possess as their own personal property a home, appliances, furniture, a car, etc. Laws and government regulations and oversight should facilitate every person's pursuit of the private ownership of a home, appliances, furniture, a car, etc. The stability and good of the economy and society itself is dependent on every person owning a home, appliances, furniture, a car, etc.

Besides personal, private property such as a home, appliances, furniture, a car, etc., there is common property which needs to be shared by many individuals. Roads, bridges, parks, beaches, lakes, oceans, forests, rivers, and water are just some of the property which is owned jointly by all people and can never be privatized without violating the rights of the people. Capitalism would privatize roads, bridges, parks, beaches, lakes, oceans, forests, rivers, and water. Laws and government regulations and oversight must guarantee that community property remains community property and as such available to all people.

Every human being has natural needs. They need to eat and drink. They need to be clothed. They need shelter. They need to be kept warm when the weather is cold and cool when the weather is hot. They need energy. They need furniture. They need transportation. They need healthcare. They need education. They need rest and recreation. They need protection. They need to be taken care of when they are very young, when they are sick and when very old. Economics involves the production, distribution and consumption of those goods and services which every human being needs to sustain mental and physical life. The economy is a system where goods are produced and distributed, services provided, goods consumed and utilized, and services received. An economy is effective to the extent to which virtually all peoples' natural needs are satisfied.

Because societies involve large numbers of people, economies need to be efficient in producing and distributing goods and efficient in providing services since the goal of an economy is helping virtually all people in their efforts to satisfy their natural needs and desires. Activities which hamper the efficient production and distribution of goods and the efficient delivery of services should be eliminated. Mass transportation, public education, health care, health insurance, public retirement plans, public unemployment insurance, life insurance, the internet, centralized processing of banking transactions, and processing of credit card and debit card transactions are some services which are more efficiently and effectively delivered by non-profit cooperatives or even by the government rather than by for-profit businesses.

There has been a movement in the United States to turn all healthcare organizations and health insurance organizations into for-profit corporations. From a Christian point of view, it is wrong for any organization involved in healthcare to be a for-profit corporation. For-profit corporations have as their objective the maximization of profits. Maximization of profits involves the maximization of revenues and the minimization of costs and expenses, both of which undermine effective healthcare. In earlier times, most healthcare organizations were non-profit and there were many hospitals run by Christian organizations. Unfortunately, today there are very large for-profit healthcare systems that are intent on dominating the entire healthcare industry and maximizing their profits and equity. This is wrong and opposed to Christian economics.

There are many situations where a corporation has to be a non-profit organization. The reason is that for-profit businesses do not seek the common good but rather personal, individual good. Economics and economies should balance the common good and individual good. While the personal good of a few can prevent many from attaining and realizing their own personal good, the common good does not prevent the attainment of personal good. Rather, the common good fosters and promotes personal good. For every human being needs both common good and personal good to be happy.

The best economic system is one which maximizes both the common good and individual good. This system combines what is best from both Capitalism and Socialism. Unfortunately, the United States is currently moving away from the proper balance between Capitalism and Socialism (capitalistic Socialism or socialistic Capitalism) toward more extreme capitalism. There are many extreme capitalists who want to eliminate virtually every aspect of socialism in the United States (Social Security, Medicare, Medicaid, un-employment insurance, the postal system, police and fire protection, social services, etc.) and privatize virtually everything. And they also promote the idea of the acquisition and control of unlimited property and wealth. These individuals hold that there is no natural, moral, social, or economic limit to how much property and wealth one person can acquire and/or control. Because of this, they hold that no one; the government, religious leaders, social leaders, or 99.9% of the population can prevent them from acquiring and controlling as much property and wealth that they want. Unfortunately, most of these people are very rich and politically very powerful. Politically very powerful means that they have significant influence on the White House, federal senators, federal representatives, federal judges, governors, state senators, state representatives and state judges.

As these individuals pursue their relentless goal of owning and/or controlling all property and wealth, supported and facilitated by their political cronies; the amount of property and wealth available to all others decreases proportionately. As the amount of property and wealth available to the vast majority of people decreases, quality of life decreases and economic growth slows and reverses. These super-rich people who already enjoy a life unparalleled by kings and queens cause a life of economic misery for millions in the United States and billions globally. This is morally wrong and must be corrected and only Christians practicing and promoting Christian economics can do so.

Fixing the US Economy

It is obvious that the United States and in fact the entire world is still in the midst of a severe economic crisis and the governments' efforts to stop this crisis have been failures. No matter what they do, almost nothing has changed. In fact, the situation is getting worse, and the economic disparity between the rich and everyone else continues to increase.

The US economy for all practical purposes is broken, that is, it does not work. While it does work for a minority of the population as well as for a minority of foreigners, it does not work for the majority of Americans—those for whom it should work. It should be emphasized that the US economy provides significant wealth and income to many non-Americans; people who are not citizens or permanent residents and who do not live within the United States. These people make no contribution to the economy of the United States; yet, they receive a significant share of the benefits from the US economy which results in the majority of Americans receiving less than their fair share.

There are four aspects involved in the fixing of the United States economy:

- Rebuilding US manufacturing capacity by creating at least 50 million new US-based manufacturing jobs
- Creating the appropriate checks and balances between banks, businesses, corporations, consumers, and the government
- Balancing wealth, income and private property among all the people
- Re-Americanizing businesses within the United States

Rebuilding the US manufacturing capacity

IT SHOULD BE CLEAR that economic growth and stability is based on jobs, jobs based in the United States and not jobs based in other countries. And these jobs need to be full-time, permanent jobs that pay a good income. The economy is in crisis because there are not enough jobs and not enough good paying, full-time, permanent jobs. The real unemployment rate is around 9 percent and the real under-employment rate is about 30 percent. That means that at least 50 million workers and their families cannot buy the products and services that they want and need. And if these 50 million people and their families are not buying what they want and need, then businesses are not selling and producing what they could if these 50 million people had full-time, permanent jobs that paid a good income.

The solution to the current economic crisis in the United States is clear at least on paper. The United States needs to create 50 million full-time, permanent jobs that pay a good income. It is simple to state the solution but difficult to implement the solution. Or is it?

Part of the problem has to do with the question, "Who can create jobs?" Businesses, corporations, and wealthy individuals hold the position and promote the doctrine (yes, this is actually a doctrine) that jobs can only and should only be created by businesses, corporations, and wealthy individuals. They hold this position because they want to control the economy. Those who own or control businesses and corporations and all wealthy individuals represent the top one percent of the wealth spectrum of the United States. They are not impacted by the current economic situation which is a crisis for the majority of the lower 99 percent. No, in fact, the current economic situation in the United States is a great opportunity for the top one percent. Their wealth and their influence and control of the economy has increased and continues to increase significantly while the wealth and influence and control of the economy for the lower 99 percent continues to decrease significantly.

Big businesses, big corporations and big banks will not create 50 million full-time, permanent jobs in the United States that pay a good income. Their objective is maximization of profits and their strategy is minimization of labor costs and maximization of prices. Big businesses, big corporations and big banks want to monopolize the economy. They do not want competition. There are millions of Americans who would like to own their own business, but big businesses, big corporations and big banks will not let them create their own businesses. They want to dominate the market. Big businesses, big corporations and big banks will not create the 50 million jobs that the United States needs to restore economic growth and stability. But if big businesses, big corporations and big banks will not create these jobs, then who will?

Can the government create jobs? Can the government create private businesses? Can the government create worker-owned businesses? Can the Federal, state and local governments create these jobs and these private businesses? Can the Federal, state and local governments create enough private, worker-owned businesses that will involve the 50 million jobs needed to restore economic growth and stability to the United States economy? Yes, yes, yes, yes, yes!

A Plan to Rebuild the US Economy—Phase 1

PHASE 1 OF THIS plan involves the creation of 40 to 50 million jobs in the United States. These jobs will not be minimum wage jobs, or temporary jobs, or jobs without benefits. No, these jobs will pay a living wage with benefits; sufficient for one person to support a family. And the jobs created by this plan will virtually eliminate unemployment and under-employment.

The basis of this plan is the rebuilding of the manufacturing base of the United States which was intentionally destroyed by the greed of free (free meaning lack of any controls or regulations) enterprise and uncontrolled, extreme capitalism. Businesses, especially large corporations, are unwilling to restore the manufacturing base of the United States. Their objective is maximization of profits and their strategy is minimization of labor costs and maximization of prices. Global corporations, no matter what the tax incentives are, want to manufacture products and deliver services at the lowest possible cost and that implies manufacturing outside of the United States and providing services from workers outside the United States.

So, if businesses will not restore the manufacturing base of the United States, then the government (Federal, state, county and local) will have to. There is no other option. The government will have to create these manufacturing jobs. The plan detailed below will outline how this could be done.

The United States needs to create at least 50 million new jobs. These jobs will extend to everything involved in the design, development, manufacture, distribution and transportation of products to be sold throughout the US retail network. In order to create these jobs, upwards of 100,000 new businesses will have to be created. These businesses will not be government owned. Rather, they will be chartered as worker cooperatives: private corporations owned entirely and solely by the active workers themselves. Furthermore, the corporate charters for these new businesses will prohibit each cooperative from being able to sell itself to a non-coop corporation or merge with a non-coop corporation. In addition, these corporate charters would mandate that these cooperatives only use US made components. It should be clear that the government creation of these privately owned, worker owned businesses is not socialistic. If the government owned the businesses, then that would be socialistic. The government creating private businesses is capitalistic.

The Federal government would be responsible for the identification of the types of manufacturing plants/businesses (textile, clothing, footwear, toys, sporting goods, small appliances, home and outdoor furniture, small tools, home improvement, etc.), the number of each type plant/business and the general location of each plant/business. The location of each business would be based entirely on population demographics and unemployment/underemployment status: the more populated areas would get more businesses. Most of these plants would be located within densely populated areas and would also be situated in areas that have high unemployment/underemployment rates.

While the Federal government would be responsible for the identification and general location of the various types of manufacturing plants, the actual planning cannot be done by government officials. For those in government are politicians; they are not planners, managers, or executives. A politician's main objective is to maintain and increase his or her power and influence. They do so by developing and maintaining a base of wealthy supporters. The program to rebuild the manufacturing base of the United States will involve trillions of dollars. Politicians cannot be allowed to use this money to develop or maintain supporters.

The planning for this program at the national level should be done by academics, professors, who would be selected at random from a pool of pre-qualified candidates who would apply to be part of this program. To qualify for this program, candidates would have to be US citizens with expertise in planning, manufacturing, supply chain management and business. These positions would be paid temporary positions and the positions would last for the duration of the program. It would be their job to do the analyses and develop the plan for the creation and location of the various manufacturing businesses which are the objective of this program. In addition, they would have the responsibility of developing the draft for the initial corporate charters and the steps in establishing and organizing the individual businesses. The Federal government would oversee the independent planning group and could disband the entire group and redo the random selection process to create a new group if necessary.

The actual creation, set up and startup of each business would be done at the local level where the business is to be located. Similar to the national planning group, a group of local professors should be randomly selected from a pool of pre-qualified candidates for each new manufacturing business to be created. The random selection process should also select the group of academics so that the group consists of an expert in management, an expert in finance, an expert in accounting, an expert in manufacturing, an expert in supply chain management, an expert in purchasing, an expert in transportation, an expert in human resources and an expert in information technology. Since these individuals will be creating, setting up and starting the business, they need to act as the initial management team.

There are many vacant factories, distribution centers and buildings which have been vacated by businesses which have moved their manufacturing operations outside the United States. If appropriate, the local government should acquire these facilities through eminent domain if necessary. For those plants, distribution centers, transportation hubs and terminals, and offices that need to be built; only US manufactured materials can be used. In addition, construction would have to be done by local contractors and not by national contractors or large regional contractors and certainly not by foreign contractors.

Each newly created business would be incorporated within the state in which the business is located. The initial management team would be comprised of the academics. They would be responsible for the site selection, construction (if necessary), acquisition of equipment, hiring and training of workers, and the actual startup of operations. As these local businesses become operational and begin to produce products, the national committee needs to be involved with respect to distribution and transportation to the retail market. These newly created businesses need to be successful both in the short run and the long run.

Over the last forty years, US based businesses have chosen to buy foreign-made products rather than American-made products. Driven by the principles of maximization of profits and "it is neither right nor wrong, it is just business"; these businesses have ignored patriotism, ignored the right of foreign workers to a living wage, and have procured products from corporations which exploit their workers for the sake of profit. Walmart, which used to advertise "made in the USA," is now the largest importer of foreign made products.

Most foreign companies that produce the products that are imported into the United States have an unfair advantage over US companies that produce in the United States. While a company that manufactures in the United States has to pay property tax, state income tax, Federal income tax, Social Security tax, Medicare tax, unemployment tax and also pay its workers at least a minimum wage; companies that manufacture in a foreign country do not have to property tax, state income tax, Federal income tax, Social Security tax, Medicare tax, unemployment tax or a minimum wage. Every product that is made outside of the United States lessens property tax revenue, state revenue, Federal revenue, revenue for Social Security, revenue for Medicare, revenue for unemployment insurance and takes away money and a job from an American.

In order to help these newly created businesses compete fairly with foreign companies, it is absolutely necessary that foreign made products be assessed a Federal tax in order to adjust for the gross inequity between US manufacturers and foreign manufacturers. This tax should be a sales tax so that consumers can choose whether to purchase a US made product with no sales tax or a foreign made product with the sales tax. The sales tax should be based on the lost revenue from property tax, state income tax, Federal income tax, Social Security tax, Medicare tax, and unemployment tax as well as the difference in the minimum wage between the US and the country where the product is made. The sales tax revenue should be split between the local government, the state government and the Federal government. As these newly created businesses become operational, this sales tax needs to be implemented. All retail items need to be clearly identified as to the country or countries of manufacture and the percentage of sales tax needs to be clearly marked as well. Most US consumers will buy American made products if given the chance and especially if they realize the significant benefits to the US economy by buying American.

As these new businesses, which are worker owned, are created, virtually all those unemployed and under-employed who are able to work will have jobs - good paying jobs. Their incomes will be used to buy food, clothing, furniture, appliances, cars, homes, education, healthcare and entertainment. Their income will be taxed and this tax revenue will be collected by Federal, state, and local governments. These new businesses and these new jobs will significantly improve the US economy and because these businesses are worker owned, the benefits to the economy will be sustainable. These worker-owned businesses will help balance the distribution of wealth and income in the United States; they will stabilize the middle class and eliminate the lower class by enabling all people to have a job that pays a good wage, has benefits and provides profit sharing.

To review, since Big Businesses, Big Corporations and Big Banks will not create the jobs critically needed to rebuild the US economy; the Federal, state and local governments will have to do this. The Federal, state and local governments can help create manufacturing jobs by helping to create US based private manufacturing businesses which are worker owned. This can be done through national and local planning by academics hired by the government. And in order to allow these US based, worker-owned businesses to compete fairly with foreign manufacturers; the Federal, state and local governments need to establish sales taxes on foreign made products and services.

One last point involves the financing of this program to create tens of millions of jobs by creating tens of thousands of private, worker-owned businesses. Obviously, it will take financing to create these businesses and since these businesses will be private, worker-owned businesses; these new businesses will have to borrow the money needed to get up and running. These loans should come from the government, primarily the Federal government, and should involve terms which will enable and facilitate the long-term sustainability of these businesses. Similar to the interest rates that the Federal Reserve charges the banks, the interest rates to these new businesses should be extremely low:.25 to.50 percent. The term of the loan should be no less than 50 years, and payments should not begin until 5 years after the business has become operational in order to allow the business to stabilize itself.

It should be clear that the above program would not be socialistic; the government would not own or control the businesses which will be created. The government's role would be coordinator, facilitator, supporter and financier.

A Plan to Rebuild the US Economy—Phase 2

THE FIRST PHASE OF the program to rebuild the US economy would involve creating US based manufacturing companies that would produce textiles, clothing, footwear, toys, sporting goods, small appliances, home and outdoor furniture, small tools, home improvement products, etc. The second phase of this program would involve continuing to create new US based manufacturing businesses which are worker owned so that 90 percent of all products that could be manufactured in the United States are in fact made in the United States.

The overall strategy for both phases of this plan is to create a US based business/worker base that will provide 90 percent of all products and materials that could be manufactured in the United States and 99 percent of all services that could be provided from the United States. The US government has allowed and helped to ruin the manufacturing base within the United States. The extremely high percentage of products that could be produced here but are imported have a significant negative effect on the economy. Besides the high percentage of imported products, there are many services which could be provided from within the US but are provided by sources outside the United States: customer service call centers, travel agency service centers, reading of x-rays and ultra-sound images, IT help desk services, engineering, computer program development, legal document development, financial services, and many others. Again, the US government is to blame for the loss of these service jobs because it has allowed corporations to outsource these jobs.

The significant downsizing of the US manufacturing base and service base is one of the main reasons for the current economic crisis in the United States. The economy is driven by consumption; not the consumption of the top 1percent of the income-wealth spectrum, but the consumption of the lower 99 percent of the income-wealth spectrum.

Who will consume cars, clothing, appliances, furniture, homes, electronics, food, entertainment, education, and healthcare at a rate and at quantities which will drive the entire US economy—the 1 percent or the 99 percent? Obviously, only the 99 percent! However, the 99 percent can only consume based on their income.

Big Businesses, Big Corporations and Big Banks, with the cooperation of the Federal government, have severely crippled the US economy by eliminating manufacturing and service jobs in the United States and creating corresponding jobs in lower wage countries. These Big Businesses, Big Corporations and Big Banks have intentionally stopped paying the property taxes, payroll taxes, unemployment taxes, and income taxes associated with the US based businesses and jobs which they have eliminated. In addition, these Big Businesses, Big Corporations and Big Banks have 'spit in the faces' of the American workers and their families who they have fired for the sake of higher profit margins, higher market share, and greater control over the economy. And the actions of these Big Businesses, Big Corporations and Big Banks have been supported by the Federal government. Have the actions of these Big Businesses, Big Corporations and Big Banks in eliminating jobs in the United States and creating jobs in other countries been patriotic? Have the actions of the Federal government in supporting the elimination of jobs in the United States been patriotic? Do Big Businesses, Big Corporations and Big Banks care about people or only their profits and market share? Do those in the Federal government who have helped Big Businesses, Big Corporations and Big Banks eliminate manufacturing and service jobs in the United States care about the people?

The US economy needs at least 50 million new jobs; good paying jobs with benefits. Fifty million new jobs could virtually eliminate unemployment and underemployment. Fifty million new jobs could stop the foreclosure and repossession crisis. Fifty million new jobs could eliminate the housing crisis. Fifty million new jobs could help reduce the budget deficits of the Federal, state and local governments. Fifty million new jobs could help families to buy homes, buy cars, buy clothes, buy appliances, buy furniture, buy healthcare, buy education, buy entertainment and realize a significant improvement in their quality of life.

The plan proposed could create at least 50 million jobs. Once implemented, 90 percent of all products that could be made in the US would be manufactured in their entirety (all materials and components) in the United States on American made machines, using American made electronics, using American developed software by American workers. Once implemented, 99 percent of all services of any and all kinds will be provided by people in the United States: citizens or permanent residents.

Economic Checks and Balances

THE ECONOMY OF THE United States needs to be viewed as an integrated system of all people living in the United States (producing goods and services and consuming goods and services) grouped into corporations, supply chains, associations and families collaborating together harmoniously for the good of each and the good of all. The United States economy should not be viewed as a disparate, disjoined collection of people, businesses and corporations each operating independently and in conflict with each other driven by the selfish pursuit of the maximization of profit and the maximization of wealth and economic control—even though that is the current model and practice within the United States. This is the very reason why the economy is unbalanced, inefficient and ineffective. In the first view the economic model is one integrated whole; one system. In the second view the economic model is a collection of competing, personal economies. The integrated economic model is based on collaboration, coordination, common goals and balance and it is rooted in true patriotism and community. The current disjoint economic model lacks collaboration, coordination, common goals and balance and is rooted in extreme selfishness.

Unfortunately, most current economic theory is based on the selfish model or as they state the self-interest model. This model has every person pursuing their own personal good and ignoring the good of others. They also hold that economic conflict or competition is both good and appropriate. The selfish doctrine and the conflict doctrine have been intentionally created to justify capitalism. However, these doctrines are false and against Christian economics.

The economy as an integrated system is similar to the human body. The human body is composed at the lowest level of cells. Each cell has two objectives: one to support its own life, and the other to support the life of the entire body. Each cell performs functions for itself and functions for the body. For the sake of efficiency, groups of cells performing similar functions form tissues and groups of tissue form organs and groups of organs form sub-systems and all sub-systems constitute the life of the body. The body is an integrated system of cells, tissues, organs and sub-systems collaborating together for the good of each and the good of all. One of the most important characteristics of the human body is balance or homeostasis. If any internal or external factor causes an imbalance in the entire system, different sub-systems act to eliminate the imbalance. While cells, tissues, organs and sub-systems regulate themselves; they are also regulated by the higher-level structures.

The economy is similar to the human body. Individuals are like cells. Individuals form groups which are called businesses or corporations to generate goods and services. These businesses or corporations form supply chains where one corporation is a supplier of another. These pairs of corporations are linked to other pairs of corporations each corporation supplying the next until the last corporation supplies the consumer. Within an integrated economy, everything is linked together and every element (individual, business, corporation, and supply chain) is dependent on the other elements (individuals, businesses, corporations, and supply chains). All the different elements of the economy interact and collaborate with the other elements. Corporations are dependent on workers and workers are dependent on corporations. Consumers are dependent on corporations and corporations are dependent on consumers. Corporations are dependent on corporations. This is especially true from a supply chain point of view. Upstream corporations are dependent on downstream corporations to sell their products or services. Downstream corporations are dependent on upstream corporations to provide goods or services. Consumers are dependent on every node or corporation in the supply chain. Every node within the supply chain needs to work with the other nodes and there needs to be coordination between all nodes (corporations) so that the entire supply chain is effective and efficient. When all the nodes collaborate together and when there is balance within the supply chain, every corporation succeeds as well as the final consumer.

The family is the basic unit or element of an economy. In fact, a family can constitute an economy. An individual is not the basic unit of an economy since an individual is born into a family and is fully supported by a family until he or she is capable of contributing to his or her own support. The individual also needs support during illnesses and during old age and this support comes from others.

A family can constitute an economy. In earlier historical times families did function as economies and in some undeveloped countries this is still true today. Every human being has natural needs. They need to eat and drink. They need to be clothed. They need shelter. They need to be kept warm when the weather is cold and cool when the weather is hot. They need energy. They need furniture. They need transportation. They need healthcare. They need education. They need rest and recreation. They need protection. They need to be taken care of when they are very young, when they are sick and when very old. Economics involves the production, distribution and consumption of those goods and services which every human being needs to sustain mental and physical life.

A family living on a farm represents an economy. The members of this economy have natural needs, they need goods and services, and these same members produce the goods and services which they need. As a production system, the family works together to produce the goods and services. It is important to note that everyone works; except for the very young, the sick and the very old—those who are incapable of working, and everyone realizes their obligation to work. No one takes the position that everyone should work for him or her and that they do not need to work. Work is divided into areas: farming, building, making clothes, making furniture, making tools, making food, caring for the young, caring for the sick, caring for old, teaching, transportation, etc.

While everyone works for their own good, they also work for the good of the economy. Each member of this mini-economy understands the relationship between them and the entire economy. They understand that they cannot do anything to undermine the economy since their good is dependent on the entire economy. Each member of the family has his or her own property and there is also property that is owned in common. The idea and practice of profit is non-existent in this mini-economy. Except for the very young, the sick and the very old, goods and services are distributed to each member based on their contribution.

While the family is a basic economic unit, it is not capable of providing for all the necessities of life. For this reason, families join together to form communities. As communities are formed, they can and should follow the integrated economic model which is based on collaboration, coordination, common goals and balance. This is the natural concept of a community and this collaborative model is the basis for true patriotism.

Communities are collections of families and the members of the community must understand that every other member of the community has the same natural needs. They need to eat and drink. They need to be clothed. They need shelter. They need to be kept warm when the weather is cold and cool when the weather is hot. They need energy. They need furniture. They need transportation. They need healthcare. They need education. They need rest and recreation. They need protection. They need to be taken of when they are very young, when they are sick and when very old. The integrated, collaborative economic model of the community involves the production, distribution and consumption of those goods and services which every human being needs to sustain mental and physical life. While every member of the community works for their own good, they also work for the good of the entire community. Each member of this economy understands the relationship between them and the entire community. They understand that they cannot do anything to undermine the economy since their good is dependent on the entire economy of the community. Each member of the community has his or her own property and there is also property that is owned in common by the entire community.

An economy, such as the United States economy, is the collection of all communities comprised of families living within the United States. There are two basic functions in the economy: production and consumption. Money is used to facilitate the exchange between producers and consumers. People produce the goods and services needed and wanted by people. And people consume the goods and services that are produced. There needs to be balance between production and consumption, between capital and labor, and between corporations and individuals. There also needs to be collaboration between production and consumption, between capital and labor and between corporations and individuals. Lastly, there needs to be coordination between production and consumption, between capital and labor and between corporations and individuals. The US economy consists of people grouped into families, communities and corporations. All people are consumers, and except for the very young, the elderly and the sick, all people are producers.

The US economy currently lacks the appropriate balance between corporations, workers, consumers, and the general public. Some big corporations and big banks have acquired such economic and political power, that they dominate other corporations, workers, consumers, and the general public. These same big corporations dominate the major supply chains of goods and services. And these same big banks and big corporations dominate the economy and the governments: Federal, state, county and local. There must be checks and balances between banks, corporations, consumers, the general public and society. Unless and until such checks and balances are created and active, this defective and deficient economy will continue to be defective and deficient.

The main problem with the economy is that the big banks and corporations are out of control, that is, there is virtually no control over them. The government is virtually helpless in controlling these out of control big banks and big corporations, because these big banks and corporations control the government. Workers are virtually helpless in controlling these out of control big banks and big corporations, because these big banks and corporations control workers. Consumers are virtually helpless in controlling these out of control big banks and big corporations, because these big banks and corporations control consumers. Basically, society is virtually helpless in controlling these out of control big banks and big corporations, because these big banks and corporations control society. Corporations set prices in order to maximize profits without concern for their customers and customers can do nothing about it. Corporations market and sell products such as genetically modified organisms GMO's, and consumers can do almost nothing about it. Corporate factory farms have taken over the farm industry in the US, and they utilize hormones and antibiotics without concern for the health of the consumer and consumers can do almost nothing about it. Corporations have closed factories and operations here in the United States and laid-off workers who have spent their entire careers at the company and the workers can do nothing about it. Private equity firms have bought companies and have dissolved the pension funds for workers and workers can do nothing about it. The greed of big banks and financial institutions has caused the economic recessions which started in 2008 and continues today without an end in sight. Banks are so powerful, that they can financially enslave cities, counties, states and even countries (the IMF and World Bank have enslaved dozens of countries). Corporations cannot be so big that they can dominate other corporations, dominate the market, dominate the economy, and dominate the government: Federal, state, county or local. For those corporations that have reached this level of influence, they must be reduced in size and be prevented from being able to influence the government, any level or any branch, in anyway whatsoever.

How is it possible to control big banks and big corporations and also to prevent other banks and corporations from getting so politically and economically powerful that they also will begin to dominate society? Big banks and big corporations are so powerful politically and economically because they are so big. Because they are so big, they control very large percentages of the money and product supply chains. They generate extremely large profits and have enormously large amounts of money with which to influence politicians through campaign contributions and lucrative salaries after politicians have left office. These big banks and big corporations intimidate and bully smaller banks and corporations. The US Federal government, state governments, and local governments are virtually controlled by big banks and big corporations. This is also true for foreign countries: big banks and big corporations control them as well. The problem is that these big banks and big corporations are too big and the solution is that they need to be significantly reduced in size. The economy requires balance and the extreme size of these big banks and corporations and their relation of dominance over the government, other corporations, workers, consumers, and society totally undermine the necessary balance within the economy.

The proper and appropriate subordination is missing in the US economic and political environments. Currently, the government (all levels; Federal, state, county and local and all branches; executive, legislative and judicial), workers, smaller corporations, consumers, and society are subordinate to big banks and big businesses. This is economically, politically and morally wrong. Yes, it is morally wrong. The proper and appropriate relation is the people, the government, and then banks and corporations.

The big banks and big corporations need to be separated and separated into much smaller entities than those that were formed when AT&T and Standard Oil were broken up. A 400 billion dollar organization, whether it is a bank or non-banking corporation, should be broken up into organizations whose annual revenues do not exceed 5 billion dollars. Every organization, whether domestic or foreign, should be limited to 5 billion dollars in annual sales. If it exceeds this limit, it needs to be broken up into smaller entities. Reducing the size of the big banks and big corporations reduces their ability to dominate the government, other corporations, workers, consumers and society. Through laws and legal force, the size and the political and economic influence of banks and corporations need to be kept in check.

While breaking up the big banks and big corporations into smaller entities and limiting the size of any corporation will help bring balance to the economy, that are other things that need to be done as well in order to bring the necessary checks and balances for there to be the correct balance in the economy between corporations, workers, consumers and society.

Today, there is virtually no balance between corporations and workers. While workers constitute the corporation and generate the revenues and profits of the corporation, they have no control over the corporation itself. Capitalists can lay off workers, close facilities, and even move operations to other countries totaling ignoring the rights of the workers. Workers need to be given shares in the corporation which will entitle them to dividends and allow them to vote for board members. The value of these shares should correspond to the compensation of the workers. There should be two types of shares: capital shares and labor shares. Every corporate board should consist of an even number of members where half of the board members would be elected by capital shareholders and half the board members would be elected by worker shareholders. Labor shares should not be transferable through sale to another individual. Capital shares can be sold as they are today. However, the sale of capital shares needs to be managed through taxes to prevent capital shareholders from 'playing the market' and to make capital shareholders true investors who have a long-term interest in the corporation.

Imagine corporations where capital shareholders and labor shareholders share the control and decision-making responsibilities of the company. The interests of the capitalists and the interests of the workers would be in balance for the benefit of both. Capitalists would be prevented from outsourcing jobs, laying-off workers to achieve financial targets, raiding the pension funds of the workers, and selling the company to private equity firms. The economy would be much healthier today if such checks and balances were in existence thirty years ago when the outsourcing of jobs began and vulturous private equity firms emerged. Giving workers shares in the company and allowing them to elect half the members of the board of directors would motivate workers to take a greater interest in the short and long-term benefits of the company.

There also needs to be better checks and balances between corporations and consumers. Consumer Protection laws in the United States are very weak especially when it comes to pharmaceuticals and food products. Consumers must be able to sue corporations both as individuals and as part of classes and the penalties associated with corporate fraud, misinformation, disinformation, and unsafe drugs and food products must be very severe.

Re-balancing Wealth, Income and Private Property

THE MAIN FACTOR UNDERLYING the current economic and political crisis facing the United States as well as the entire world is the great and ever-widening disparity in wealth, income and private property within the population. The wealthiest 20% of people in the US own 93% of all US wealth. Twenty-five percent of the people in the US have negative or zero wealth, that is, their liabilities (what they owe) exceed their assets (what they own). These percentages have been increasing for the past thirty years since the Reagan presidency and continue to increase which means that there is a continuous movement of wealth from the lower economic levels of the population to the upper levels especially the top one percent. In other words, the disparity in wealth, income and private property which is the main factor underlying the current economic and political crisis is increasing. That means things are actually getting worse not better.

The economy is based on production and consumption and production is directly proportional to demand for consumption. When demand declines, production declines proportionately. When demand rises, production rises proportionately. Production of goods produces property which has value and therefore production produces wealth. Currently, actual demand is less than it should and could be. People want to buy homes, cars, furniture, appliances, education, medical care, and entertainment; but they cannot because they do not have the money. People do not have the money to buy these things which drive the economy for many reasons. Many people who want to work are not able to work because jobs and job creation are controlled by the Capitalists. Many people have jobs which do not pay a living wage. Many people do not receive their fair share of the profits which they generate through their labor. Many people have been tricked and manipulated into financial arrangements where they are paying an unjust, immoral, and un-American interest rate. And every one of these reasons represents a scheme or mechanism whereby the wealthy and super-wealthy take money and wealth away from the working-class majority and place it under their control and ownership. This movement of wealth away from the working class, those that generate the wealth, to the non-working capitalist class has to be stopped. And the significant inequity in the distribution of wealth, income and private property which is the result of this scheme of the wealthy and super-wealthy to take wealth away from the working class needs to be corrected. Equity not equality needs to be restored to the distribution of wealth, income and private property throughout the population based on the contribution made to the generation of wealth—wealth is generated through work; physical and intellectual. Investment or capital facilitates the generation but does not generate wealth itself.

The super-wealthy and the very wealthy have such great political and economic power that they have significant influence with the various levels and branches of government. The super-wealthy and the very wealthy are able to have laws passed, judicial decisions made and executive actions taken that support and facilitate their activities that take wealth away from the working class. This is a very important point. Because of the influence of the super-wealthy and the very wealthy within the various levels and branches of government; most laws, many judicial decisions, and most executive actions involving both domestic and foreign policy favor and benefit the super-wealthy and the very wealthy to the detriment of everyone else. It is for this reason that it can be claimed the United States government is a plutocracy and the United States economy is a plutonomy. The capitalist class exploits the working class legally though unethically and immorally for its own benefit. Fixing the gross imbalance in the economy and political system involves reducing the control that the capitalist class has over the economy and the political system.

Reducing the capitalist class's control of the economy is straight forward, at least from a theoretical point of view. From a practical point of view, it is much more difficult because of the significant influence that they have within the political system. For the changes that need to be made to the economy can only happen through the political system. Minimizing the flow of wealth from the working class to the capitalist class needs to happen and can happen by the following means. The capitalist class exerts its influence within the economy and political system through their control of corporations and financial institutions. Through their influence within the political system, capitalists have been able to have judicial decisions made and laws passed that give them absolute control over corporations and this influence has also been instrumental in having the courts falsely define a corporation in a way that allows the capitalist absolute control over the corporation and immunity from legal harm (limited liability). It is the definition of the corporation which needs to be changed and made to represent what the corporation actually is. The corporation is the collection of people who operate together to perform the functions of the organization. The corporation needs to have a legal identity but that identity should not be different from the people who activate the company. There must be limits and controls on what they corporation can and cannot do and it must be liable for its actions. There should not be any ownership distinction between those people who carry out the activities of the organization and those who are true long-term investors—they are both co-owners.

Reducing the capitalist class's control of the economy would involve the following:

- Changing the income tax system

    - Restore the graduated tax rates to the same levels as during the Eisenhower Administration

    - Capital gains tax rates must equal the individual income tax rates

    - Corporate tax rate must equal the individual income tax rates

- Creating a graduated asset tax on financial assets greater than $1 million
- Eliminating corporate tax subsidies
- Increase the minimum wage and define the minimum wage as a living wage
- Make workers co-owners with capital shareholders by giving them labor shares in the corporation and allowing them voting rights
- Create jobs as explained above
- Strictly regulate interest rates, terms on loans and fees associated with loans

- A usury interest rate needs to be defined and interest rates regulated accordingly

Making the super-wealthy and the very wealthy pay significantly more income tax would help to reduce the flow of wealth from the working class to the capitalist class. CEO's, CFO's and other senior managers within corporations making tens of millions of dollars a year are paid significantly more than the value that they provide to the corporation. CEO's and CFO's do not create, do not design, do not sell, do not take orders, do not make products, do not ship products, do not deliver services, do not nurse, do not doctor; yet they often make 2000 to 3000 times the lowest paid worker in the corporation who does in fact add value. This difference between the top managers within a company and the lowest paid workers has increased significantly in the last thirty years. Imagine what the compensation packages would be for upper managers within corporations if half the members of the board of directors were elected by the worker shareholders. The worker shareholders would obviously work to restore equity (not equality) in the compensation for all levels of the corporation.

Many of the super-wealthy and the very wealthy do not work but play the markets; stock, bond, commodity, etc. They are not investors but gamblers for they do not provide money to companies but rather buy and sell from other traders. Many of these individuals have extremely high incomes from these activities and currently they pay only up to 15 percent in capital gains tax. Because of this their wealth grows and grows as well as their economic and political power. Having the same Eisenhower tax rates as the individual income tax rates would help reduce the flow of wealth from the working class to the capitalist class. Because these individuals are good players they win while others, the people from the lower levels of the economic scale, lose. Most people are led to believe that they can benefit from playing the markets. Unfortunately, just like gambling in a casino, most people in the stock, bond and commodity markets are losers and the super-wealthy and very wealthy are the winners who win at the expense of the losers—money flows from the losers to the winners.

While reducing, minimizing or stopping the flow of wealth from the working class to the capitalist class will help the economy, it will not significantly reduce the economic and political power of the super-wealthy and the very wealthy. The vast wealth accumulated by the super-wealthy and the very wealthy needs to be reduced and can be reduced by asset taxes. Most of the wealth accumulated by the super-wealthy and the very wealthy has come at the expense of the working class and the economy itself. They have acquired this wealth by taking it away from the working class through legal but immoral means. An asset tax on financial assets would reduce the wealth of the super-wealthy and the very wealthy and reduce their economic and political power. Financial assets are assets which an individual has which are or can be invested in stocks, bonds, commodities, currencies, and real estate which is not used for their own personal use. There are over 5 million people in the United States who have at least 1 million dollars in financial assets. Taxing financial assets over $1 million would over time reduce the excess financial assets of these individuals and reduce their economic and political power.

Re-balancing wealth, income and private property among all the people involves the reduction and possible elimination of the extremes in the distribution of wealth, income and private property. Restoring the Eisenhower era graduated tax rates, making the capital gains taxes the same as individual tax rates and creating a graduated asset tax on financial assets over $1 million would reduce the extremes on the high side of the socio-economic range. Efforts must also be undertaken to reduce the extremes on the low side as well. 25% of the people in the US have negative or zero wealth. Virtually everyone should have a positive net worth. Helping these 80 million people (25% of the US population) achieve and maintain a positive net worth will not only help them, improving their quality of life, it will also significantly help the economy. The first way to help people who have zero or negative net worth is to increase the minimum wage first to a living wage and then to a respectable wage. A living wage is a wage based on full-time employment (40 hours per week) that is sufficient to allow the person to afford housing, utilities, food, clothing, furniture, appliances, transportation, medical care, personal care (care of clothes (washing and drying), hair care, bodily care), an education and some money for contingencies. A respectable wage is a wage that provides the individual with a living wage income but also allows the individual to buy their own home and save money for retirement. A respectable wage is best for all individuals and for the economy.

Making workers co-owners with capital shareholders by giving them labor shares in the corporation and allowing them voting rights is also necessary to re-balancing the wealth, income and private property among the population. Making workers shareholders will eventually increase their income and prevent those periods of unemployment resulting from layoffs which significantly impact an individual's wealth. Unemployment can quickly wipe out a person's wealth and force the individual into a negative net worth position which can take years or even a lifetime to recover from. Empowering workers within a corporation and giving them shared decision-making ability can minimize layoffs and unemployment since it forces the capital shareholders into a position of being investors with long-term interests in the corporation rather than short-term interests. Giving workers within a corporation shared decision-making ability would also reduce if not eliminate the take-overs of corporations by private-equity firms, hostile take-overs by other corporations and the outsourcing of jobs; all of which lead to unemployment for workers within the corporation.

Creating 40 to 50 million jobs in the US as explained above would also significantly help re-balance the distribution of wealth, income and private property within the United States. These jobs would pay good wages, have good benefits and provide long-term if not lifetime employment for these people. Lifetime employment prevents unemployment which severely impacts an individual's wealth and the economy. The state where virtually all workers have good paying jobs is best for the economy since it leads to maximum consumption which drives maximum production. Achieving the state where virtually all workers have good paying jobs requires a more equitable distribution of the profits from businesses. Today, virtually all the profits go to top management and those that control the corporation even though both groups make little to no contribution to the process of producing the goods and services which generate the profits.

Financial interest is one of the greatest means used by capitalists to take wealth, income and private property from workers. It is not interest in itself, but interest charged at a rate or over a term which is so high that it severely impacts an individual's financial stability and leads to their financial ruin. Payday loans, title loans, and other types of personal loans have exorbitant interest rates, terms and conditions such that a person who takes out such a loan usually falls deeper and deeper into debt. People who take out such loans usually have negative net worth and these loans put them further into debt often without the hope of ever achieving a positive net worth position. Mortgage rates can also be excessively high and put the borrower into a lifelong debt position. It was the American dream of owning a home; buying a home and paying off the mortgage before retirement. Over the past thirty years, this, dream has been ruined because of high mortgage rates and vulturous mortgage holders who seek to benefit by repossessing people's homes. Interest rates, all interest rates, must be strictly regulated, as well as the terms, conditions and fees associated with loans. A usury interest rate needs to be defined and interest rates regulated accordingly for mortgage loans, car loans, personal loans and every other type of loan.

Re-Americanizing American Businesses

WHAT DOES IT MEAN to pledge allegiance to the United States of America? This phrase is contained in the US pledge of allegiance and embodies the basis of patriotism. But what is the United States of America? Most definitions point to the governmental structure; the state government and the Federal government. These definitions are both incorrect and misleading. The United States of America is first and foremost a corporation of people within its borders grouped into families and communities. People, families, and communities existed in this country before any state government and before the Federal government. This corporation of people forms first and foremost an economy, an economic system where the people work together for both individual and common interests. The government of these people, families and communities is secondary in importance and is subordinate to the people of the United States. It is a great error and deceit to subordinate the people of the United States to the government of the United States.

The US economy should comprise of individuals and corporations which seek to add value to the entire economy. It should not include individuals and corporations which seek to extract wealth and private property from the US economy for their own selfish purposes and this includes individuals and corporations who seek to withdraw wealth and private property from the US economy and place it within another economy. American property: land, water, natural resources, buildings, equipment, roads, bridges, dams, power plants, etc. must remain under the control of the US economy which means that these things must be owned by US citizens or US corporations. Businesses and corporations must be owned by US citizens. As a house divided against itself cannot stand, so an economy divided against itself cannot stand. The US economy needs to grow. That means that it needs to generate new wealth.

This new wealth must stay within the US economy otherwise there is no growth.

Over the past forty years there has been a significant increase in the number of foreigners who bought and now own and control US property (land, buildings, roads, bridges) and US businesses, that is, businesses which operate within the United States. In fact, the US government has actually helped foreigners to acquire US businesses. And the percentage of foreign-owned US businesses continues to rise and most of the profits of these businesses go back into the economies where these individuals are citizens. All of this impacts the US economy. The economy of the United States is for the people of the United States. The land, roads, bridges, apartment buildings, shopping malls, lakes, etc. are for the people of the United States. The property of the United States is for the people of the United States. The property of the United States is not for the British, not for the French, not for the Germans, not for the Spanish, not for the Greeks, not for the Italians, not for the Russians, not for the Israelis, not for the Japanese, not for the Indians, and not for any other country. The wealth generated by US businesses is for the people in the United States. The wealth generated by US businesses is not for the British, not for the French, not for the Germans, not for the Spanish, not for the Greeks, not for the Italians, not for the Russians, not for the Israelis, not for the Japanese, not for the Indians, and not for any other country. Other countries limit the ability of foreigners to own their property and businesses and this makes economic sense. The United States needs to do the same thing. While the US Federal, state and local governments talk about patriotism, they do not practice patriotism.

The Federal, state and local governments must stop helping foreigners to buy or gain control over US businesses and US property. It makes absolutely no sense and it is unpatriotic for the Federal, state or local government to help a foreigner buy or gain control over US property or a US business. Who does the government serve, the people of the United States or the people of other countries? Congress needs to change the tax system to severely tax people who take money out of the United States economy and place it in foreign banks or financial institutions. And laws must be passed that restrict ownership by individuals and corporations which not American. The US economy is for the people of the United States. Family takes care of family!

PART III

The Solution—Christians Applying Christian Economics

Who Can Solve this Crisis?

THERE ARE MANY BOOKS detailing the problems relative to out of control capitalism : its drive for a global empire, its control of governments, its exploitation of nations, its subjugation of the working class, etc. Yet none of these books offer any real, effective solution to the problem of inordinate capitalism. And because of this readers and people in general have lost hope and they don't think things will ever change. Is that true? Is there no hope for change, for justice, and for true democracy?

Capitalism has been out of control for the last 2000 years. The super-rich have unjustly controlled economies and governments for their benefit virtually ignoring the rights, needs and dignity of almost everyone else. While these super rich have been and are few in numbers, they have been able to manipulate, control and exploit the masses of people. They have done so by using four means. First, they have created and propagated a false economic and political philosophy based on principles that are contrary to the Natural Law and Christian Economics principles. Secondly, they have created a hierarchical structure among the people and use the people in the higher levels of this hierarchy to control the people in the lower levels rewarding them for their actions and loyalty. Thirdly, the super-rich have been able to manipulate the military and police through a false patriotism and blind obedience into controlling the non-super rich majority. Lastly, the super-rich have been able to control Christian leaders and use Christian leaders to manipulate and control the people. The solution to the problem of the economic injustices that exist within the United States as well as the entire world is found in undermining these four tools of the super-rich minority.

Inordinate capitalism has been and is based on principles that are counter to the Natural Law and Christian Economics principles. Unfortunately, people have been taught to accept these inconsistencies. Starting in the 4th Century, Christian leaders manipulated by governments started to teach that a person could have two different lives based on two contradictory sets of principles: one their private life and the other their business, political and economic life. The practice of Christianity was limited to praying, attending services, and participating in Christian rituals. The practice of Christian principles was precluded from one's business, work, economic and political life. Prior to the 4th Century, Christians did not engage in military activities and avoided being used by governments to extend their empires. Starting in the 4th Century, Christians began to participate in military engagements with all the injustices and atrocities associated with wars especially wars of aggression and imperialism. And Christian leaders condoned such behavior in spite of the clear conflict with Christian principles. Since the 4th Century Christians have been pawns of governments and the super-rich who control these governments in waging wars to expand the empires of these super rich. Christians have placed crosses on their uniforms, Christians have fought against and killed other Christians, and Christians have engaged in acts of genocide in spite of the clear inconsistency of these actions with Christian principles.

Christians have done so and continue to do so because Christian leaders have been silent. Christian leaders starting in the 4th Century have abandoned their responsibility of proclaiming Christian principles and pointing out the errors in political, economic and business philosophies and practices. Christian leaders are supposed to be the conscience of society. Instead, they have chosen to lead lives of comfort and privilege by currying favor with the power elite: the leaders of government and the super-rich. Every once in a while a Christian leader has made some vague statement concerning an injustice in society, but then they do nothing more. The super-rich have pursued wars of aggression and imperialism and Christian leaders have said nothing. In the last Century, what did Christian leaders say and do about the wars that made the 20th Century the most costly and destructive century in all of history? What did Christian leaders say and do about the Spanish-American war, the Second Boer War, the Somali Jihad, the Philippine-American War, the Boxer Rebellion, the Italo-Ottoman War, the First Balkan War, the Second Balkan War, World War 1, the Turkish War of Independence, the Greco-Turkish War, the Russian Civil War, the Polish-Soviet War, the Sino-Japanese War, the Second Italo-Ethiopian War, the Spanish Civil War, World War 2, the Cold War, the Greek Civil War, the First Kashmir War, the First Arab-Israeli War, the Malayan War, the Korean War, the Algerian War of Independence, the Suez War of 1956, the Vietnam War, the Laotian Civil War, the Cambodian Civil War, the Yemen Civil War, the Sino-Indian War, the Second Kashmir War, the Six-Day War, the Warsaw Pact Invasion of Czechoslovakia, the Bengali War of Independence, the Yom Kippur War/Ramadan War, the Lebanese Civil War, the Falkland Islands War, the Israeli Invasion and Occupation of Southern Lebanon, the Invasion of Grenada, the Gulf War, the Third Balkan War, the Second Chechen War, the US attack of Panama, the Congo War, the Gulf War, the war in Afghanistan, the Iraq War, the Yugoslav War, and the War in Yemen?

If Christian leaders had collectively claimed as nations prepared for each of these wars that these wars were morally wrong and that participation in these wars by Christians was immoral, could some if not many of these wars have been avoided? If Jesus is called the Prince of Peace, then shouldn't Christians promote and pursue peace? If Jesus is the Prince of Peace, then isn't war incompatible with Christianity? Since the time of Christ, Christianity has been an absolute failure with respect to wars, genocides, military actions, and police actions. Christian leaders have said nothing while Christians have been used as pawns in wars to extend financial empires; for money and economics are behind every war—every war. Why have Christian leaders since the 4th Century been silent with respect to wars, genocides, slavery, disregard for human rights, and the exploitation of the majority by the super-rich? Why have Christian leaders been silent as the super-rich become richer at the expense of billions of people many of whom live lives of poverty, some extreme poverty, due to machinations by the super-rich? Is it because Christian leaders have been controlled by the super-rich and have been allowed by the super-rich to live rather comfortable lives?

The US economy will not improve until Christian leaders begin to act like Christian leaders, individuals who lead Christians in the practice of Christianity in every aspect of their lives: their social lives, their business lives, their economic lives and their political lives. The world economy will not improve until Christian leaders begin to act like Christian leaders, individuals who lead Christians in the practice of Christianity in every aspect of their lives: their social lives, their business lives, their economic lives and their political lives. What will it take for Christian leaders to act like Christian leaders?

Christian leaders, Christian schools, Christian writers and Christian academics must begin to address the inconsistencies between the current philosophies and practices of economics, business and politics and Christian principles. These inconsistencies must be clearly articulated and published through all possible media to all Christians. Every Christian high school student, every Christian college student, every Christian worker, every Christian politician, every Christian judge, every Christian in the military, and every Christian in law enforcement must understand the inconsistencies between the current philosophies and practices of economics, business, the military, law enforcement, the justice system and politics and Christian principles. These same people must understand their social, business, economic and political responsibilities as Christians to promote Christian principles: love your neighbor as yourself, do good and avoid evil, and absolute respect for the rights of all people.

Christian CEO's, vice-presidents, directors, and managers must begin to apply Christian principles in their business lives. They must recognize that many business practices are contrary to Christian principles. They must understand that going to Church, singing hymns, saying prayers and praising Jesus is not what Christianity is about. Christianity is about the practice of Christian principles in one's social, business, economic and political life. Doing good and avoiding evil in everything including business, economics and politics is what Christianity is about. Christianity is all about loving your neighbor as yourself and extends to all people including workers, tenants, customers, the unemployed, the under-employed, the sick, those without insurance, the homeless, people from other countries, etc. Christianity is all about respecting the rights of all others.

The current political system involves the government of the people, by the rich and for the rich. With this system in place, the unbalanced and disordered economy is not going to change, the dominance of the market and economy by the Wealthy Elite is not going to change, the composition of government by the wealthy is not going to change, and the change from a plutocratic government to a truly representative and democratic government is not going to occur. It is up to Christians to bring about these changes and this will be an extremely difficult task in spite of the fact that the majority of people in the United States claim to be Christians. For those in power will resist any attempt to reduce their control. The Wealthy Elite will do all in their power and will resort to any means to prevent the people from exercising their right to govern and to bring about a government and economy "of the people, by the people, and for the people."

Big Business owns most of the media; the television news media, the radio news media, the printed news media and the electronic news media. They don't want things to change, they like being in control, they like receiving a disproportionate share of the benefits of the US and world economies. The news media controlled by big corporations is biased and not objective. They will not provide news or information which is not supportive of their goals and objectives: the maximization of profits.

The most difficult part of the solution is getting people to realize that something can be done, change is possible. Equally difficult is getting Christians to realize that only they can solve the problem for the problem is that Christian principles are not applied to business, economics and politics: do good and avoid evil, love your neighbor as yourself and respect the rights of all others. The President is not going to solve the problem because he is part of the problem - he does not represent the people, he serves the Wealthy Elite. The senators and representatives are not going to solve the problem because they also are part of the problem—they do not represent the people, they serve the Wealthy Elite. The news media is not going to solve the problem for they are part of the problem—they are controlled by the wealthy power elite. Who can solve the problem of a government and an economy which serves primarily the wealthiest people of the United States and which supports and facilitates the exploitation of the majority of citizens as well as the majority of people throughout the world? It is only the people who can help themselves. It is only the people who can correct the deficiencies in the economy. It is only the people who can make the government serve them the people.

The political and economic crisis within the United States will only be solved when a majority of the working class realize that those who are currently governing; the President, his Administration, Congress, the Supreme Court, Federal judges, state governors, state legislatures, state judges, county administrators, county judges, and local mayors and city councils; are not serving the majority but rather the small class of wealthy. Once the majority of the working class realizes that only they can fix the political and economic problems confronting the United States, then they must take the necessary actions to restore the appropriate order and balance to the political system and the economy which involves the application of Christian Economics.

In order for the majority of people to realize that only they can solve the current political and economic problems facing the United States, they must be re-educated with respect to economic principles and democratic principles. For too long the general public have been like sheep, told what to think. People need to start thinking for themselves, asking questions, and validating the answers that they are given by their teachers, by the media, by politicians and by the so-called experts.

The people must realize that they have the power to bring about the changes needed to make the government and the economy serve all the people and not just a select group of people.

People must become politically active. Voting alone will not bring about any change whatsoever because of the problems with the election laws, the election process, the campaign laws, and the campaign process; all of which are designed to support the current plutocratic political system. The people must exercise their rights of initiative, referendum, and recall.

Political activism must start at the state, county, municipal and local levels before it can effectively enter the Federal arena. And the first objective of the people's political activism needs to be the effective exercise of recall. In a democracy with a representative government, people elect those who should serve them and they have the right and the power to recall any official whom they no longer want to have represent them. Unfortunately, this right and power has been rarely exercised. Recall will make officials listen to the people.

Every official is subject to being recalled by a majority vote of the people. At the state and local level; the governor, the attorney general, state senators, state representatives, state Supreme Court judges, any judge whatsoever, mayors, aldermen, and city council members among others are all subject to recall. At the Federal level, the president, the vice-president, senators, representatives and judges, even Supreme Court judges are all subject to recall. It does not matter that this right is not expressed either in the US constitution or any state constitution; it is a natural right of the people.

Current elected officials will vehemently resist any attempts by voters to exercise their right of recall. Because recalls of elected officials have been rare, it will be necessary for the people to be persistent and adamant about exercising their right of recall until the practice of recall is accepted, utilized, and the appropriate policies and laws are in place that support and facilitate the process. And this will probably involve amending state and the Federal constitutions—difficult but absolutely necessary. The process for recall would start with a petition signed by one percent of the number of voters in the last election in a particular jurisdiction. Once the petition has been validated by the specific election office, the recall vote would be scheduled to take place within 90 days and appropriate notification would go out to voters. If the majority of those voting approve the recall, the position of the official being recalled would terminate once the vote count is confirmed.

The first obstacle to be overcome will be the claim that the right of recall is not explicitly stated in the US constitution or in most state constitutions. Over two hundred years ago, the Declaration of Independence of the United States was written. It stated the basis for which the People were able to establish a new government and the reasons why it was necessary to do so. The Laws of Nature give people the right (the natural right) to establish a society to safeguard their rights, promote their welfare, and facilitate the efficient and effective collaboration of all citizens for the common good of all citizens. The Natural Law allows the people to establish a nation consisting of a government, an economy, a set of laws, and an array of operating practices which will promote the goals of society and the good of all. The People have the natural right of recall and they can and should use it.

"We hold these truths to be self-evident, that all men are created equal, that they are endowed by their Creator with certain unalienable Rights, that among these are Life, Liberty and the pursuit of Happiness. — That to secure these rights, Governments are instituted among Men, deriving their just powers from the consent of the governed, — That whenever any Form of Government becomes destructive of these ends, it is the Right of the People to alter or to abolish it, and to institute new Government, laying its foundation on such principles and organizing its powers in such form, as to them shall seem most likely to affect their Safety and Happiness. Prudence, indeed, will dictate that Governments long established should not be changed for light and transient causes; and accordingly, all experience hath shown that mankind are more disposed to suffer, while evils are sufferable than to right themselves by abolishing the forms to which they are accustomed. But when a long train of abuses and usurpations, pursuing invariably the same Object evinces a design to reduce them under absolute Despotism, it is their right, it is their duty, to throw off such Government, and to provide new Guards for their future security. . .." Declaration of the United States

The United States has reached a point where its government does not represent the people. Its government does not promote the general welfare or the common good of the people. The government of the United States in all its facets; the executive branch, the legislative branch and the judicial branch represent a small and select group of individuals and seek and promote the welfare and interests of that select group ignoring and excluding the welfare and interests of the general population. In fact, the good of the people is sacrificed for the good of a select few. This select few consists of those who have accumulated great wealth and power and numerically represents a small percentage of the total population.

Besides the right of recall, people need to exercise their rights of initiative and referendum. An initiative is the natural right of the people in a democracy to introduce and propose legislation; a new law or a change to an existing law. Initiative is also considered the procedure itself in which the proposed new law or change in law is submitted to a vote for approval by the people. A referendum is the natural right of the people to enact new laws including amendments to the constitution (federal and state) by a vote. Initiative and referendum are natural rights and belong to the people by nature.

There are two problems with respect to the rights of initiative and referendum. First, most people do not realize that these rights exist and that it is their patriotic duty and responsibility to exercise them. People need to understand that participation in a democracy is a duty and not a privilege. Unfortunately, people have intentionally been misled by those in government and those in control of government that only a selected few have an active role in government. This is absolutely wrong. Dictators, kings, and totalitarian governments can only be prevented through the active participation of the people in government through initiatives, referendums, votes and recalls. The main problem with the current governments in the United States; federal, state, and local; is that those in government do not represent the people, do not serve the people and do not promote the good of the people.

The second problem with respect to the rights of initiative and referendum has to do with the intentional and active efforts on the part of those in government and those in control of government to deny and or limit the natural rights of the people to initiative, referendum and recall. State and local governments make the initiative process extremely, extremely difficult by requiring so large a number of petitions to be signed and verified that the time and expense make the process virtually impossible to pursue. In addition, many state governments that allow initiatives do not allow binding referendums. In other words, the voters can vote on an initiative but their votes do not really count. The state legislatures can ignore the will of the people, the people whom they are supposed to serve. Many state governments actually deny the rights of the people to initiative, referendum and recall and this is also true in the vast majority of local governments: county, city, etc. And the Federal government totally denies the rights of the people to initiative, referendum and recall.

Obviously, the Federal government, most state governments and most local governments do not believe in real democracy. Despite all the protestations of democracy by government officials, the United States is only a nominal democracy, not a real democracy. And this is the intention of those in control of the government. For those in government and those who control the government do not want the people to exercise their rights of initiative, referendum and recall. For if the people were to exercise their rights of initiative, referendum and recall, then governments would serve the people and not the select few which it now serves.

While there could be a quick solution to the economic crisis that the US is experiencing, there will not and cannot be one because those who are responsible for this crisis are in control of the government. Because of this, the solution will take a long time and will be very difficult.

The People

THE FIRST PART OF the solution lies in the people who need to be educated, motivated, and inspired to force those in government to represent the majority of the people and do what is necessary to bring about the common good and the maximum good for the majority of the people. The real solution to the current economic crisis lies in the people. It lies in the common people. It lies in the working people. It lies in men and women. It lies in the young, the middle-aged and the old—but especially the young.

First of all, people need to question and question critically! They must not blindly accept anything from the government, the news media or any authority whatsoever without questioning it. Blind obedience is a vice and not a virtue. The people have been deceived and misled by the government and the major media organizations for so long that they cannot be trusted. People have been lied to by virtually every president for the last fifty years. Because the President, his administration and Congress are controlled by Big Business to the point where they are pawns and puppets of Big Business, their agenda involves serving Big Business and doing what is in the best interests of Big Business with respect to both domestic and foreign affairs. People must not believe the president because he is the president. People must not believe senators and congressmen because of their position. People must not believe something just because it is on the news or in the newspapers. People must not believe a Republican because they are republicans. People must not believe a Democrat because they are a democrat. People must not believe the CEO because he or she is CEO. A soldier must not believe their commanding officer because of their position. People must not believe a person because of their authority, their looks, their popularity or their sincerity. People need to find alternate sources of news to keep informed. People need to question and question critically!

For too long the people, the majority of the people in the United States have left government and economics up to a very select minority. The people have trusted this select minority to represent them and make decisions in the best interests of all the people. That has been a serious mistake. The government and economy of the United States is and must be democratic. No matter what arguments some people might bring up trying to undermine this idea, the United States must be a democracy both in its government and in its economy. Unfortunately, the democratic nature of the United States government and economy has been only theoretical and that needs to change and change immediately.

The vast majority of people are totally frustrated and apathetic when it comes to the government and the economy. While the vast majority of people disagree with the government and the economy, they feel that there is nothing that they can do to change things. Most people think that voting is the only way that they can affect change in the government. And they are frustrated with the voting process itself because there are virtually no laws restricting the dominance of Big Money in the election process. In addition, people do not have choices when it comes to voting. Their only choices are millionaire candidate A or millionaire candidate B. Because of this many people do not even vote at all. In the elections of 2016 only 58 percent of eligible voters did vote. That means that over 95 million people did not vote. Most of these 95 million people have given up home in the United States government and the US economy.

The people of the United States must have hope. It is possible for the people to change things; to change the government and to change the economy. It will not be easy, but it is possible. And the hope for change lies in the people. It is up to the people, the 250 million people who represent the lower 80 percent of the economic distribution to make change happen.

The first thing that people need to do is to stop being indifferent to what is going on in government and in the economy and start to do something. People need to take action. And this means that virtually everyone needs to take action. Social activism by a few thousand people will not accomplish anything. Social activism by a few hundred thousand people will accomplish something. Social activism by a few million of people will accomplish more. Social activism by tens of millions of people will accomplish much more. But imagine what social activism by 100 million people could do? Imagine what social activism by 200 million people could do? There is nothing that cannot be accomplished in the United States by the activism of 200 million people.

The activism of 100 or 200 million people could force the President and Congress to serve the people instead of Big Business and Big Wealth. The activism of 100 or 200 million people could change the constitution, clearly expressing the right of the people to initiative, referendum and recall. The activism of 100 or 200 million people could put in place campaign finance reform, term limits, and very strict controls on lobbying. The activism of 100 or 200 million people could amend the constitution to require a popular vote to decide when to enter and when to end a war.

Imagine a demonstration of 2 million people descending peacefully on Washington demanding that the President and Congress balance the budget. Imagine demonstrations of millions of people in every major city within the United States peacefully demanding that the officers and boards of directors of corporations be held criminally responsible for physical and financial injuries caused by their corporations. Imagine mass demonstrations throughout the United States involving 150 million people demanding the immediate resignation of the president or they will remove him by a recall vote.

Imagine what would happen if the government attempted to stop the peaceful demonstrations of millions of people demonstrating in every major city by having the police breakup the demonstrations and the police men and police women refuse because they serve the people before they serve those in government. Imagine what would happen if the government attempted to stop the peaceful demonstrations of millions of people demonstrating in every major city by having the National Guard breakup the demonstrations and the National Guard soldiers refuse because they serve the people before they serve those in government. Imagine what would happen if the government attempted to stop the peaceful demonstrations of millions of people demonstrating in every major city by having the Army breakup the demonstrations and the soldiers refuse because they serve the people before they serve those in government. What would the government do? The government would do what the people wanted them to do.

The 250 to 280 million people of the United States who are not really represented by the government need to stop complaining and stop being indifferent. They need to take action to force the government to serve them. They need to take action to fix the economy. Activism is the solution, activism by the vast majority of Americans. What kind of activism is needed to succeed? Petitions are a form of activism which are only useful in unifying people. Petitions either written or electronic are ineffective unless they are backed up by the more appropriate forms of activism, boycotts and demonstrations. It should be clearly understood that petitions, boycotts, and demonstrations are not only natural rights but also expressions of true patriotism.

Boycotts are a very effective form of activism when engaged in by millions or tens of millions of people. People can and should boycott newspapers, television stations, banks, and businesses. Demonstrations are also a very effective form of activism. But demonstrations need to involve millions of people to be truly effective.

Students

PEOPLE NEED TO BE educated starting first with college students, high school students and junior high students. Unfortunately, education in the United States does not promote critical thinking, questioning, discussing, analyzing or philosophizing. Most school systems in the US employ indoctrination instead of education. Lectures are the dominant teaching technique and students are expected to memorize the content of the lectures and are tested on their understanding of the content. Questioning and open discussions on the subject matter is discouraged and even forbidden. While indoctrination may work (and that can be argued as well) in mathematics and the physical sciences, it is absolutely wrong with respect to the social sciences; history, sociology, economics, law, education, geography, political science, public administration, and psychology. The social sciences are totally different from mathematics and the physical sciences.

The teaching of the social sciences through indoctrination is biased towards the views and opinions of the teacher and or text book. There are differing views and interpretations of historical events, social events, social behaviors, economic dynamics and interactions, etc. It is wrong to teach only one view, the view of the teacher or textbook. It is wrong to prevent students from developing critical and analytical abilities in regards to how they view history, society, economics, politics, law, and psychology.

For example, the depiction of the characters of the early history of the 'New World" is that of virtuous individuals; adventurous and filled with the spirit of freedom. Little to nothing is said of the exploitation of the Native Americans by these individuals. Students are taught virtually every war, conflict and military action involving the United States was justifiable and the United States was always right and the 'good guy' and the opposing party was always wrong and the 'bad guy'. Students need to be allowed to hear all the facts, views and opinions on US history in order to make up their own minds and they should not be tested and graded on the biased views of their teachers and their textbooks. Students should actually be encouraged to question history, economics, politics, etc.

Students are indoctrinated in the Federal and state constitutions. They are not allowed to discuss the underlying principles of these constitutions. They are not taught about the constitutions of other countries and how they contain democratic principles that should be found in the US constitution. Students are not allowed to discuss human rights, all human rights including the right to initiative, the right to referendum, the right to recall, the right to a livelihood, etc.

Schools are not going to change on their own. Teachers are not going to change on their own. The students themselves will need to bring about change. Students need to educate themselves in the social sciences. Students need to question their teachers. Students need to refuse to be indoctrinated. Students need to form groups and take action to change the school system.

Students represent the hope for change in society in the future. Changes in government and changes in the economy will only come about through the education and activism of students. Young people today will be most affected by the problems in the economy. They are the hope for the future.

Unions

CAPITALISTS HATE UNIONS BECAUSE they want to dominate workers. Capitalists do not consider workers as partners or as equals but rather they see themselves as superior and workers as inferior. Capitalists think that they own workers, a notion that is contrary to Natural Law. Again, it must be clearly understood that Labor represents all those individuals involved in creating, designing, selling, making, assembling, delivering, repairing, instructing, nursing, entertaining, etc.—over 150 million people in the United States.

Capital currently has a dominant position over Labor facilitated by the government: executive, legislative and judicial; at every level; Federal, state, county, municipal, and local. This dominant position has led to an extremely unbalanced distribution of income and wealth between the minority capitalists and the majority workers. This imbalance has reached such a point that the ability of laborers (312 million people including their families) to buy the goods and services that they want and need for life, liberty and the pursuit of happiness is severely limited—limited to the point where the entire economy has been affected. The economy can only be fixed by correcting the imbalance in income and wealth between Capital and Labor; capitalists and workers. The only way to correct the economic imbalance between Capital and Labor is to balance the political power between Capital and Labor. And the only way to balance the political power between capitalists and workers is for workers to organize into unions and associations of workers who will be able to exert their combined and collaborative political power through voting, recalls, referendums, boycotts, protests and strikes.

The state of the economy is best measured in terms of the size of and the standard of living of the lowest level of the socio-economic spectrum. The lowest level of the socio-economic spectrum is most affected by poverty, homelessness, unemployment, low wages, and average life expectancy. The state of the economy cannot and must not be measured in terms of the top 1 percent of the socio-economic spectrum or the top 5 percent or the top 10 percent or even the top 20 percent.

If the bottom level of the socio-economic spectrum is small in relation to the rest of the socio-economic spectrum and the standard of living for the bottom level of the socio-economic spectrum is high (virtually no poverty, no homelessness, no unemployment, living wages, high life expectancy, etc.), then all of the higher levels of the socio-economic spectrum have to be realizing even higher standards of living and the economy is functioning well and meeting its goal of pursuing the highest standard of living for the majority of the population. On the other hand, if the top 1 percent or top 5 percent or top 10 percent or even the top 20 percent of the socio-economic spectrum is realizing an exceptionally high standard of living, nothing can be concluded about the standard of living for all the groups below.

Taking the size and standard of living of the bottom level of the socio-economic spectrum as the real indicator of the state of the economy and applying this criterion as the metric of the health of the US economy from a historical point of view, it will be seen that the US economy has been the strongest and healthiest when the number of and political power of the unions was the greatest.

Many of the benefits that US workers have today are due to the efforts of the unions of the last hundred years. Five-day work weeks, eight-hour work days, overtime pay, health insurance, vacations, pensions, etc. are among the many worker benefits that can be attributed directly to the efforts of unions. And the fact that worker benefits have eroded over the last forty years is an indication of the shrinking of unions and the loss of political power of the unions.

Unions and only unions can balance the extreme power wielded by Big Business, Big Finance, and Big Wealth. Unions and only unions can balance the extreme power of the capitalists. In any system there must be balance. The economic system of the United States, the economy, must be balanced. Capital and Labor are two components of the economy that must balance each other. Unions act as the check and balance to Capital for the good of the economy and the good of all the people.

There are approximately 150 million workers in the United States of which only 15 million are union workers, approximately 10% of the total work force. The number of unemployed workers is approximately equal to the number of union workers and the number of under-employed and those who have given up looking for work because they are in despair of finding a job are twice the number of union workers.

One of the main causes of the current economic crisis is the small number of unions and the lack of political power of unions. Capitalists have been waging an aggressive campaign against unions for the last forty years and their campaign has been successful. The capitalists have waged a 'smear' campaign against the unions depicting them as corrupt. The capitalists have worked to both break up unions and reduce the number of union members. And the capitalists have succeeded in transforming the United States from the most powerful and productive manufacturing nation in the world into a type of 3rd world country with respect to manufacturing.

The United States needs more unions, and more unionized workers within both the public and private sectors. Nurses and hospital workers need to be unionized. Retail workers need to be unionized. Grocery workers need to be unionized. Restaurant workers need to be unionized. Bank tellers and all those working in banks need to be unionized. Sales workers need to be unionized. Customer service representatives need to be unionized. Architects, engineers, planners, cab drivers, truck drivers, warehouse workers, policemen, firemen, teachers, lawyers, doctors, pharmacists and every worker in the United States needs to be part of a union so that collectively and collaboratively all workers can offset the extreme views and policies of the capitalists, restore economic balance between Capital and Labor, and fix the problems in both the government and in the economy that is the result of the lack of balance between Capital and Labor. The restoration of a healthy economy and the future of the United States as a nation are dependent on politically strong and effective unions that can represent the majority of the people, the 150 million workers and their families.

The 150 million workers in the United States as individuals are virtually powerless. However, 150 million workers as a collective group working together for the common cause of all workers; fair wages, living wages, stable work, health insurance, pensions, safe working environments, and working hours balanced with time off, are powerful enough to succeed even in the current political and economic environment which is grossly slanted in favor of the capitalists.

Imagine fifty percent of all US workers joined together as unions of workers. That would be 75 million people which together with their families would represent a voting block of 125 to 150 million people.

Every president, every senator, every congressman, every governor, every judge, every mayor and every other elected official would be a representative of Labor, the majority of the people. Laws would favor Labor, the majority of the people. Treaties would favor Labor, the majority of the people.

All workers must realize that it is their responsibility to fix the economy, to correct the imbalance in the economy caused by exaggerated capitalism, to offset the extreme political and economic power of Capital, and to restore balance to both government and the economy. All workers must realize that the solution is to form unions and associations with their fellow workers and to collectively and collaboratively exert the necessary political influence to make the government, all of branches and levels of government, represent and serve the workers, the majority of the population, and not just the minority capitalists. It is in fact the patriotic duty of every worker to serve their country by doing what is necessary to promote the common good of all the people of the United States.

For too long workers have been used and financially abused by Capital, their rights ignored and their needs unmet. Workers must realize that in order to achieve and maintain equality with capitalists, they must join together to exercise, defend and protect their human, political and economic rights. Unions are the solution. Workers must get off their couches, turn off their TV sets and take an active role in turning this country around. The President and his administration will not solve the problem with the economy ; they are puppets of Big Business, Big Finance and Big Wealth. Congress will not solve the problem with the economy; they are puppets of Big Business, Big Finance and Big Wealth. The Courts will not solve the problem with the economy; they are puppets of Big Business, Big Finance and Big Wealth. Governors will not solve the problem with the economy; they are puppets of Big Business, Big Finance and Big Wealth. Mayors will not solve the problem with the economy; they are puppets of Big Business, Big Finance and Big Wealth.

Workers and only unionized workers can solve the problems affecting the economy. It is up to them. No one else is going to do it for them. They must do it themselves.

A New Political Party

UNFORTUNATELY, THERE IS NOT much difference between the Republican and Democratic parties. The majority of members of both parties have similar political and economic philosophical views and most members have become puppets of Big Business, Big Finance and Big Wealth through their lobbies. The vast majority of the members of both major political parties do not represent the people; instead they represent the special interests of Business, Finance and Wealth of all sizes. Because the vast majority of republicans and democrats rely on the campaign contributions of Business, Finance and Wealth to get into office and stay in office; they are indebted and obligated to their benefactors. This applies to all levels of government; Federal, state, county, and local; as well as all branches of government including the judiciary.

Any attempts to change the current political structure and system where government is run by Big Business, Big Finance and Big Wealth through their influence and control of government are futile. There is almost no hope of changing the current system as long as Business, Finance and Wealth can influence and control government through campaign contributions. And there is almost no hope of changing the Republican Party and a large part of the Democratic Party which condones, supports and facilitates the control of government by Business, Finance and Wealth. Is it hopeless? Is there no chance to change the current political system and rectify the current economic crisis ? If there is virtually no hope of changing the current Republican and Democratic parties, then the only solution is to form a new national political party which is not controlled and cannot be controlled by Business, Finance and Wealth.

Another aspect of the solution to the political and economic crisis that the United States is facing is to create a new political party - a new political party that will rival the Democratic and Republican parties and will surpass these parties in size, organization, depth and commitment

- a new political party that is neither controlled nor influenced by Big Business, Big Finance and Big Wealth and their lobbies - a new political party consisting of workers and students, the backbone of the nation and the future of the nation. This new political party would bring about real democracy within the United States and not the nominal democracy which exists today. This new political party would replace the current government of the rich, by the rich and for the rich with a government of the people, by the people and for people. This new political party would represent the working class, students, and all those social groups who have been excluded from the American political system because they lack wealth.

The Republican Party is dominated by Big Business, Big Finance and Big Wealth and espouses the philosophy of extreme and pure capitalism. Because of this, it is controlled by special interest groups at all levels: national, state, county and local. It is clearly the party of billionaires, multi-millionaires and millionaires and as such only represents the goals of the upper 1 percent of the population. Over the past year, the Republican Party has become almost militant in their tactics and vehemently resists any attempts to restore any kind of balance to the US economy.

While the Democratic Party is nominally the party of the people, many democrats are now greatly influenced by Big Business, Big Finance and Big Wealth through their lobbies. Sometimes referred to as 'corporate' democrats, these party members are very much like Republicans and they promote and support the same upper-class objectives and policies as the Republicans. Unfortunately, both Bill Clinton and Barack Obama were corporate democrats and their administrations, policies, and goals supported most corporate goals and objectives.

There have been many attempts to create new political parties that rival the Democratic and Republican parties, but all have failed. The Republican and Democratic parties are well organized, well-funded and will resist any attempt by any new party to encroach on their dominant national, state and local positions.

In the United States a little over 55 percent of the voting age population vote in election years when the president is being elected. In election years when the president is not being elected, less than 40 percent of the voting age population vote. In general, about 30 percent of the voting age population does not even register to vote. The majority of people who either do not register to vote or who do not vote even though they are registered to vote have lost faith in the system. These people feel that the process of voting does not produce any real change. They feel that there is virtually no difference between the candidates and that no matter who is elected there will be no effective change in the American political system; a system that represents the rich and exploits the working class—the majority of the US population.

The United States is not a real democracy when less than 50 percent of the people eligible to vote do vote. Despite all the rhetoric by politicians, public officials and teachers; the United States of America is not a democracy. That does not mean that it should not be a democracy for the essence of the US constitution is embodied in the words "We the People." These words imply that the United States as a nation, the basis for the constitution and the basis for the government of the United States are the people of the United States. While the United States is theoretically a democracy, from a practical point of view it is not a democracy.

In order for the United States to fix its economic problems, it needs to fix its political problems. And in order to fix its political problems, the United States needs to become a true working democracy where the government represents the people, the majority of the people, and executes the will of the people, the majority of the people. The people of the United States cannot fix the economic and political problems affecting this nation without becoming the dominant political force. Unfortunately, the dominant political force in the US today is the top 1 percent of the population who exert almost absolute control over every facet of the United States economy and government, virtually all branches and levels.

The people of the United States will only be able to exert the necessary political power to fix the problems underlying the current economic and governmental crises by establishing a new political party. This party needs to be truly the party of the people, the majority of the people. The charter and bylaws of this party need to specifically prevent any attempts to allow it to be infiltrated and controlled by Big Business, Big Finance and Big Wealth. There cannot be any contributions to this party from business, lobbies, foreign governments or political action committees affiliated with a business or foreign government.

This new political party must be comprised of the people, working people and students. It must be comprised of teachers, nurses, plumbers, carpenters, electricians, construction workers, laborers, retail workers, restaurant workers, farm workers, engineers, architects, entertainers, college students, high school students, truck drivers, taxi drivers, doctors, and warehouse workers—every category of worker and student needs to be part of this new party. This new party needs to be comprised of every ethnic group, every age group, and every group of any background whatsoever. This new party needs to be comprised of people from all economic groups but especially the middle class and the lower class. This new party needs to be truly the party of the people and it needs to be a grassroots organization.

This new political party needs to engage in both informal and formal education programs in order train its members to run for political office. It must train its members in democratic and Natural Law economic principals. It must train its members to be able to debate, to campaign, and to organize. It must train its members in the principles of management, accounting and finance so that they can become effective members of government. This new party must have regular meetings at every level to discuss actions and strategies.

This new political party needs to support its members to run for every political office at every level of government. This party needs to re-constitute the representative branches of all levels of government (national, state, county and local) with individuals so that the diversity and demographics of the nation are statistically reflected.

If fifty percent of the population is women, then fifty percent of the senators and representatives (national, state, county and local) need to be women. Fifty percent of judges need to be women. Fifty percent of all those in government at any and every level need to be women.

If eight percent of the population is between 18 and 24 years of age, then eight percent of the senators and representatives (national, state, county and local) need to be between 18 and 24 years of age. Eight percent of judges need to be between 18 and 24 years of age. Eight percent of all those in government at any and every level need to be between 18 and 24 years of age.

If thirteen percent of the population is Latino, then thirteen percent of the senators and representatives (national, state, county and local) need to be Latino. Thirteen percent of judges need to be Latino. Thirteen percent of all those in government at any and every level need to be Latino.

If twelve percent of the population is Black, then twelve percent of the senators and representatives (national, state, county and local) need to be Black. Twelve percent of judges need to be Black. Twelve percent of all those in government at any and every level need to be Black.

If fifty percent of the population has an income less than $32,000 a year, then fifty percent of the senators and representatives (national, state, county and local) need to be elected from those whose income is less than $32,000 a year. Fifty percent of judges need to be elected or appointed from those whose income is less than $32,000 a year. Fifty percent of all those in government at any and every level need to be selected from those whose income is less than $32,000 a year.

Only when the diversity and demographics of the nation are statistically reflected in the presidency, the administration, the Senate, the House of Representatives, the federal court system, the Supreme Court, state governments, county governments and local governments will the United States become a true government of the people, by the people and for the people and only then will the government represent the people and serve their best interests.

Organized Religions

THE CAUSE OF THE present economic crisis is in fact a moral crisis. Uncontrolled greed, which has been masked by the business philosophy that "it is neither right nor wrong, it is just business," is the direct and only cause of the current economic crisis. Foreclosures, layoffs, usurious finance charges and terms, and unjustly high prices are the direct result of a greed which totally ignores the rights of others.

People have no choice; they have to eat and they have to heat their homes. Two thirds of US families live from paycheck to paycheck. That means that they do not have any money left over after paying all their expenses. Their expenses either equal or exceed their income. And they do not have savings, stocks, bonds, or any other type of investment. There is no just reason why healthcare, education and prescription drug prices should so drastically have risen in the last ten years. The only reason why they have risen so high is greed.

When the government borrows money, is there any collateral? When corporations borrow money, is there any collateral? When banks borrow money, is there any collateral? No! No! No! Then why is there collateral on home loans? For most people who fall behind on their mortgage payments, it is only a temporary situation. Is it necessary to foreclose on a family's home, repossess it, and displace the family from their home? Certainly not! Why can't banks accept partial mortgage payments until the family's financial situation improves? The answer is greed of course.

And yet, the people who are responsible for the economically crippling prices, the unjust interest rates, the unnecessary layoffs, and the dishonest foreclosures do not think that they are doing anything wrong. People in business have embraced the philosophy expressed in the phrase "it is neither right nor wrong, it is just business." Of course, every conscious deliberate action is either morally right or morally wrong. This amoral philosophy permeating the business world allows people to act without conscience, without guilt, and with total disregard for the rights of others. But whose duty and responsibility is it to teach, instruct and admonish on moral matters?

All the major religious organizations, Catholics, non-Catholic Christians, Orthodox Christians, Jews, Muslims, Hindus, Buddhists, etc.; exist to provide moral leadership, moral direction and moral guidance to their members and society in general. Their common position is that all deliberate human actions are either good (moral) or bad (immoral). The primary purpose of the executives, directors, and managers of these religious organizations (pope, ayatollahs, cardinals, bishops, priests, ministers, rabbis, sheiks, etc.) is to instruct members and society in general concerning moral matters. Unfortunately, virtually every major religious organization has abandoned their responsibility of moral leadership and has focused almost exclusively on culture and rituals.

Virtually every religion believes in Heaven, obviously something that they have in common. Unfortunately, they all hold that membership in their religion is a requirement to gain Heaven—a major point of diversity and disharmony. Catholics hold, in general, that you have to be Catholic to go to Heaven. Protestants hold that you have to believe in Jesus Christ to go to Heaven. Judaism holds that you have to be Jewish to go to Heaven. Muslims, Hindus, and Buddhists (and every other organized religion) hold pretty much the same. What makes things worse is that not only is membership in a particular organized religion a requirement for Heaven but also is the practice of rituals and rules unique to the various religions. You cannot eat pork, you have to say these prayers, you have to attend these ceremonies; these and countless other practices and mechanics are specified by organized religions. Membership and rituals seem to be all that is required for a person to go to Heaven.

It seems as though all organized religions have lost the understanding of what is truly important in life and what is absolutely necessary to go to Heaven and that is living a good life. Living a good life transcends all of the practices, beliefs, and rituals of all organized religions. It's really so simple, yet seemingly beyond the grasp of the leadership of organized religions: a person needs to live a good life. Religious leadership will pay lip-service to the "good life" principle, yet in practice they ignore it.

The religious leaders of all organized religions (pope, ayatollahs, cardinals, bishops, priests, ministers, rabbis, sheiks, etc.) are very much to blame for the economic crisis that the United States and the entire world are in. Religious leaders must fulfill their duty to be the moral leaders of society, for there is no one else who will state that greed is wrong and that every greed-based business practice, no matter what it is called, is wrong. Religious leaders have been silent for too long and have not and are not fulfilling their duty. More than a hundred million people in the United States are suffering economic hardship, and the leaders of the religious organizations say and do nothing to stop this crisis.

Is it too hard to state that interest rates of 35 to 400 percent (pay-day loan rates can exceed 400 percent) are morally wrong? Is it too hard to say that foreclosures and repossessions in the context of a family who is able to make significant partial payments are wrong? Is it too hard to say that layoffs which occur because the CEO wants to receive his or her bonus or the corporation wants to increase profits are wrong? Is it too hard to state that every conscious, deliberate action, even business actions and activities, are morally right or morally wrong? Is it too hard to say that price increases which are 5 or more times higher than the average increase in family income are wrong?

The pope, ayatollahs, cardinals, bishops, priests, ministers, rabbis, sheiks, etc. need to speak out and address this uncontrollable greed which is crippling the country and the world. They need to draft comprehensive and detailed statements which address the moral causes of this economic breakdown. These statements need to be read at all churches, synagogues, mosques, and religious high schools and colleges. These religious leaders need to organize series of conferences/discussions/debates in which the present economic catastrophe is seen as the failure of following basic, moral principles. People need to be taught that there are other principles on price, such as the just price principle and the balanced economy price principle, besides the principle of "whatever the market will bear." People need to be taught about the living wage principle. People need to be taught about the proper role of the government. People need to be taught about the equality of capital and labor, and the equality of all people without regard to income, nationality, gender, age, education, etc.

Again, this terrible economic situation is the direct result of a moral breakdown in the business and governmental spheres of society. And the pope, ayatollahs, cardinals, bishops, priests, ministers, rabbis, sheiks, etc. must address the underlying moral causes of this economic crisis. They must take action. It is their duty. It is their moral obligation.

The Military, the CIA, the FBI and the Police

MOST PEOPLE ENTER THE military, the CIA, the FBI, and state and local police departments to serve their country. Service of one's country is an expression of patriotism. Once a person has joined the military, the CIA, the FBI or a police department they do not comprehend their acts within the context of the principles of true patriotism, social justice or Christianity. They assume that anything done by and for the military, the CIA, the FBI, or the police is patriotic and moral. They do not consider that the actions pursued by their leaders are not to benefit the majority of Americans but rather the wealthy minority.

Who arrested and killed Jesus Christ? Was it the Jewish people? Was it the Roman people? Jesus was arrested by the Temple guards, the police controlled by the Jewish leaders. Jesus was tortured and executed by Roman soldiers. Obviously, the temple police could have refused to arrest Jesus based on their own moral judgment that Jesus did nothing wrong. Obviously, the Roman soldiers could have refused to torture Jesus based on their own moral judgment that Jesus did nothing wrong, was falsely accused, was a political pawn and certainly did not merit torture. And obviously the Roman soldiers could have refused to execute Jesus based on their own moral judgment that Jesus was an innocent man. It is stated in the Bible that when the Centurion pierced the side of Jesus to make sure that he was dead, he said that surely Jesus was a righteous man. Since the Centurion had been involved with Jesus for many hours up to this point, he must have come to the conclusion that Jesus did not deserve to be executed much earlier than this. And if the Centurion had realized that Jesus was innocent and not deserving of death, why did the Centurion proceed to execute him? The Temple police and the Roman soldiers acted based on the false principles of blind obedience and false patriotism.

The military, the CIA, the FBI and police departments operate on the principle of blind obedience. Subordinates are required to blindly obey the orders of their superiors. In the case of refusal, a soldier could be immediately put to death. There is a hierarchy to blind obedience that corresponds to the organizational hierarchy of the branch of service. A police officer ultimately is subordinate to the mayor or the state governor. Soldiers and members of the CIA and FBI are subordinate to the President, who is referred to as the commander in chief. While this is not a bad thing, it is true that mayors, governors and presidents are politicians who often have political agendas. That is, their actions are not always about what is best for the city, the state or the nation, but rather about their career, political power, and personal benefit.

The good of society is dependent on individuals within the military, the CIA, the FBI and police departments doing what is right and not blindly following the orders of their superiors. Service of one's country is serving the people of one's country and doing what is best for the people of one's country. It happens often, especially within matters of foreign affairs, that the government is not acting in the best interests of the people of the country but rather in the interests of the wealthiest minority of the people and the corporations which they control.

What is patriotism? Is patriotism blindly following the orders of a superior: the commander-in-chief, a general, a captain, a police-chief, etc.? Does patriotism hold that your country is superior to every other country and that the rights and privileges of your citizens do not apply to the citizens of any other country? Is every action performed out of patriotism morally correct? "I was only following orders"; "I was only doing my job": are these legitimate excuses for any type of behavior? Are there any limits to or constraints on patriotism? Are acts which are contrary to Christian morals patriotic?

If a superior orders a subordinate to assassinate a person in another country, is the order a sufficient reason to make such an action morally correct? If a superior orders a subordinate to torture a person (even a citizen in one's own country), is the order a sufficient reason to make such an action morally correct? If a superior orders a subordinate to bomb a city knowing that there is the certainty that civilians will be killed, is the order a sufficient reason to make such an action morally correct? If a superior orders a subordinate to forcefully enter a persons' house, is the order a sufficient reason to make such an action morally correct? If a superior orders a subordinate to infiltrate a citizen's group organized to protest the war or the economy, is the order a sufficient reason to make such an action morally correct? If a superior orders a subordinate to forcefully break up a peaceful demonstration, is the order a sufficient reason to make such an action morally correct? The answer to each of these questions is 'no'. An order does not justify the morality of the act that is ordered. "I was only following orders," "I did what I was told to do," "I did what I had to do," do not excuse an individual from doing what is wrong. For a person's first mandate is to do good and avoid evil.

True patriotism means love, respect, support, and protection of those around you. The last part of the definition needs to be discussed for it is the source of the most problems. First, patriotism extends to the family - family takes care of family. First the immediate family and then the extended family (grandparents, aunts, uncles, cousins), patriotism moves individuals to mutually love, respect, support, and protect one another. This circle of patriotism grows from extended family to community to society. In its widest context, patriotism extends to the entire human family. Patriotism is synonymous with brotherhood.

True patriotism does not consist in blind obedience. Imagine how different history would be if there was no blind obedience. How many wars could have been avoided? How many deaths prevented? How much destruction avoided?

What does blind obedience and patriotism have to do with the solution to the economic crisis ? The economic crisis is not going to be solved by the current president, Congress, the Federal Reserve Board, banks or any other organization. The economic crisis can only be solved by the people; the social activism of the people through demonstrations, boycotts, initiatives, referendums and recalls. Currently, the government is virtually a puppet of Big Business and Big Wealth. Because of this, the government, Big Business and Big Wealth will resist any attempt by the people to exercise their natural rights to correct the problems within the economy. And the government will attempt to use the military, the FBI, the CIA, and police officers to do so. Police officers, the military, members of the FBI, and members of the CIA must not blindly obey orders by their superiors that deny the exercise of the people's rights to demonstrate, to boycott, to initiate, vote on referendums and vote on recalls. Individuals within the military, the CIA, the FBI and police departments need to act based on true patriotism (love of and service to family, community and the people of the United States) and ignore blind obedience to the commands of superiors when those commands are counter to true patriotism and the Natural Law.

Blind Obedience and Blind Patriotism—Virtues or Vices?

MAO TSE-TUNG, JOSEPH STALIN, and Adolph Hitler are perhaps the most infamous individuals in history, responsible for the deaths of millions of people. And yet, how many people did Mao Tse-Tung, Joseph Stalin, or Adolph Hitler personally and directly kill? Perhaps none! They acted through their subordinates. Their subordinates were directly responsible for killing these millions of people. And there were obviously thousands of subordinates. These subordinates: soldiers, security/prison guards and police officers; followed the orders and carried out the directives of their superiors. It is amazing to consider how a superior can order a subordinate to commit an atrocity and the subordinate obeys without question. Why is it that a superior can give a command to kill innocent people, even women and children (non-combatants), and no one says "no, this is absolutely wrong and I am not going to do it"? How is it that a command can be given to shoot an unarmed person in the back and the soldier or police officer does exactly that without question? When a person is ordered to bomb a city of non-combatants, knowing full-well that he will be killing women, children and the elderly, why does that person not stop and ask himself, "Is this right or is this wrong?" In the case of Mao Tse-Tung, Joseph Stalin, and Adolph Hitler, they gave orders to kill millions of people and tens of thousands of people executed their orders without question. Imagine what would happen if their subordinates refused. Of course, the first subordinates who refused their orders would probably have been put to death but what if more and more subordinates refused. Obviously, there would have come a point where Mao Tse-Tung, Joseph Stalin, and Adolph Hitler could not have committed their atrocities because their subordinates refused to obey their orders and millions and millions of lives would have been saved.

The subordinates of Mao Tse-tung, Joseph Stalin, and Adolph Hitler obviously acted through 'blind obedience' when they followed the orders of their superiors; an act where one focuses entirely and exclusively on what is commanded ignoring any other consideration. They did not question their orders—they blindly followed them. Without any real understanding of why people should be killed; these soldiers, guards and police officers blindly proceeded to follow the order to torture and kill. Their obedience was truly blind. However, was their obedience a good thing or a bad thing? Were they acting morally? Were they being truly patriotic? Is blind obedience a virtue or a vice? What is the relationship between blind obedience and true patriotism? Should it apply to soldiers, policemen, and government officials? Should it apply to citizens? Are there more abuses of blind obedience than good uses? Can abuses be prevented?

Blind obedience has been practiced since the beginning of history. It usually applied to situations involving the king, where the king's orders were supposed to be obeyed without question. Such orders passed through a hierarchy. The king's orders first passed through the so-called nobles, from the nobles through the various ranks of soldiers, all the way to the end person who was to execute the orders. While every level of this process was blind or ignorant of the reason(s) underlying the order, the final person on this chain of command was most ignorant and this was done intentionally. In fact, the whole scheme of blind obedience was a construct to provide the king with almost unlimited power. Any attempt to disobey the king's orders was dealt with extreme punishment, oftentimes death. No one dared question the king or disobey his commands through fear of punishment.

Most types of governments and many associations and societies hold, promote and practice some type of "blind obedience." In addition, many religious orders within the Catholic Church have practiced forms of blind obedience. Most recently the blind obedience of Opus Dei has gotten much publicity because of alleged abuses.

A human being is by nature rational, having intellect and free will. Also, because of its nature, a human being naturally seeks what is perceived to be good. This process involves first conceiving something as good and therefore desirable within the intellect, and then the will is moved by choice towards that good. The target or goal must be known or conceived to be good in order for the will to be moved towards that good. It is clear that the act of the will follows the act of the intellect. The intellect perceives something as good, and the will desires it.

In the case of blind obedience, the natural process between the intellect and will is broken. While on one hand, the will of the superior is considered by the intellect to be good, the intellect is often confronted with many inconsistencies between what it perceives is good and the actions ordered by the superior. In other words, the individual perceives some act as bad while at the same time it is ordered by the superior and obeying the order of the superior is considered to be good. Hence, there is a conflict.

While there are times when there is no conflict between what the superior orders and what is perceived as good, very often there is a conflict. This is especially true when the superior makes no attempt to justify the action ordered and hence allow the subordinate to form the perception that the act ordered is good on its own merit and not because it is ordered by the superior. The will naturally follows the intellect or works in conjunction with the intellect. It is abhorrent to nature, that is, to the natural order of things (the Natural Law), for the will to move an individual to do something that it perceives is wrong. Yet, with blind obedience, it happens often.

Blind obedience, in fact, requires the subordinate to totally subject his/her will to the superior and suspend the act of the intellect which evaluates whether an action is right or wrong. In the past within the Catholic Church, within most kingdoms and within most societies in general, the will of the superior was taught to be the will of God. This is certainly an exaggeration and a deceit obviously developed and promoted by those in authority. And such views especially within the context of civil authority generally lead to abuse.

If an immoral order is not to be obeyed, it is implied that the order must be evaluated and judged within the context of a moral system. In other words, every order must be evaluated and judged to be right or wrong, at least from a moral point of view. This implies that obedience cannot be blind.

People, all people, must reject blind obedience and always seek to do good, avoid/overcome evil (the absence of good), love all others and treat all others in words and actions with respect and dignity.

Power Tends to Corrupt

Power tends to corrupt at every level: what does that mean? A person in a position of authority over others is tempted to think that he or she is better than those over whom this authority is exercised. The teacher is tempted to think, "I am better than my students." The policeman is tempted to think, "I am better than these citizens." The boss is tempted to think, "I am better than those people that report to me." The judge is tempted to think, "I am better than those I am to judge." The mayor, the governor, the congressman, and the president are all tempted to think, "I am better than all those over whom I have authority." These thoughts come because of the prestige surrounding such positions. And if these thoughts are not overcome with the truth that the person in authority is meant to serve others and is subordinate to the needs of all those to be served, then the person with authority (teacher, policeman, boss, judge, mayor, governor, congressman, president) will first begin to think that they are better than others and then begin to act as though they are better than others. Unfortunately, most people with authority succumb to this temptation and consider themselves superior to those over whom they have authority. This is true historically and is still true today.

As the person in authority begins to think that they are better than their subordinates, they also begin to reverse the relationship between themselves and their subordinates. That is, they begin to think that their subordinates should serve them rather than they serve their subordinates. This, unfortunately, happens most often and leads to unjust effects. In fact, in the vast majority of cases, the superior believes that his or her subordinates are meant to serve him or her instead of him or her serving their subordinates.

Because of this, it is necessary that there be strict limits on the period of time that a person has authority for. It is absurd for a person to have authority for life. Whether that person is king, president, Supreme Court justice, or whatever; their term of rule must be strictly limited. In fact, every person in any capacity of authority must be limited in terms of the duration of their power over others. Congressmen, senators, governors, mayors, judges, police chiefs, police officers, CEO's, superintendents, teachers, etc. should have very limited terms of power.

The Role of the Leader

FROM A NATURAL LAW point of view, an organization is a group of people, bonded together by a common set of goals that collaborates with each other to achieve those goals. The common set of goals is referred to as the common good because the good of all those comprising the organization is what is most important. The common good does not preclude nor exclude the good of the individual, but rather assumes and supports it. However, if the good of one individual is so great that it prevents the common or collective good of all others, then it is out of order and needs to be subordinated to the common good.

In very small organizations, it may not be necessary for there to be one individual who functions as a leader since it is possible for everyone in the group to identify the strategies and tactics necessary to achieve the common goals. As organizations increase in size, it usually makes sense to have one individual dedicated to the task of promoting the goals of the organization. According to the Natural Law, this individual is selected from and elected by the majority of the organization. Again, depending on the size of the organization, it is also possible and even beneficial to have a small group function in the overall leadership role. In such a case, there is no one individual who has total responsibility and authority but instead total responsibility and authority resides collectively in the hands of a group which is again selected from and elected by the majority.

As organizations grow in size, it becomes necessary for the sake of effectiveness and efficiency that the leadership takes on a certain structure. As in the case of the United States which is similar to other countries, there are two separate branches: the executive and the legislative. Because of the carry-over from the days of monarchies, the executive branch of leadership is vested in one individual. However, there is no reason why there should not be more than one president, that is, there could be co-presidents. In fact, there are many advantages to there being three individuals (three co-presidents) constituting the executive branch. With three individuals, consensus must be reached among the three in order for a decision to be made. Having three individuals tends to prevent the problems associated with the limitations resulting from one individual vested with extensive or extreme power and authority.

The authority to rule is granted by the people to those selected and elected to rule for a specified, limited period of time. Because the authority of those within a leadership position comes from the people, it can be taken away by the people at any time.

Leaders; the president, congress people, CEO's, vice-presidents, managers, teachers, generals, etc.; must understand their true role according to the Natural Law is to serve the people, all the people, that they oversee. Serving the people means acting in the best interests of the people and promoting both the common good and the individual goods of each and every person.

Musicians, Artists and Celebrities

AN EXTREMELY GREAT VEHICLE for social change is music. Because songs are heard by tens of millions of people and heard dozens of times, lyrics can be used to instruct and inspire people. Recall the many songs in the 1960's that inspired people to take a stand against the war in Vietnam.

Musicians have a great opportunity and a corresponding responsibility to write songs whose lyrics have social themes. Imagine the power and effect that a song on unemployment, foreclosures and repossessions would have. Songs are needed that highlight the greed of banks and multinational corporations. Songs are needed to motivate people to become active in politics, to demonstrate, to boycott, to form initiatives and to start recalls. Musicians are needed to fight the good fight and help restore the economy and to bring tens of millions of people out of a financially desperate situation. Musicians are part of the solution to the problems in the economy and represent the greatest communications medium that exists. Music lyrics can have greater credibility than textbooks, sermons and political speeches. What will it take to get musicians to do their part to help restore the US economy?

In a similar manner artists and celebrities can use their notoriety and artistic expressions to comment on social issues. Art and drama must have communication value and the message that is conveyed must be socially beneficial and productive.

Christian Family Economics

BANKS, CREDIT CARD COMPANIES, home loan companies and finance companies have a stranglehold on the majority of the population. Well over a hundred million people have become financially enslaved by these ruthless corporations. These corporations have become a cancer sucking the financial life out of these well over a hundred million people. These people are enslaved by excessively high interest rates, late fees, and over-limit fees that consume so much of their income that they have virtually no discretionary income. What can people do to overcome this cruel slave-like situation?

It will take a concerted, national, majority effort to force banks and finance companies to do business fairly, justly and patriotically. The idea is to hit banks and finance companies where it hurts; in their revenues and profits. Except for checking accounts and debit card accounts, people must stop doing business with banks and finance companies. People (all people) must avoid all types and kinds of loans from banks and finance companies as much as possible. People must avoid credit cards, auto loans, personal loans and if possible even home loans. The principle that must be followed to avoid loans from banks and financial institutions is 'family takes care of family'. Families can and should loan money to each other. Families can draw up contracts similar to mortgage contracts, auto liens, etc. but with fair interest rates and terms. Most extended families have a group of mature members who have paid off their homes and have money invested in money markets, CD's, etc. They don't earn much from these investments. If a younger member of the extended family needs to borrow money for a car, for furniture, for appliances, for college, for a home improvement, or even for a home; the older member can loan them the money at an interest rate 2 percentage points higher than what they are receiving on their investments. It ends up being a win-win arrangement; the borrower benefits and the lender benefits. The lender who is getting less than a 2 percent return on their money will be earning 4 percent. The borrower will be paying 4 percent interest instead of 7 percent or more for an auto loan, 12 percent or more for a loan to buy furniture or appliances, and 6 percent or more to buy a home.

Small credit unions can also be used to avoid the financial traps of big banking as long as they remain small, very small so that they can remain true to the social, equitable and cooperative principles which formed the basis for the first credit unions.

What would happen to the banks and financial corporations, if millions of people or even tens of millions of people took their money out of their systems and used it in family banking or in credit unions? What would happen to the banks and financial corporations, if millions of people or tens of millions of people did not borrow money from them? What would happen to the banks and financial corporations, if millions of people or tens of millions of people paid off their loans and there was no steady stream of high interest revenue, late-fee revenue, and over-limit revenue?

Would banks collapse and go out of business? Would the credit card companies collapse and go out of business? Would finance companies collapse and go out of business? Would home loan companies collapse and go out of business? Certainly not! Banks, credit companies, finance companies and home loan companies would raise the raise the interest rates that they pay people who deposit money with them and lower interest rates on auto loans, credit cards, and home loans. They would also get rid of late fees and over-limit fees. And they would still make money.

The only companies that could go out of business if tens of millions of people engaged in family banking and credit union banking would be payday loan companies, personal finance companies, auto title loan companies and pawn shops. And they should go out of business. The financial abuses perpetrated by payday loan companies, personal finance companies, auto-title loan companies and pawn shops are crimes against humanity and the fact that these abuses are legal shows the extreme bias of the Federal, state, and local governments in favor of businesses and the wealthy and against the common people.

More people need to start their own business. More family farms are needed that serve the local area and region. More co-ops need to be formed for buying food. People should buy from small, local, and independent businesses. People should create backyard gardens. They should walk more and drive less. Bike more and drive less. Take mass transportation and avoid owning a car. Young people should not be so eager to move out on their own and get their own apartment. They should live with their parents, save money for a significant down payment and buy a home or a townhouse when they move out.

People should avoid renting a home or an apartment. People should not lease cars, furniture or appliances. People should buy used furniture and appliances and purchase from other individuals through the newspapers. People should shop at resale stores. Don't throw things away, give them away. Share your excess with those who have less to none. Use less air conditioning in the summer and less heat in the winter. Avoid, avoid fast foods; cook at home—it is much, much cheaper and much, much healthier. By preparing a lunch at home and bringing it to work or school, a person can save over $1200 a year. Avoid, avoid buying coffee at coffee shops.

Avoid attending professional sporting events. Don't go to a baseball game, play baseball. Don't go to a soccer game, play soccer. Don't go to a football game, play football. Don't go to a basketball game, play basketball. Don't go to a concert, play music. Forest preserves are free; beaches are free; bicycling is free. Don't go to movie theaters, get movies from the library.

The working class has to regain financial stability and it can only do so by avoiding Big Business and Big Finance as much as possible. People have to change their lifestyles and don't give money away to businesses which only care about themselves. If people want to give money away, they should donate to the poor and needy—not to businesses.

The List of Critical Actions

ALL ENERGY MUST BE declared national resources subject to oversight and management by the Federal government. Energy consists of electricity, crude oil, gasoline, diesel fuel, heating oil, jet fuel, natural gas, propane, butane, bio-diesel, ethanol, nuclear-based and others. There should be an immediate limit placed on all changes to prices of energy—energy prices cannot change more than the annual growth rate of the economy.

- There needs to be an immediate limit placed on all changes to prices of wholesale products and commodities—wholesale prices and commodity prices cannot change more than the annual growth rate of the economy.
- There needs to be an immediate limit placed on all changes to retail prices—retail prices cannot change more than the annual growth rate of the economy.
- There needs to be an immediate freeze on all foreclosures and repossessions.
- Any home that has been repossessed and is currently on the market unoccupied should be re-possessed by the original owners subject to a forbearance program.
- There needs to be an immediate ceiling on all interest rates as well as an adjustment in interest rates back to the ceiling. The ceiling must be three times the average personal savings account interest rate and no more than ten percent.
- All late fees and over-limit fees must be terminated.
- The whole process of assessing personal credit scores should be taken away from for-profit organizations and managed by the government.

- There needs to be an immediate change in the graduated income tax program:
  - All personal income must be taxed
  - Capital gains must be taxed at the same rates as other income
  - The lowest income bracket tax rate should be 4%
  - The highest income bracket tax rate should be 95%
  - Corporate income should be taxed like personal income
  - There should be an asset tax on personal assets over $1,000,000
  - There should be a graduated sales tax on the sale of stocks, bonds and other monetary instruments
  - There should be a graduated sales tax on the sale of property, assets and businesses over $1,000,000
- There needs to be a high corporate tax on layoffs.
- All trade treaties need to be terminated and tariffs needed to be placed on all imported goods and outsourced services
- Patents and copy-rights must be limited to 10 years after which they fall under the public domain

The Federal government

- Must immediately balance its budget
- It cannot borrow any money whatsoever
- All foreign aid to cease immediately except for aid involving natural disasters
- All foreign expenditures by the Federal government must not exceed 5% of the Federal budget
- The Federal Government must monitor and report weekly to the People through the news media on Economic Key Performance Indicators KPI such as
  - The trade imbalance

- The growth rate

- The jobless rate

- The distribution of wealth variance

- The price index

- The interest rate index

- The GDP

- The percentage of workforce earning minimum wage

- The annualized minimum wage as percent of average income

- The poverty level and the homeless level

Conclusion

ALL THAT IS GOOD about the United States, all the good accomplished by the United States, all the successes of the United States can be attributed to the people of the United States. All that is bad about the United States, all the harm and injustices perpetrated by the United States on the peoples of other countries can be attributed to the government, Big Business and the very wealthy of the United States. Slavery, the Mexican War, the imperial conquest of the Philippines, the exploitation of most of the LATAM countries, the attach on Panama, and the ruin of most of the national economies through the World Bank and the International Monetary Fund are attributable to the government, Big Business and the very wealthy of the United States. The people's role in these events and activities has been that of pawns who unknowingly were used by Big Business and the very wealthy to achieve their unjust objectives.

The people must refuse to be the pawns any longer. The government must serve the people. Big Business must serve the people. The rich are equal to and no better than the people. The people must refuse to be exploited any more by Big Business and Big Wealth. They must seek justice and their fair share. There is currently a class war. It is and has been a pre-emptive attack by the rich minority on the working majority. And the working majority has naively done nothing. Nikita Khrushchev, the First Secretary of the Communist Party of the Soviet Union from 1953 to 1964, once stated regarding the American people, 'we spit in your face and you call it dew." Big Business and Big Wealth spit in the face of the American people—and the American people have done nothing. That has to change. That has to end. It is every American's patriotic responsibility to bring Big Business and Big Wealth into control by non-violent, principled means. The people need to engage in continuous, aggressive social activism. They must exercise their rights of initiative, referendum and recall. They must demonstrate, they must boycott, and they must demand equality between the rich and everyone else. They must demand that the government represent all the people. And they must demand that the government seek the common good and the maximum benefit of the economy for all people.

The economic crisis can only be solved by the people. It will not be solved by the President or Congress, for they are a major part of the problem because they are pawns and puppets of Big Business and Big Wealth. The people cannot sit back. They must act. The future of the United States depends on the actions of the people to rectify the problems in the economy and force the government to serve all the people.

The phrase 'evil exists because good people do nothing' is false. Evil exits because there are too few good people to counter the evil. Evil is countered or offset by goodness. The prevalence and extent of evil in the world indicates the lack of good people to counter that evil. Good people need to remove the evil in evil people, not destroy evil people. The evils affecting the economy are in fact moral evils and they must be countered by moral means. These means are Christian principles applied to economics and are based on the three Christian axioms of do good and avoid evil, love your neighbor as yourself and absolute respect for the rights of all people.

What is the essence of Christianity and how will God judge people when they die?

At the end of the world when God judges everyone, he will separate the good from the bad based on the commandment to 'love your neighbor as yourself'. He will say to the good, 'Come you blessed and inherit the kingdom prepared for you from the beginning of time. For I was poor and you helped Me out of poverty. I was unemployed and you helped Me to find a job or you gave Me a job or you created a job for Me. I did not have health insurance and you helped to obtain insurance. I was not making a living wage and you worked to have My employer pay a living wage. I was homeless and you helped me find a place to live. My house was in foreclosure and you helped prevent it from being repossessed. I was old and you helped Me with a socially-based income and health insurance. I was uneducated and you helped to educate Me. I was in prison and you helped change the system from retribution based to restorative based. I was discriminated against and you helped stop the discrimination.' And the righteous will ask Him, 'Lord, when did we see You in poverty or unemployed or without insurance or making less than a living wage or homeless? When did we see Your home in foreclosure or You uneducated or old and without an income or health insurance? When did we see you in prison or being discriminated against?' And God will answer, 'Whatever you did for any of my brothers or sisters, you did for me.' Then he will say to the others, 'Depart from me. For I was poor and you ignored Me. I was unemployed and you did nothing but say that is was My fault. I did not have health insurance and you resisted any means to provide Me with public health insurance. I was not making a living wage and you said that My employer should determine how much I was worth and that there should not be a minimum wage let alone a living wage. I was homeless and you crossed the street so that you would not have to walk by Me. My house was in foreclosure and you did nothing. My house was re-possessed and you helped with My eviction. I was old and you worked to take away my government mandated pension and health insurance. I was uneducated and you said that only those that can afford an education should be educated. I was in prison and you threw away the key. I was discriminated against and you did nothing to stop the discrimination.' And the unrighteous will ask Him, 'Lord, when did we act this way to you?' And God will answer, 'What you did or did not do to your fellow human beings, you did to Me.'

www.ingramcontent.com/pod-product-compliance
Lightning Source LLC
Chambersburg PA
CBHW071312150426
43191CB00007B/601